The Future of Finance

How Private Equity and Venture Capital Will Shape the Global Economy

3/2010

Betty,

Thanks for your comments.

Hope you enjoy the book!

The Future of Finance

How Private Equity and Venture Capital Will Shape the Global Economy

DAN SCHWARTZ

WILEY

John Wiley & Sons (Asia) Pte. Ltd.

Published in 2010 by John Wiley & Sons (Asia) Pte. Ltd.
2 Clementi Loop, #02-01, Singapore 129809

Other Wiley Editorial Offices

John Wiley & Sons, 111 River Street, Hoboken, NJ 07030, USA

John Wiley & Sons, The Atrium, Southern Gate, Chichester, West Sussex, P019 8SQ, United Kingdom

John Wiley & Sons (Canada) Ltd., 5353 Dundas Street West, Suite 400, Toronto, Ontario, M9B 6HB, Canada

John Wiley & Sons Australia Ltd, 42 McDougall Street, Milton, Queensland 4064, Australia

Wiley-VCH, Boschstrasse 12, D-69469 Weinheim, Germany

Library of Congress Cataloging-in-Publication Data

ISBN 978-0-470-82511-2

Typeset in 10/12 pt Sabon by Thomson Digital

Printed in Singapore by Toppan Security Printing Pte. Ltd.

10 9 8 7 6 5 4 3 2 1

For my daughters, Allison and Dana, and to Karen,
who took care of them while I was away.

Contents

Foreword

From embryonic starts in the United States in the 1960s and 1970s, the separate, but inextricably linked investment disciplines of venture capital and private equity grew, by the early part of the twenty-first century, into a significant, global (and at times controversial) industry managing trillions of dollars and employing tens of millions of workers.

The good times for these firms—and their ever-growing set of institutional and individual investors—seemed likely to extend for many years, if not decades, into the future.

And then came the Great Recession of 2008–2009, with its devastating effects on so many of the largest, most vibrant economies in the world.

Although the venture capital and private equity industries were generally not blamed for causing the Great Recession, they were nonetheless severely and adversely impacted by it—to the point that many serious observers openly wondered whether these once seemingly infallible investment forces might become a relic of the past.

Their magic was gone. Their investor allure had waned. Their images had been impaired.

How had this happened—and so quickly? Could venture capital and private equity recover, perhaps by reinventing themselves as they had following previous, though far less severe, economic downturns? And what if they did not? Who in the future might provide entrepreneurial capital for innovation or enhanced corporate productivity?

The answers to these questions and related ones are still unknown, for the Great Recession is only beginning to recede, and its full, and perhaps permanent impact on the world of investing—especially in the higher-risk but higher-return areas of venture capital and private equity—is difficult to accurately predict.

To be sure, many of us who have worked through prior ups and downs in the investment cycle believe that venture capital and private equity will indeed return, and in many ways stronger than ever—chastened by earlier excesses and focused anew on helping entrepreneurs, managers, and investors achieve their goals. But that is admittedly a biased perspective.

To those who have not lived in the trenches of venture capital and private equity, but would nonetheless like to have answers to the key questions about the future of venture capital and private equity, a less biased—but fully informed—perspective might be in order. And that is precisely what Dan Schwartz has provided in *The Future of Finance*, a book that, because of the author's clear objectivity and unquestioned knowledge of the subject, is certain to be widely read and thoroughly commented on.

One of the many problems that venture capital, to some extent, and private equity, to a greater extent, have faced in recent years is the general public's general lack of understanding of these disciplines: how they work, why they have grown, what they achieve, and who they impact. Regrettably few works by well-informed writers have appeared in recent years to provide answers to these basic questions. And the most recent turmoil in the venture capital and private equity worlds has no doubt exacerbated this general lack of understanding.

Dan Schwartz has therefore provided a real public service by not only carefully researching and skillfully writing this book, but by doing so in a way that can truly inform the layperson, as well as investment professionals, about what has happened, is happening, and is likely to happen in the increasingly important—but rapidly changing—worlds of venture capital and private equity.

And the author has done this while holding down a day job of running a business he headed for more than 15 years—the *Asian Venture Capital Journal*, which has grown from its modest beginnings to a position of enormous influence in the burgeoning Asia venture and private equity worlds.

That perch has put Dan Schwartz into frequent contact with the leading professionals in both the Asian and the global venture capital and private equity industries. This is made abundantly clear in *The Future of Finance*, for the author has been able to obtain many frank (and invaluable) observations and insights from those professionals.

Stated simply, a nonprofessional interested in learning about the seeming mysteries—and likely future—of venture capital and private equity would be hard pressed to find a more useful, up-to-date primer than *The Future of Finance*. But, to the author's credit, he has also written a book that provides a great deal of information likely to be unknown to even the most seasoned of venture capital and private equity professionals. And they are therefore likely to benefit as well from reading *The Future of Finance*. I already know one who has so benefited.

David Rubenstein
Cofounder and Managing Director
The Carlyle Group

Acknowledgments

As anyone who has done so will tell you, writing a book is no small feat. It has occupied the greater part of my attention for the past year, and I have enjoyed the process. A number of people who assisted with the project have made it easier, and I wish to thank them profusely.

First, I would like to thank those who agreed to share their thoughts for the book. Not only did they spend time speaking with me, but they checked quotes, found photos, and signed forms. Despite busy days and hectic travel schedules, their time on the phone or in person discussing and describing the industry was most appreciated. You were great. I hope the book meets your expectations.

Most of those with whom I spoke or met had personal assistants, secretaries, or significant others who made it all happen. Your names do not appear in the book, but you know who you are. And so do I. Thank you!

Next, I would like to thank David Rubenstein for writing the Foreword. He is a busy man. His taking the time to write a substantive introduction is much appreciated. Those who know David and are familiar with his reputation as a hard-working and insightful man would, of course, expect no less.

I would like to thank my associate at the *Asian Venture Capital Journal*, Harmony Heung, for her assistance in putting this book together as well as everything else she has taken care of for me in Hong Kong over the past 18 years. You have been invaluable. Many others at *AVCJ* have also helped, including Allen Lee, Anil Nathani, Paul Mackintosh, Ying Jiang, Amelie Poon, and Helen Lee. I would also like to thank Jonathon Whiteley and his Incisive Media colleagues. They purchased the company in 2006. Good luck, and don't forget us in Asia!

I wish to extend my appreciation to the many others for your indulgence over the past year as I lugged my laptop around the world to talk, gather information, and to write. That includes my family, girlfriend(s), and friends from all over who graciously allowed me the time and space to think and write.

Finally, my sincere appreciation to Nick Wallwork and the crew at John Wiley & Sons (Asia) in Singapore, who have agreed to publish this book. May it be a winner!

The book contains a lot of information and facts. I have done my best to ensure that they are correct and timely. Mistakes will happen, though, and for these, please accept my sincere apologies. They are my own.

Dan Schwartz
Hong Kong
January 2010

CHAPTER 1

Tomorrow Will Be Different than Today

Private equity is a people business. Some people you love to hate. But most are smart, work hard, and deliver the goods. They live in New York, Hong Kong, and London. They complete transactions ranging from large buyouts of public companies to restructuring failed banks to funding dorm-room start-ups. They run on ambition, greed, talent, and the challenge of finding new ways to finance and run a company.

Over the past 17 years, I have managed the *Asian Venture Capital Journal* in Hong Kong. In 1992 we started with one monthly, one conference, and one guidebook. *AVCJ* now boasts a weekly and two other magazines, organizes 11 conferences on four continents, and offers online directories, databases, and consulting services. This growth took place in the same period that saw the print magazine industry implode, as ad revenues dried up and titles folded.

It was a period in which the Internet was born and exploded onto the world scene, China and India grew from remote destinations to pillars of the global economy, and an expanding debt bubble in the West finally burst, leaving the world looking for answers. It was a time in which private equity and venture capital grew out of offices on Park Avenue and Sand Hill Road to become a global phenomenon.

AVCJ was there. We watched it from the front porch and inevitably became part of it. We survived the 1997 Asian financial crisis and rode the Internet boom and bust. We watched as the trickle of U.S. and European firms setting up shop in Asia became a torrent. We saw the private equity world explode in size with come-and-get-it debt, and then freeze-frame when the lending markets imploded. And we kept asking for more, as a nonstop stream of crises played out in front of us. I vividly recall peering over the chasm of SARS and thinking it was all over, as people and businesses bolted out of Hong Kong in April 2003. Some never came back.

This story is about what happened then and what will happen in the future: private equity and venture capital's people, their firms, and their customers—billion-dollar pension plans, endowments, and sovereign wealth funds. It is also a story about the stage on which they play: the world's economies—chiefly the United States, Europe, and Asia. You'll see where the industry is today and where it will be tomorrow, and you'll look into the possibilities that lie ahead. The story is about the many challenges the industry faces: the plunge in distributions, looming government regulation, and the issues of succession and business models, among others. The story is also about the opportunities—from overleveraged companies to what's happening in alternative energy, digital media, and new markets. The words are mostly those of industry leaders: a global story about an important industry.

For all the many hurdles that private equity and venture face, however, I think the industry has a bright future. It is testing a new corporate norm, one that aligns the interests of owners and managers and alters the way in which they report corporate earnings. It's a future that offers a superior form of corporate governance—one that ultimately, I believe, leads to superior performance.

Accordingly, this drama is framed by a larger context—the global economy and the role these two communities will play in it. The system is on the mend, but the credit market collapse in the United States and Europe has taken its toll on both the general economy and private equity in particular: portfolio companies are struggling, new investments have been stymied, and all important exits are nonexistent. The IPO and M&A markets are slowly reviving but remain largely closed, with three exceptions: corporate acquisitions, bankruptcies, and fire sales. The recovery will be different in different places, reflecting each country's financial infrastructure, government policies, and corporate dynamics.

The relationship between general partners (those who invest) and their limited partners (those who supply the money to invest) is sure to change. The limiteds like the asset class, but there's a problem: returns on their investments have dried up. Many are facing large write-downs. Although they may be "in disarray," they are starting to talk to each other for the first time. And the financial arrangement that has governed the relationship between the two parties for the past 25 years is being questioned. As one economist notes, "We can show that private equity has outperformed public markets over a long period of time. There is an issue, though, in terms of distributing excess returns."

It's easy to point the finger at the United States as the origin of the economic maelstrom. The country's easy mortgage policies, toxic securities, and consumer spending lit the fire. (Its political shouting matches and fractured decision-making processes didn't help.) But a lot more happened around the world: the push toward global free trade meant that national markets were no longer isolated, China's emergence as a global power called into question its exchange rate policies, and the inflated asset bubble that gripped places as diverse as Dubai and London points to causes on a much broader scale.

Wilbur Ross, Jr., chairman of WL Ross & Co., says, "Historic modeling implicitly assumed that tomorrow would look a lot like yesterday. But the truth is, major credit crises come about when tomorrow turns out very different from yesterday." Howard Marks, chairman of Oaktree Capital Management, notes, "There's a lot of discussion now on models which have small tails. Most everything takes place within two standard deviations. But everything interesting takes place outside of two standard deviations."

Of any recovery, Ross says, "We will do well to be out of this recession by the second quarter of 2010, and even then the recovery is likely to be slow because of the permanent change in consumers' ability and desire to spend. This is not like the V-shaped recoveries from recessions that had been caused mainly by inventory reductions and tight money. The question is whether it will be a wobbly 'W' or more 'L' shaped." Marks agrees: "I see a saucer-like recovery, not a V-shaped recovery. Eventually, things will get better."

The world's economies are in a transition period. The public equity markets have rebounded from their lows in the period from late 2008 to early 2009. Many U.S. and European banks have reported better profits; multiple technology and consumer-driven companies are also making money. But collapses in the number of jobs, housing prices, and consumer credit markets have yet to be repaired. Western governments have taken many of the losses and defaults and put them on their own balance sheets. That's surely helpful, but now the same governments must begin to unwind the massive flows of capital they have pumped into the system. Whether these programs will alter fundamental purchasing decisions, reverse wealth destruction, or delay the shift of economic growth from West to East remains to be seen. Like many others, I also believe that we are seeing a delinking—a separation of high-cost, older, and mature economies from low-cost, younger, and growing markets. Tomorrow will be different from today for many reasons. The consequences for global economies are serious and far reaching.

A CHANGING WORLD

The numbers alone tell us that the world will change. In October 2009, U.S. unemployment rose to 10.2 percent—over 15 million jobless. Eurostat reported a September 2009 unemployment rate of 9.7 percent or 22 million in the 27 countries of the European Union. That's 37 million people without jobs on a workforce of about 385 million. Reemploying these people will take years. And many factory doors will not reopen. In Chapter Seven's discussion of new technology, I suggest there are still areas of innovation and new products. Though the great ideas may happen in the West, the products will be built elsewhere. The reasons are not hard to discern: lower manufacturing costs, growing demand, and the ability to pay for—not borrow—the costs.

The U.S. consumer will be less hardy than before, if for no other reason than they will have less money to spend. Without jobs, with retirement savings depleted, and with their home values deflated, American consumers will be doing what they should have been doing all along—saving. That's the good news. The bad news is that consumption accounted for close to three-quarters of U.S. GDP. One industry executive estimates that if U.S. consumer activity drops from 72 percent to 65 percent of GDP, $1 trillion of purchases will be lost from the economy. Two-and-a-half billion consumers in India and China will not replace them in the near future. Many banks have exited consumer lending, the mainstay of America's consumption-driven economy. And those funding the country's spending habits have likely learned their lesson. Securitizations that provide funding for credit cards and car loans remain moribund.

Corporate lending will revive, but on different terms and pricing. Western governments will pass regulatory legislation enabling them to tinker with important swatches of the industrial landscape. The United States will have a national debt whose $500 billion annual interest payments will consume 15 percent of an already inflated national budget.

The financial community has changed dramatically from two years ago. Gone are stand-alone U.S. investment banks. Hedge funds have fallen victim to redemptions, and securitization markets have yet to reopen. What started out as a crisis in the subprime mortgage market has infected the financial system and global economy as a whole—the downside of free trade, which is oblivious to national boundaries. And although the United States is slowly coming to its feet and Europe by and large remains static, the Asian economies are reporting robust growth. Their financial systems were largely unaffected by toxic securities, and their domestic demand has nowhere to go but up.

ENTER PRIVATE EQUITY AND VENTURE CAPITAL

What seems most likely to happen is also the most obvious possibility: for now, the global economy will shrink. An economic surge won't happen overnight, because the means to that boom—the credit markets and consumer demand—have also contracted. The progress of private equity and venture capital will reflect these macro conditions. The industry will have to deal with its own excesses, but it potentially has a tool in its arsenal to work through the downturn: a new model that combines accountability, focus, and financial structure to succeed. If you are unfamiliar with how the industry works, you can jump to the next chapter for a brief introduction.

There will be fewer billionaire private equity fund managers. The days of $20 billion funds are over until the industry better understands its needs and the new model evolves. The venture industry is in for a profound makeover as well: despite venture's inherent optimism about new technologies and new businesses, "institutional venture" is not funding the same technology businesses that it did in the 1980s and 1990s. Its investment profile has already become far more sophisticated. It will develop a new profile and new leaders.

This book looks at private equity and venture from a global perspective. Asia, Australia, and the Middle East have all begun to develop nascent industries on the back of growing economies. Though the larger private equity firms have grown global through the interdependence of free trade and industry expertise, by its very nature private equity remains local in terms of deal sourcing and portfolio company management. European and, to a lesser extent, American firms have had a hard time breaking into new markets. That will change over time, and the Western firms will learn to adapt.

What forces are driving global and national economies? What is the purpose of private equity? Why is venture capital facing an historic makeover? Who are the world's principal private equity and venture players? What issues does the industry face? Where are the opportunities? How could the industry alter the way in which corporations are governed and operated? Once the economy returns to "normal"—whatever that is—what will the world and, in particular, the private equity and venture worlds look like? Read on!

The World in Which We Live

Today's world is marked by economic, political, and social uncertainties. The economics speaks for themselves: massive deleveraging, a fall in consumer demand, and a freeze in bank lending are all apparent. Politically, many eyes have been on the United States—that is, on the Obama administration and Congress. There was considerable optimism as the new president took office in January 2009, but there remained a number of unknowns: administration policies and their effectiveness, the rate of U.S.

consumers' spending and banks' willingness to lend to them, non-U.S. investors' appetite for U.S. borrowing, and the fate of corporate America.

More seriously, the epicenter of global capitalism, Wall Street, is no longer held in the same esteem as it was before the meltdown. Many of its practices and relationships are being questioned. Certainly, other nations have looked at the salaries, bonuses, and options that many American corporate CEOs and financial executives have received and wondered whether the United States got its money's worth. The bailout of financial institutions seemed more a function of the Treasury Department's choices than of economic necessity. A popular "cash for clunkers" program spent $2.88 billion, while Goldman Sachs received $13 billion from the AIG bailout, $10 billion under the Troubled Asset Relief Program (TARP), and multiple regulatory benefits. Goldman partners and alumni count among the richest people on the planet, whereas most of those receiving their $4,500 rebates are, by definition, just able to afford a new car. Whether valid or not, other nations have looked at the numbers and decided to try it their way.

In March 2009, China's Prime Minister Wen Jiabao publicly wondered about the safety of holding U.S. government securities: "We have lent a huge amount of money [$1 trillion] to the United States. Of course we are concerned about the safety of our assets. To be honest, I am definitely a little worried." Whether that was intended as a joke or signaled a policy change is still an open question. The U.S. treasury secretary made a trip to China in May 2009 to confirm that the Chinese prime minister was only kidding. Secretary Geithner's assurances aside, my opinion is that he was not kidding. The Chinese intend to make their yuan a global currency as well as foster trade settlements in other non-dollar script. Socially and culturally, the disparity between the haves and have-nots has not gone away. The selection of *Slumdog Millionaire* as the Best Picture of 2008 by Academy Awards voters was more than a Hollywood moment: it was a profound symptom of these changes. But this is an economics book, so we will leave these and similar issues for others to resolve.

Prolonging the government guarantees and backstops that have been handed to financial and industrial corporations will be tough because of the deficits. Reversing them will be equally hard because companies have come to depend on them. Moreover, the sums may be insufficient to the task at hand, while disbursement potentially floods the United States economy with currency. For now, these amounts will live mostly on bank balance sheets or pay for small fixes or transfer payments—reimbursement for healthcare, highway repairs, or unemployment compensation. Instead of building an interstate highway system, the United States will paint bridges and fill in potholes. Despite the promise of a more comprehensive healthcare plan, the country will struggle to keep up with ballooning Medicare and Medicaid entitlements. Whether U.S. consumers can actually save is an open question. But as they do, with the national debt at $12 trillion and budget deficits expected to reach a further $10 trillion over the next decade, the private investments needed to rebuild the industrial infrastructure and to provide jobs will stall. Loading up the government's balance sheet with debt could simply kick the can down the street.

Is inflation inevitable? Not necessarily, if the economy remains depressed. But with the cash poised precariously for disbursement, it is difficult to see how it can ultimately be avoided. A dynamic and decentralized U.S. economy may rebound in other ways, but the late William Seidman, former chairman of the FDIC and the Resolution Trust Corp., said, "One of the great problems is that when we start to reduce these guarantees, how the private sector will react? We have so many programs, the results will be different."

Europe has built an enviable infrastructure and can look toward the East for new markets and manufacturing capacity. Education is solid and living standards high. But governments will bicker over work weeks and termination benefits rather than encouraging entrepreneurs and risk-taking corporations. In the United States (and in Asia), an entrepreneur loses, but then gets up and tries again. In Europe, he loses and he's out. Maybe that is inevitable in a region where personal wealth tends to be inherited and an easy lifestyle has become the ultimate objective. Brussels will expand, but without the cultural impetus to innovate and grow, it remains to be seen how the underlying economies will keep pace with global expansion.

Asian markets may well fare the best of all. Their economies will feel the impact of lower exports, but their financial institutions remain solid, their citizens solvent, and their economies growing. Clearly, the commodities markets were hit by the recession, as were export-driven economies. But commodities have rebounded. As one Chinese economist pointed out, "There is no financial crisis in China." Nor is there one in India. For several reasons, including government regulation, Asian banks did not buy the toxic assets or engage in risky lending that affected major banks in the United States and Europe. As a result, these economies seem to be emerging more quickly from the downturn than others.

Toward a New Corporate Norm?

At the end of the day, corporations conduct business; governments do not. Stephen Diamond, a law professor at Santa Clara University in California, writes, "The arrival of a potentially new stage in the history of capitalism is, without doubt, an unusual and perhaps perplexing event. The last such moment was marked 75 years ago by the publication of *The Modern*

Corporation and Private Property in 1932 by legal scholar Adolf Berle and economist Gardiner Means. Their book is now recognized as a critical, if flawed, study of the publicly traded corporation, which was then still a relatively new and little understood institution."[1]

To a large extent, as Berle and Means predicted, the modern corporation has become a captive of management. The fault lies largely with distracted boards of directors and dispersed shareholders. Nominally, the board of directors represents the shareholders. Sometimes that works; many times it doesn't. All too often, the board's members are nominated by the CEO. He or she remains the person in charge. Directors are reluctant to buck the chief. Other factors also affect management behavior. These include activist institutional shareholders, who are increasingly vocal, and security analysts, whose forecasts are tuned to quarterly earnings. The all-important, albeit invisible, third man—"better than expected" or "worse than expected"—also shapes stock market reaction.

Are the accepted divides between shareholders, managers, and employees still viable? Does the private equity and venture industry provide a model for successful corporate behavior different from that of Berle and Means? The answer, I believe, is yes—from both a financial and an operations standpoint.

Financially, private equity and venture capital may well be one of the only institutions left standing. With investment banks operating as bank holding companies, and bank holding companies dominated by a handful of giants, the field looks increasingly bare. Capital markets' trading has driven their profits, but banks' core lending activities remain frozen. Advisory houses and hedge funds will endure, but few with institutional funding or a "hundred day plan" to lead the financial field will be around.

By contrast, private equity firms have a robust funding structure: "long-term deposits"—investments—from their limited partners. Their capital and investment horizons are premised on future goals. They are flexible in their approach to potential opportunities. Though resting on an illiquid base, they offer higher returns to their investors in good times. Although their portfolio companies are suffering from the same downturn afflicting the rest of the economy, the owners control both the balance sheet and the business. General partners can perform their own triage on companies that will succeed, those that need help to survive, and those that should be left to fail. Many private equity houses have losses in their portfolios, but they are also sitting on large amounts of uninvested capital.

Operationally, that underscores the most profound reason why I believe the industry will change but the art form will remain: accountability and the alignment of interests. As private equity (in its saner moments) has shown, aligning business ownership with business management produces profitable results. Separating ownership and management doesn't always produce a debacle, but many of the recent busts in the financial, automotive, and retailing sectors have proven exactly that. Venture will be different as well, but the fundamental reason for its existence remains: sourcing institutional capital, investing in new ideas, and bringing them to market.

Despite the current reliance on government intervention, private equity and venture nominally solve the problem of modern corporations by aligning the interests of owners and managers. By demanding accountability to the owners of the business, these firms provide incentives to operate in today's highly competitive global economy. At the same time, successful general partners are involved in the businesses they fund. As a result, private equity could well emerge as a model for corporate governance and as a weathervane for the underlying economy. If large, centrally controlled companies are breaking down, then the answer could be an economic model based on more flexible entities, direct links between ownership and management, a corporate structure that is less leveraged, the input of banks and LPs, and recognition of the role played by motivated employees. Private equity and venture may have formalized the interdependence of owners, managers, debt providers, and labor. They work as a team to ensure a profitable and successful corporation. If that's the case, then issues of accountability, ownership, and ultimate rewards should be revisited by the corporate community as a whole.

Will private equity and venture save the western world's economies as we know them today? No. As successive chapters show, the industry must first save itself before it can save others. The model for the past 35 years, with few if any modifications, has been unchanged. Investors (LPs) have seen their returns dwindle, whereas fund managers (GPs) have watched their bank accounts soar. That may or may not change, but there will be questions about how "excess returns" are rewarded. There are regulatory and tax hurdles to be overcome. And there are serious structural questions—including succession issues, the dearth of credit and exits, and choice of business model—that the funds will have to address soon. If not, then Boston Consulting Group's 2008 study[2] could well prove true. They reckon that as many as 40 percent of the private equity and venture partnerships that began in 2003–2007 will go out of business in the next two to three years because they cannot get funding.

Private equity and venture are approaching the end of their first generational life cycle. What current leaders leave behind and how they handle the transition will determine the industry's contribution to the financial system and ultimately to the future global economy. As the book suggests, the potential is large.

The intent here is not to lionize private equity or venture capital, but to recognize their strengths for what they are: in their finest hour, they provide generally successful ways to rehabilitate companies or build businesses through a more efficient means of corporate governance. Many wealthy people have made their money though private equity and venture. They don't own oil wells, they didn't get it from Dad, and they are not in jail. A lot of public and private institutions have given them money to invest—state pension funds, private endowments, and corporate bankers. These dollars represent the retirement savings and pensions of millions of people. There must be something to it, and that something is the story this book tells.

American-Anglo Institutions

Although my experience at the *Asian Venture Capital Journal* in Hong Kong begins in Asia, it has required a global perspective. That's because in their formative years in the 1970s and 1980s, Asia's financial and legal institutions had just begun to develop. As such, the Tokyo or Hong Kong offices of Western institutions were effectively run out of New York and London. That began to change in the 1980s as overseas firms rented offices in Tokyo, and continued in the 1990s as they sent managing directors to Hong Kong and Singapore. At the same time, Asians schooled in the United States, United Kingdom, and continental Europe came home to run local operations. Thus to understand Asia required an understanding of events in the United States, United Kingdom, and Europe. Today the Middle East and parts of Africa and South America should be added to that list.

It is my opinion that private equity and venture capital in their modern guise are largely American-Anglo institutions that have been brought to and adapted by Asian markets. The reasons for their U.S. and U.K. origins are straightforward: they rely on a partnership structure that has its foundations in American and English common and statutory law; they are funded through widely held capital pools that had previously existed only in the United States and United Kingdom—public and private pension funds, endowments, and foundations—and they earn their returns through highly liquid public securities and M&A markets whose existence is facilitated by Western institutions. That is not to say that Asia and the Middle East don't have similar activities through the role played by prominent families and nascent funds. They do. But the industry's hard edge, legal structure, and financial distributions are all Western at heart.

Beyond that, the structure of private equity and venture capital reflects American-Anglo free markets. Private equity has enabled individuals with little more than their smarts and a good name to borrow and build vast financial empires. Venture capital as we know it depended on cultural, educational, and legal foundations that were initially found only along Route 128 (Boston) and in Silicon Valley (San Francisco Bay Area). The model has been brought to and adapted by European and Asian markets. Much has certainly changed on these continents. They cannot be the same there. But the concept survives largely intact. That testifies to private equity's and venture's underlying strengths, which are explored in this book.

The book is divided into eight chapters. After this Introduction, the next chapter is a primer on private equity and venture capital. Not necessary for those in the business, useful for those who aren't. It also asks the question, "What is the purpose of private equity?" The third chapter discusses the private equity and venture capital industries in the context of the macro/economic forces that affect how they operate. Economists, general partners, and limited partners provide their thoughts. This chapter also discusses the banks, sovereign wealth funds, and the limited partners. The economic crisis has given added impetus to their concerns, and the market may well be looking at some fundamental changes in the agreements between the general partners and their customers. Issues and opportunities in venture capital are also discussed. The venture focus is mostly on Silicon Valley and China, though important markets in Australia, India, and Europe are also covered.

The fourth chapter surveys today's private equity and venture capital landscape by looking at the league tables. Although they capture only a small segment of the industry, that's probably the best way to see who's doing what. The fifth chapter looks at private equity and venture capital through the prism of world markets. It covers the United States, Europe, and countries in Asia (including Australia) and discusses issues and opportunities in the venture community. The emphasis is mostly on Silicon Valley and China, with a look at Europe as well. If private equity will need to rescale and rethink its internal dynamics, then venture capital may well be looking at a different organizational model altogether.

The sixth chapter covers industry issues. There are many, among them tax, regulatory, and internal questions. Internal issues involve publicly held partnerships, succession, the public face of private equity, business models, and the split between private equity and venture. And then there are the issues that venture capital firms must resolve. These center mostly on returns—improving the IPO process, for starters.

The seventh chapter gazes into the crystal ball. It is about the new landscape, the model for private equity and venture capital. It discusses investment opportunities for private equity and its partners—pension funds, endowments, and high-net-worth individuals. It looks at opportunities in distressed and secondary markets as well as the many ideas and emerging industries in which venture capital can invest. The chapter concludes with a sobering thought: however private equity and venture capital invest, their new technologies and energy-saving devices may not be made in the United States or Europe under current conditions. There will be some relief if the United States and Europe devote more dollars to research and development. But the underlying trend will be hard to change: Asia's cost, population, and financial attributes will increasingly make it the world's manufacturing and consumer center. The United States and Europe will hold their own, but future growth will narrow to certain sectors, leaving governments with the problem of what to do with persistent structural unemployment.

The final chapter proposes a new model for corporate governance. If private equity and venture capital offer a path superior to the large corporation as it exists today, what are the implications for Western corporate culture? What lessons does this hold for more traditional European and Asian companies? Do we need to think in terms of an incentive-driven management and workforce accountable to involved ownership and directors, rather than the traditional corporate pyramid with an all-powerful CEO, passive board, and dispersed shareholders? The answer is undoubtedly yes. But no one knows whether or when that will happen.

This is not a casebook, a "how to," or a "confessions of" book. Nor is it a social commentary. This book highlights one important corner of the financial world. My purpose is to consider the world's economy and financial backdrop on a global scale, to suggest what may lie ahead, and to outline a role for private equity and venture capital among the many changes that will occur in the years ahead.

CHAPTER 2

Private Equity and Venture Capital: A Primer

To understand the game, you need a scorecard. If you are already familiar with private equity and venture capital, you can skip this chapter. For those of you who aren't, it is worth a read if for no other reason than to better grasp one of the less well understood but potentially more important components of the financial world. In the course of explaining the industry, I include much that is relevant to understanding the economic crisis, its aftermath, and the regulatory actions that European governments are contemplating or have enacted.

To begin, the financial world is divided into two broad categories of securities: equity (ownership) and debt (loans). Equity commands higher returns because the risks are greater: equity investors (or shareholders) can earn a lot as the company grows or they can lose everything if the company fails. Debt holders recover a lot less, but the return of their capital is more certain: financial derivatives aside, they receive an ongoing coupon (interest) and will own the company's assets if the business goes bad.

Both equity and debt are also divided into two: primary markets and secondary markets. For equity, these are private equity and the public exchanges. On the debt side, the primary market is private placements and the secondary, public bond markets. The secondary, public market is, of course, enormous. To become a publicly traded security, the shares or bonds must meet certain disclosure requirements prescribed by governments. The public markets are what most people know and refer to when they talk about "the market."

The primary markets—private placements and private equity—are less visible. These are not registered with the exchanges, though they still must meet specific disclosure requirements. These securities are subject to certain restrictions prescribed by national regulatory agencies, generally following the "smart or rich" rule: the holder has to be either wealthy or experienced to own them. They are traded "by appointment only" and are not listed on public stock or bond exchanges such as the New York, London, or Shanghai exchanges. But they represent the ownership interests or debt of small businesses that organize themselves as corporations as well as holdings of many nascent businesses by venture capitalists. Of course, they include the securities of larger enterprises held by the private equity firms.

Private equity and venture capital are first cousins—or maybe brother and sister. But they are different. They are becoming more different as time progresses. As discussed in this book, both private equity and venture capital are "institutional"; that is, they are funded by large (wealthy) investors and have to meet certain reporting requirements. Their structure adheres to certain governance standards. There are certainly private equity and venture capital firms that fall outside these parameters. A lot of people say they "do private equity," which generally means they acquire small businesses and hold them for resale. Those who "do venture capital" invest in new ideas or start-ups. What I have to say in this book certainly relates to what non-institutional individuals or groups do, but the focus is on how the larger funds operate.

For both private equity and venture capital, the ownership structure in the West is the same: a limited partnership. The ultimate goal is also the same: an exit. That is, the private equity partnerships and venture capitalists sell their equity interests to earn a profit. They seek a return on their capital, referred to as rate of return (ROR) or return on investment (ROI). Because their investments are illiquid, these investors expect this return to be higher than for publicly traded securities. For both, exits can be achieved through either an initial public offering (IPO) or a trade sale to another investor or revaluing the business at a higher multiple ("recap").

The limited partnership agreements that enable both the private equity and venture partnerships to raise money have a limited shelf life, usually 10 years to an eventual winding-up. Listing (or relisting) the company on a public exchange or selling the company in a trade sale to another corporation (or private equity fund) is the way to accomplish this. Before they buy, most industry practitioners have thought through how they will sell.

But beyond that similarity, major differences emerge. Private equity focuses on larger deals and older companies, with healthy cash flows, tangible assets, and room for improvement. A lot of debt is (was) used to structure the transaction. Many see private equity as the temporary stewardship of a company that can be fixed up. In the words of Leonard Harlan, chairman of Castle Harlan, "There are a lot of broken balance sheets, not broken companies." Most private equity firms take a hands-off approach to management unless there's a problem.

Venture capital likes new ideas and start-ups, particularly in technology, the life sciences, and more recently alternative energy. It starts with smaller deals, no cash flow, few assets, and a business plan. There is no debt. A business plan creates milestones and raises new money as each hurdle is met. The venture capitalist is (or should be) deeply involved in the company and its management from inception to exit.

THE STRUCTURE OF THE INDUSTRY

In theory, private equity and venture capital can exist anywhere that an individual can raise money, invest it, and then dispose of the investment at a profit. Each has its own structures and communities.

Three principal parties inhabit the private equity world: general partners (GPs), limited partners (LPs), and debt providers (banks and mezzanine—mezzanine debt is subordinate to but earns more interest than the bank debt). Two other groups—management and service providers—play important but ancillary roles. Among the general partners are the global funds, those firms that have evolved into asset managers, and the pure play, those who invest opportunistically in deals. The global funds have offices around the world and invest locally. Regional funds are mostly found in Asia, where they invest across the continent. The global funds have dedicated funds that invest in specific transactions, but they also engage in other activities such as hedge funds, real estate, and capital markets.

The size of the deal is another differentiator; that is, how much of its own cash can a fund invest and leverage in a specific transaction? Geographically, the firms can be either regional or national; their role and form can also vary in different parts of the world. They may have an industry specialty; for example, infrastructure, real estate, or media. Or they may focus on types of investments; for example, fund-of-funds, distressed, or secondaries. These classifications are good indicators of how the funds disperse their capital. Many private equity firms are located in New York and London—and, increasingly, Hong Kong, Sydney, and Mumbai.

The venture capital world is also divided into three constituencies: general partners, limited partners, and entrepreneurs. Venture capital does not depend on external debt to fund its investments. Venture firms are generally classed by the stage of investment in which they put their money: seed/startup, early stage, later stage, and pre-IPO. Some specialize in specific industries; for example, telecoms or life sciences. They have also expanded to different countries. Menlo Park (California) and, increasingly, Beijing, Singapore, Bangalore, and Tel Aviv are venture capital centers. Historically, Boston (Massachusetts) has played a role.

The limited partners form the next group of participants. They are the GP's customers, the groups that provide the capital that enables GPs to close transactions. Among them are state and corporate pension funds, endowments, sovereign wealth funds, and high-net-worth individuals.

Finally, for private equity, there are the debt providers. Although they rarely make headlines, they have in the past contributed 80 to 90 percent of the money required to complete a private equity transaction. That percentage will come down in the future, probably hitting 50 percent at its limit. Commercial banks and mezzanine funds are the two big players in this group.

And for venture capital, entrepreneurs are vital to the process. They have the ideas, start the companies, and bring their business plans to the venture capitalists. Venture capitalists will know a particular sector in depth, but individuals like Steve Jobs, Sergey Brin, Jeffrey Bezos, Jack Ma, and their peers are the ones who drive venture capital.

All are explained in the following section.

General Partners (GPs)

Private equity and venture capital firms are organized as partnerships in the United States and Europe. In countries that do not recognize partnerships—Taiwan, for example—they can take the form of corporations. The main reason is taxation: partnerships enable the managers to pass through their gains (or losses) to investors, tax free; that is, the capital gains tax on profits is paid at the investor level and not subject to double taxation at the fund level.

In the United States, the private equity industry is centered in New York, with outposts in Washington and Boston. (One firm, TPG, is located in Fort Worth, Texas.) Local firms exist in Chicago and on the West Coast. The United Kingdom and Europe have a handful of players, virtually all headquartered in London. (There's one firm in France and another in Sweden.)

The Middle East is composed of Middle East-North Africa (MENA) and the Gulf Cooperation Council (GCC), with investment activity centered in the United Arab Emirates and Saudi Arabia. Egypt, Turkey, and Jordan are important investment destinations. Israel is also located in the Middle East, but its politics have made this nation the odd man out in a region that is its natural investment partner. It's an emerging area, with large sovereign wealth funds in Abu Dhabi (Abu Dhabi Investment Authority, ADIA) and Saudi Arabia (Saudi Arabian Monetary Agency, SAMA). Other countries—such as Kuwait, Qatar, and Bahrain—have large cash holdings as well. Most of the activity in this region is driven by the price of oil. The 2008–2009 recession has largely taken these investors out of the market, though when oil rises above $70 to $75 a barrel, their surpluses once again make them viable international investors. It is a region that will increasingly use its funds to build domestic infrastructure as well as invest selectively overseas.

Asia will continue to expand. And, more important, investors will begin to recognize that there is no one Asia, but multiple markets within the continent. China and India have both grown into their own, as have Australia, Japan, and South Korea. Thailand and Taiwan also have locally based industries. Hong Kong has become Asia's "private equity central," whereas Singapore is home to institutional investors Government of Singapore Investment Corporation (GIC) and Temasek Holdings. Outside of China, these are the region's major sovereign wealth funds (SWFs). Vietnam, Malaysia, and Sri Lanka have considerably smaller and more focused investment communities.

Joe Bae, managing partner, KKR Asia, sees a bright future. "If you took a 10-year view of the world, Asia will become more and more important. The macro economic trends are headed in that direction." He adds, "We continue to see reasonably attractive deals in China. Valuations have come down and access to capital is difficult. But the best franchises still need capital to grow." Also, he notes, "There's an interesting role for private equity to play in Australia, whether it's in the form of a major refinancing or working with companies to restructure."

South America and Africa remain on the fringe, though the Republic of South Africa and Brazil have become increasingly viable markets.

General partners manage the fund: they raise the money, hire staff, select investments, manage their portfolio companies, and ultimately choose the exit. For taking on this responsibility, they are paid a management fee (generally 2 percent) and are entitled to "the carry"—a cut of the profits once the investors' money is repaid. Traditionally the carry is 20 percent, but 30 percent is not unknown in venture. Frequently there is also a "hurdle rate," an annual percentage payback to the LPs that the partnership must achieve before its carried interest is activated. And there are a variety of other terms, including "catch-ups" (enabling the GP to catch up with the return to LPs) and "clawbacks" (if the GP makes money on one deal but loses it on another).

If deals go bad on the private equity side, it's usually because the general partner made certain flawed assumptions and cannot service the debt. On the venture capital side, it's usually because the product or markets never evolved in the way the original business plan envisioned. Bad people are factors in both.

In the world to come, many expect these arrangements to be challenged. AlpInvest economist Peter Cornelius says the core issues center on distributing what he terms "excess returns." "It looks pretty clear to me that the underlying distribution model will change. From our perspective, with significantly higher risk, we want to be compensated. If we got the same returns from public equity, we wouldn't invest. Which takes me back to the question of how returns get distributed. Investors are expecting the pendulum to swing back in their favor."

Specialized Niches

Among the special niches are middle market and growth capital; infrastructure and real estate; and fund-of-funds, distressed, and secondary funds. These will be discussed in greater detail in Chapter Four, but following are some general comments as they relate to the overall business.

Middle Market Carl Ferenbach, managing director, Berkshire Partners, suggests, "The middle market is probably best defined by fund size. We are a firm that can write a $100- to $400-million check, and we focus on what assets we can purchase with that check." Leonard Harlan says, "The middle market roughly translates to an enterprise value of $100 to $200 million at the bottom end, to $700 to $800 million at the upper end. The statistics, however, always show $250 to $500 million. But we would rather define middle market by EBITDA [pre-tax earnings, less interest, depreciation, and amortization], from $25 million to $100 million. Multiples can change, but the measure of the size of the companies is the EBITDA."

Growth Capital Many private equity fund managers specialize in "growth capital." What is this? In short, it means taking a minority as opposed to a control position in a company. There are other elements involved as well; for example, what is the reason for taking the minority position: is it a first step in acquiring control or just a matter of participating in a growth story? Though the investor lacks a shareholder majority, what provisions has he included in the shareholder agreement to protect himself? Are there board seats, or board seats with a blocking minority? What is the exit strategy: an eventual IPO or a sale to a third party? For some, a growth capital strategy is a matter of necessity: the owner of the company in which the fund wants to invest will offer only a minority position. For others, it's a core strategy that enables the fund to tap into markets and expertise with which it is otherwise unfamiliar but eager to be a participant.

Infrastructure Infrastructure finance was popular in the mid-1990s in Asia but came a cropper after the 1997 financial crisis. Large projects were started that couldn't get additional funding or became victims of currency devaluations. It's aimed at funding structural improvements, including toll roads, ports, airports, mass transit, utilities, and telecommunications. Today it still exists in certain areas; for example, Australia, India, and the Middle East. Governments have played a significant role, as strategically they like to see the assets built and are willing to accept a lower but steady rate of return.

Business in this field is again booming. Despite offering lower growth than traditional private equity deals, infrastructure assets are attractive due to their stable cash flow in an uncertain financial environment. The unlisted infrastructure market has mushroomed by a staggering 429 percent in two years, according to London-based Private Equity Intelligence (Preqin), an alternative assets data and analysis provider. In its 2008 "Preqin Infrastructure Review," the group finds that in 2006, a total of $34.9 billion was raised by 18 funds, up from $6.6 billion raised in 2005 by 11 funds.

It "has grown from being a niche sector of the private equity industry into being what many now regard as a separate asset class," reports Preqin. "Many investors now treat the sector completely independently [of] other private equity and unlisted fund investments, with a significant 47 percent of active investors in the asset class establishing a separate allocation for infrastructure, while 43 percent include infrastructure funds in their private equity portfolio and 10 percent include it in their real assets portfolio."

Real Estate Private Equity Real estate private equity, as the name suggests, is focused on acquiring real estate. Michael Pralle, former global CEO, GE Real Estate Investing and Lending, explains that the industry's partnership structures parallel those of private equity. He says, "There was a time when there were very few global investors. Ten or 15 years ago there were only three truly global firms: Morgan Stanley, GE Capital, and ING Clarion. That has changed now, with firms like Macquarie, Goldman, and others who have real estate offices around the world." The investment parameters are also similar to mainstream private equity: cap rates—the ratio between the annual net operating income (or cash flow) and the price paid for a property (or market value)—is the equivalent of the price-to-earnings ratio, and the resulting valuation is priced in terms of both the potential appreciation of the building and the anticipated future rent increases (annual income).

Fund-of-Funds Fund-of-funds invest in other funds not in the underlying portfolio company securities. They offer investors (limited partners) with small staffs an opportunity to diversify across the asset class, and they can provide newcomers a chance to dip their toes into the water with limited risk. The downside is that fund-of-funds charge an additional fee for their services. Therefore much depends on how well the fund-of-funds have selected their fund managers.

Distressed Funds Distressed private equity (often referred to as simply "distressed") focuses on companies that are insolvent or bankrupt. Its purpose is to gain control of a company through purchasing its debt securities at a discount. These funds use their creditor rights to squeeze out the shareholders and then effectively run the company by converting their debt into equity. (The capitalist jungle is a mean place.)

Distressed occupies a central place in the 2010 investment pantheon. Many have raised specific funds for distressed investing, and the total amount of capital available for such deals is $51 billion, according to Preqin. To some extent that is being spent—in the first quarter of 2009, firms spent $1.8 billion buying assets out of bankruptcy in the United States, compared with $340 million the same time a year earlier, according to data from Thomson Reuters. For 2008, deals totaled $1.9 billion, up from $1 billion in 2007.

Even governments have gotten into the action. Wilbur Ross points out that "Treasury acted like a true distressed investor in GM, offering a last-minute sweetener to induce a pre-negotiated bankruptcy."

Secondary Funds Secondary funds purchase illiquid LP interests from investors who want out of the asset class. The interests are purchased at a discount and then, if all goes as hoped, redeemed at a profit when the partnership exits the portfolio company. This type of investment has increased in popularity during the 2008–2010 economic downturn, with an estimated $15 to $20 billion of purchasing power. Though this has proved a small amount in comparison with the amount of partnership interests that have been offered for sale, the spread between what sellers want and buyers are willing to pay has kept deal volume low.

Venture Capital

Venture capital is a different beast: to begin with, smaller funds invest smaller amounts. But then, the deal sizes are smaller. The target companies are not public and are in the early stages of their growth. There is no cash flow from the business for two to four years, so borrowing is out. If all goes according to plan, the business is financed through successive rounds of funding at increasingly higher valuations. That can be done through the use of milestones—that is, progress goals marking the company's advance along the way to profitability. When times are tough—as they were, for example, in 2002–03 and 2008–10—the company's value may be headed downhill.

Investors will demand a "down round" to put in additional funds; that is, the previous investors are diluted as the new investors get better terms at a lower valuation.

Venture deals have reflected industries popular at the time, but have been mostly technology plays: computers, semiconductors, the Internet, and search. Today they are focused on mobile platforms, green tech, alternative energy, and life sciences. Social networking investments are popular, though the industry has yet to figure out how to make money with them. Most recently, alternative energy and cash-saving devices have been added to the venture menu. Venture has been most comfortable with investing relatively smaller amounts early in a company's history. That said, corporate venture capitalists have been known to put in larger amounts. Intel Capital, for example, has invested over $1.6 billion in Clearwire, a carrier of WiMAX (broadband wireless) technology.

When the day comes for the venture capitalist to exit, the leverage may be small but the multiples are high. For a successful venture deal, the returns can be galactic. In June 1999, Google raised $25 million from Sequoia Capital and Kleiner Perkins. At the August 2004 IPO, their shares were worth about $5.4 billion on a market cap of $27.2 billion. In November 2009, Google's market capitalization was more than $175 billion. Average net returns to investors should be a percentage rate in the high teens, though certain vintage-year funds have returned up to 50 percent. (The Google returns were obviously higher.)

Venture funds also have certain geographic and industry-specific features, but by and large they are classified by the investment stage in which their funds are allocated. There's the "family and friends" round in which the budding entrepreneur asks Uncle Bob for a loan to get his idea off the ground. The "seed" round is next; that's when the fund invests early on, just after the entrepreneur has moved from his garage to an office. "Early stage" looks at deals in which the product or service exists in some format. "Later stage" invests when the product has been deployed and proven but needs to build market presence. Finally, pre-IPO money provides a stable shareholder base for companies that will soon list on a public exchange. In an ideal world, each round goes out at a higher valuation.

Venture Proverbs Venture capital has its own lore and lessons. There are, however, several sayings that are frequently cited as general partners go about their daily business of sourcing, investing in, managing, and exiting from their portfolio companies. Of the many one-liners, here are five.

What is your unfair advantage/competitive differential? Private equity certainly likes to see a competitive advantage, but it is imperative in venture capital. Businesses that start small are more open to competitors. Barriers to entry can be low, and the "me too" urge is strong. That's why you will often hear about venture-backed companies operating in stealth mode—they don't want to attract a lot of attention while they are proving and debugging their products and services. More often than not, this unfair advantage takes the form of a patent. But it can also mean being first to market with a new product idea or service.

What business are you in? Understanding the business is crucial: drawing the wrong lines around a product or service can be fatal. This axiom is best understood from a tale told by a marketing professor at Columbia Business School in 1977. In the late 1940s, if someone wanted to travel from New York to Chicago or across the country, he or she took the train. It was the principal means of long-distance transportation in the United States. The Pennsylvania Railroad and New York Central were among the dominant railroad businesses in the United States. They both thought they were in the train business. Along came the airlines, who effectively wiped out the trains. The reason: the airlines understood they were in the *transportation* business, not the plane business.

There's an epilogue to the professor's story. In the 1970s, the airline industry thought that, seeing as they were in the transportation business, they could also be in the transportation *services* business—that is, the hotel and rental car businesses. United Airlines bought Westin Hotels and Hertz rental cars, Air France founded Le Meridien Hotels, and Pan Am started Intercontinental Hotels. The airlines failed to understand that the hospitality industry and rental vehicle businesses were only partially connected to the airline business. They had overlapping but very different customer, product, and financing profiles. In the end, the airlines sold off all these businesses to concentrate on their core strength—itself a full-time occupation.

That is not to say that businesses can't evolve. When Google began, the company thought its main revenues would come from the search and appliance business; that is, they sold their algorithms to generate search revenues. Once they began experimenting with advertising, they realized they were in the media business: selling ads against content. And that they had the perfect model: no cost for the content and only minor rebates for the advertising. The rest is financial history.

Is the business scalable? Certainly, a good business has a core competence. But to become successful, it requires scalability: the ability to move to a much larger distribution network at low relative cost. Any of the large commercial enterprises provide a good example—restaurants, hotels, retail, and computers are just a few. More commonly for venture than for private equity, fund managers look for businesses that can scale with only marginal incremental costs. The Internet has proved particularly suitable for growing small enterprises very quickly.

Who are the CEO and the management team? The world is full of good people with bright ideas. But the ideas have to be executed and the people hired. The key to a successful investment is a competent CEO coupled with a team that he or she assembles to implement a great idea. In the late 1950s, the world had many competing hamburger chains: O'Henry's, White Castle, Wimpy, and McDonald's among them. Only one—McDonald's—grew into a Dow Jones Industrial Average component. "Management, management, management" is the fund managers' version of real estate investors' vaunted "location, location, location."

"I never did a bad deal—it just turned out that way" No general partner ever goes into a deal knowing it will fail. But, inevitably, many do. Some of the reasons: good people leave, unforeseen lawsuits occur, a better product is introduced, or market whims change. Fund managers must then decide the best course of action: close down the company, salvage valuable parts, sell it, or invest additional capital in the hope of better times to come. Bad deals are never a sunny day, but there's always tomorrow.

Limited Partners (LPs)

Limited partners are the customers of the private equity and venture funds. They invest large sums of money in the partnership that are locked up for 10 years; in return, they expect above-market returns. They have certain rights, spelled out in the partnership agreement. Limited partners are generally sophisticated investors and have a financial rather than a strategic role; that is, their intent is to generate a financial return rather than to operate a business. Among them are pension funds, insurance companies, endowments, high-net-worth individuals, and sovereign wealth funds. There are, however, strategic venture companies—such as Intel, Cisco, Nokia (Helsinki), and Jarir (Riyadh)—whose priorities and programs are more strategically oriented.

Limited partners make up a multi-trillion dollar universe. According to the 2008 Institutional Investment Report, in the United States alone, the latest available year-end 2006 data show that total institutional investors—defined as pension funds, investment companies, insurance companies, banks, and foundations—controlled assets totaling \$27.1 trillion, up from \$24.4 trillion in 2005. Their 2006 level represents a tenfold increase from \$2.7 trillion in 1980, and an increase from \$7.6 trillion in 1990 and

$19.7 trillion in 2000. Pension funds represent the largest single category in 2006, with $10.4 trillion in assets. Much more will be said in the next chapter about limited partners and the issues they are currently facing.

Debt Providers

Traditional private equity has relied on vast amounts of debt to earn the returns promised to investors. Providers of debt include banks, insurance companies, mezzanine funds, and even hedge funds. But it is mainly the commercial banks that fund the purchases.

Banks Says Joseph Ferrigno, managing partner, Asia Mezzanine Capital Group, "The public markets are ignoring that credit markets will require further write-downs." In June 2009 *The Deal* magazine reported that, according to Thomson Reuters' Loan Pricing Corp, the banks lent $375 billion to fund leveraged buyouts completed between 2005 and 2007.[1] "But right now, the leveraged loan market is fixated on one number: $430 billion, the amount in leveraged loans due to mature between 2012 and 2014." The article continues, "according to Standard & Poor's Leveraged Commentary & Data unit, about $10.8 billion worth of loans will mature in 2010. In 2011, the total more than doubles, to $26.5 billion. Then, it almost triples in 2012, when it reaches $73.6 billion. But in 2013 and 2014, the volume of maturing loans surges to $152.5 billion, then surges again to $203.1 billion, before falling back to $27.7 billion in 2015." Some of these amounts have been renegotiated, but given the equity base on which they were written, these are staggering amounts.

This debt is owed by companies that are owned by private equity. But Warren Hellman, chairman and cofounder of San Francisco–based Hellman & Friedman, says, "Private equity has many really smart people. They will find ways to recap or refinance. All are at interest levels that are very high. And there's a gamble that the economy will improve. There is a huge debt overhang from 2011–2015."

Mezzanine Finance Between the buyout fund's equity and the bank's debt are a group of investors known as "mezzanine funds." As the name implies, "mezz" (as it is frequently called) lies between the senior bond holders and the shareholders in its claim on the company's assets. It carries a higher coupon and frequently incorporates warrants or other features that are convertible into the company's equity, potentially providing an even higher return—if things work out. Matthew Chanin, senior managing director, Prudential Investment Management (which has a large mezzanine fund), explains, "Prudential and other insurance companies have been at the forefront of doing leveraged finance for over 30 years. Given the nature of the liabilities that are long term and relatively stable—life insurance policies, annuities, and structured finance—we're looking for yield and willing to trade off on liquidity." He adds, "Mezzanine evolved as a way to get current return on as big a part as you could, while acknowledging that equity carries some types of equity risk."

Management and Entrepreneurs Management and entrepreneurs run the portfolio companies in which the GPs and LPs have invested. On the private equity side, they are compensated with a salary and an allotment of stock that varies from 10 percent to 20 percent of a company. On the venture side, they are the individuals who started the company. Initially, they have a large percentage ownership. If all goes well, their percentage is reduced as more money comes in, but they still make out well as the value of their shares continues to increase.

Good management can come from a variety of sources. Mega-funds such as Texas Pacific Group (TPG) and Kohlberg Kravis Roberts & Co. (KKR) use professional recruiters. Frequently the CEO and management team are part of existing management, waiting for the opportunity to unleash their dreams. Or they can be part of a fund's network, having successfully led previous deals for the general partners.

China and India have become the quintessential homes to today's entrepreneurs. Many entrepreneurs certainly exist in the United States and less so in Europe. But China's exploding economy and the well-reported success stories of companies such as Alibaba and Baidu have made it the "wild east" of launching companies. Gary Rieschel, founder and managing director at Qiming Venture Partners in Shanghai, says that the skill sets of Chinese entrepreneurs have improved considerably. "The relative skills of the Chinese entrepreneur are getting better year after year. More people who have been in the workforce are signing on, and the completeness of teams is getting better." The other side of the coin, says Rieschel, "is dealing with the Chinese entrepreneur. He will trade off maintaining control versus doing the right thing for the business. If you're in a good company, it's not a problem. But a guy with a great idea who has difficulty growing the company poses a problem." A related issue is middle management: running the company after it's been launched. By and large, Chinese companies are started by dynamic entrepreneurs and run by competent CEOs, but the middle levels of management are still in the maturation stage.

Service Providers Service providers include lawyers, accountants, investment bankers, and even consulting firms. Lawyers put the deals together, the accountants keep track of the books, and investment banks underwrite the exit. They are paid on a fee basis.

The service industry had its good days and is now facing a major consolidation. Investment banks such as Bear Stearns and Lehman Brothers have closed their doors. A June 2009 *New York Times* article reports that, in the first quarter of 2009, demand for legal services in New York decreased by nearly 10 percent over 2008.[2] The story explains, "[A]t the root of the law-firm crisis is the credit crisis, which has pulverized the need for traditional practice areas like structured finance, mergers and acquisitions and private-equity transactions. The downward trend has been unrelenting: fewer Wall Street deals mean fewer Wall Street lawyers." The industry "is facing a potential paradigm shift as fundamental as the one that has hit investment banks and the auto industry. Big, as a business model, seems bound for obsolescence."[2]

In his blog, American Lawyer Media (ALM) president William Pollak writes,

> As the impact of the economic tsunami continues to play out in the industries we cover, it becomes clearer that the future will not look like the past. That is, the structural changes in law and real estate will not go away when the economy improves—the impact will be long-lasting. One of those potential long-term changes will be to law firms, and how they are organized and financed. There are dozens of different ways in which that will play itself out. But one of the most intriguing is the idea that law firms will be financed and owned much like other kinds of businesses—with outside investors and, possibly, publicly traded shares. That's already happening in Australia, and there is evidence of similar moves in the U.K.[3]

Private equity and venture capital general partners are very different from other financial industry players. Though their deals are structured to maximize returns, they are also strategically oriented: the GPs invest funds, take a management role, and (ideally) make their compensation through the successful sale or exit of the investment.

Investment bankers are transaction-oriented: they are agents, offering advice and taking a fee for their work. This can be in the form of an underwriting spread, M&A fee, or other fixed commission. They then move on to the next deal. Morgan Stanley and Goldman Sachs have converted to bank holding companies. But, says Stephen Roach of Morgan Stanley, "I see no diminution of our core corporate finance activities. That is the essence of how our franchise is defined."

Hedge fund managers are traders: their funding structure is generally short-term (for example, 45 days), and they can be in and out of a deal in a day. Though they branched out to provide equity and debt financing during the 2004–2007 period, most have now retreated to their core activity: buying and selling public securities to deliver a return superior to the market. Then there are the management consultants whose primary task is consultancy—that is, working with their corporate clients to understand and improve their operations. They are paid on a fee or project basis.

THE GAME

Private equity and venture capital use similar plays in running their businesses. How they execute makes all the difference between the top 10 percent and those whose next fund will be a nonstarter. The first step is to establish a fund, generally a limited partnership. The individuals who set up the fund are key to its success: prior experience, particularly successful deals, is the main criterion. Where do general partners get that experience? Almost invariably they earn their stripes by working for another fund, though corporate executives, lawyers, and investment bankers have also been successful.

Next, the general partners get funded. The suppliers of capital are the LPs. Fund raising is a difficult and torturous process. In most instances it takes anywhere from one to two years, although well-known names can raise funds in three to six months. Generally, the partners will hold a first close on funds they've raised, followed by a final close when all of the commitments have been obtained. Some GPs raise their own funds; others hire placement agents who assist them with contacting LPs and selling the funds. Either way, a confidential document—the placement memorandum—is circulated among LPs to interest them in the fund. Limited partners sign the LP agreement, which contains the terms and conditions of their investment. (See "Limited Partners: When Access Is No Longer Enough" in Chapter Three.)

Once the GP has the money, it's time to invest. Deal sourcing—the "deal pipeline"—is the key ingredient. This means finding "good deals": it's different for private equity and venture capital. Most GPs brag that they have "proprietary deal flow"; that is, access to deals that no one else has. Others invest based on "the book," a memorandum written by an investment banker or other broker with the salient facts about the target company. Occasionally they "build a platform," which entails consolidating an inefficient industry.

What is a "good deal"? Private equity and venture capital general partners diverge in the nature and size of the transactions they undertake. Private equity invests in large deals and has traditionally used anywhere from 50 to 90 percent debt. The hallmarks of a good private equity deal are solid cash flows, moderate growth, and unrealized profit potential. Stable cash flows are extremely important, as these transactions tend to be highly leveraged.

For private equity, deal structure is also important in determining final returns. That is a function of the debt structure. In today's market, for example, Leonard Harlan thinks that for a typical deal, "In terms of financing structure, you're talking about 50 percent equity. In the mid-sized range, lenders are willing to talk two to three times [2x to 3x, in industry parlance] on EBITDA, including one-half to one times on mezzanine. Totally, that gets you up to a six times multiple [for the purchase price]."

There's usually only one financing round. Investment preferences are generally reflected in the debt structure; for example, senior, subordinated, and mezzanine. Then comes the exit—payday. This occurs when the general partner lists or sells the business: it can be an IPO or a trade sale. Exits are a function of improved operation, multiple expansion, and financial structure. Says Henry Kravis, cofounder of KKR, "Eighty-five percent of our returns come from operational improvements in our portfolio companies, not multiple expansion. Obviously, if we manage the companies better, we throw off more cash, which in turn pays down the debt faster and improves the earnings."

The exit—trade sale or listing—takes place at reasonable multiples; for example, 10 to 15 times EBITDA. This figure—again, the result of pre-tax earnings, less interest, depreciation and amortization—is used to approximate free cash flow for leveraged companies. Once the debt had been paid off, returns to investors can be high. For example, assume the market value of a company is $750,000. Private equity pays $1,000,000 to purchase it—a 25-percent premium to current shareholders. But it structures the purchase price as a $750,000 loan and invests $250,000 in equity. The private equity firm pays down the debt, makes operational improvements, and relists the company for $1,500,000. Although the market value of the company has increased 50 percent, the investors have made 300 percent on their capital: $750,000/$250,000 = three times the original investment.

For a brief period, general partners also used the "recap" to get their money back. A recap involves convincing the banks that the business has grown in value and is worth more than when the initial funding went in. The banks then lend the money at the new multiple ("cap rate"), which goes out to general and limited partners. In today's environment, the recap is probably a legacy technique, more appropriate for the private equity historic display in the Smithsonian than for today's market.

Daniel Mintz, founding managing director, Olympus Capital, notes an interesting point on trade sales to other firms in the industry: "If you can deliver control of a company, there's a very robust market among private equity firms. Firms are willing to pay full prices in order to access a true control deal. There's a reason that firms will pay that premium—with control, you can actually effectuate change instead of just recommend it."

As a rule, venture capital tends to look at smaller or start-up deals, uses little or no debt in the financial structure, and requires multiple rounds of financing at higher valuations to complete the deal. It has many stages, from friends and family at the start, to seed money, to early round, to late round, to pre-IPO. Different venture capitalists specialize in different industries and different phases of the investment process. What they like are deals that have a proprietary product, are scalable (can grow to an enormous size), and have a hard-working and committed CEO and management team. Cash flow is negative in the early years.

Exits are done at large multiples on a growing capital base, which can translate into big returns for early investors. The sign of a good venture capital deal is a successful exit as measured by times money earned. A good exit is 3 times, a very good exit is 5 times, and a home run is 10 times or greater.

A BRIEF HISTORY

Much has been written about private equity and venture capital, mostly by practitioners who tell their own story, academics who analyze databases, or journalists who read Bryan Burrough and John Helyar's *Barbarians at the Gate: The Fall of RJR Nabisco* (HarperCollins, 1990). *Barbarians* is an excellent book and still a great read. But it's 20 years old. The industry has moved on.

In the United States, private equity and venture began with several wealthy families who were looking to diversify their investments. Asia and the Middle East had long been home to wealthy families who made investments for their own account. Europe incubated private banks, which again were largely extensions of family wealth. The United States was the first to start institutionalizing this process.

In the beginning, there was venture capital. Venture capital provided seed money to launch technology-related deals in the Boston suburbs on the East Coast and in greater Palo Alto on the West Coast. Early investors included the Rockefellers, Whitneys, Hewletts, and Packards. In 1946, Harvard professor George Doriot started American

Research and Development, considered the first non-family-owned venture capital firm. Both Apple Computer and Genentech launched their IPOs in 1980. The Internet bubble and bust took place in 1995–2000; many—if not most—of the deals that imploded were venture-backed.

Private equity traces its lineage to the "bootstrap" deals done shortly after the Second World War. These were the activities of financiers in the late 1940s and 1950s, who bootstrapped acquisitions of public companies by borrowing against their assets. These became "leveraged buyouts" in the 1980s. But the industry really began with three employees of Bear Stearns—Jerome Kohlberg, Henry Kravis, and George Roberts. They understood risk, cash flow, and people. A good book to read on the subject is *The New Financial Capitalists* by George Baker and George David Smith. Kohlberg Kravis Roberts & Co. (KKR) did their first major public-to-private buyout of Houdaille Industries in 1978. The term "private equity" wasn't invented until the early 1990s. It was principally a means to distinguish the industry from the leveraged buyouts (LBOs) that had given everyone a bad name in the press. Private equity flourished through a "golden period," 2004–2007. The lights went out in early 2008.

Different time periods have generated different objectives, particularly in private equity. In the 1970s, when stock prices were low, transactions turned on privatizing the company and generating returns based on undervalued assets not reflected in the balance sheet. This decade gave way to the 1980s, in which private equity went into high gear. Corporate raiders saw the bear-market valuations of the 1970s and "greenmailed" large companies into either selling out or buying the raiders' shares. In the 1990s and early 2000, public-to-private buyouts (PIPEs) gradually came into vogue. In these transactions, funds reached an agreement with the management of large public corporations and bought out the public shareholders. The funds would then streamline operations and improve earnings. The funds would list them on a public exchange, sell them to a competitor, or transfer them to another private equity fund—and then take home the multiples of cash invested as described earlier.

About the time *Barbarians* was written, the industry began to change. The financial engineering-driven structure of the 1980s collapsed, and competitors arrived. Where KKR had had the market to itself, The Carlyle Group, Blackstone, and Texas Pacific Group emerged as global competitors. And then there was Forstmann Little; Hicks, Muse, Tate, & Furst; Clayton, Dubilier, & Rice; Hellman & Friedman; Thomas H. Lee Partners; Welsh, Carson, Anderson & Stowe; and Castle Harlan.

The list continued to grow. Dow Jones advertised its 2009 private equity and venture directory as including "more than 2,900 *active* private capital firms in the U.S. and overseas." Buying assets at undervalued prices or waging proxy fights with large amounts of debt was no longer enough.

Not only did the financing package change, but so did the way the funds made investments. In the 1970s and 1980s, underpriced assets, "highly confident" funding letters, and financial manipulation all were key to closing transactions. The bull market of the 1980s built on the undervalued markets of the 1970s. The 1990s saw a period of consolidation in which venture capitalists basked in the supernova glow of the Internet revolution.

Private equity firms had to create value in a business; that is, they had to improve the earnings process. They did that through some unpopular means; for example, firing redundant staff or shutting down surplus factories or closing unprofitable stores. They did it through more acceptable techniques: hiring capable managers, improving marketing, and streamlining the production and sales process. They upgraded their own returns by borrowing large portions of the purchase price and by ladling collateral fees onto portfolio companies.

The decade beginning in 2000 was a period of $20-billion funds and "covenant lite" debt instruments. "Covenant lite" debentures were bonds without the traditional terms that required borrowers to maintain certain liquidity and operating ratios. All that began to unravel in July 2007, when a new term, "subprime debt," entered the public vocabulary. In essence, subprime debt was mortgages given to people who couldn't afford them, then repackaged by Wall Street bankers into strips of bonds secured by these original (bad) mortgages. "Rating agencies"—S&P and Moody's among them—were then persuaded to rate them "AAA." They were then sold around the world to yield-hungry investors. At the tipping point in March 2007, the Associated Press estimated that approximately $1.3 trillion in subprime mortgages were outstanding. The crisis that continues as of this writing began three months later, in July 2007. The results are well known: the fourth quarter of 2008 saw the financial markets and consumer demand spin into free fall, finally beginning to stabilize at 50 percent of their previous highs in fall 2009.

Against this backdrop, private equity retrenched. Exits were barred, bank loans evaporated, and many LPs saw their capital bases reduced by 25 to 40 percent. Private equity firms reported major losses. KKR lost $1.19 billion before taxes in 2008, compared with a pretax net income of about $815 million in 2007. In its 2008 annual report, Carlyle said "The year 2008 was a humbling experience for us and most of the financial services industry. After several years of unprecedented growth, product innovation, geographic expansion, capital deployment and investment gains, our world changed dramatically." It went on, "Deal flow has slackened, exits are fewer, investors are hesitant to commit fresh capital, stock prices are down, and debt and equity valuations have been hard hit." In fact, the results reported by KKR and Carlyle were repeated by most other firms in the industry as mark-to-market valuations (as described in Chapter Six) and portfolio company losses took their toll. With the public stock markets rallying in 2009, portfolio company valuations that were marked down for 2008 were marked up in 2009.

LIFE AFTER THE LIQUIDITY BUBBLE: PRIVATE EQUITY

Today, in 2010, the private equity world is facing a new set of rules and economic conditions. It has, for example, long relied on private debt to improve the returns that it has generated. Tight credit markets have meant that it cannot get the debt it wants on the terms it needs. Banks are willing to lend, but in smaller amounts and on tougher terms. IPO markets have dried up, so fund managers have been unable to exit. Many portfolio companies have been pushed to get the working capital they need. And their investors, the LPs, have been trying to unload their positions through the secondary market rather than take on new ones.

The United States, the epicenter of the global blowout, will remain a cauldron of conflicting forces despite the federal government's efforts to tamp down the excesses of free market capitalism. Europe, having destroyed itself in two world wars, has sought to rebuild and remold itself through the European Union (EU). It has succeeded in building stable and prosperous economies, but ones that largely take comfort in safety and security rather than in growth and innovation. Asian nations, with two-thirds of the world's population and three-fifths of its land mass, will continue to expand. Asian countries will confront the challenge of widespread poverty and illiteracy with disciplined and well-educated populations intent on bettering their lives.

Will the years 2004 through 2007 simply define a time and place, the grand finale to a 60-year epic of post-war growth, available credit, and lax regulation? Douglas Lowenstein, president/CEO, Private Equity Council, says, "Industry leaders like Rubenstein and Kravis have been quite public that the 2004–2007 period was an anomaly. It is not likely to see this convergence of forces for some time to come. How far the pendulum swings back is unknown." The period was indeed—or appeared to be—a "golden age." But the deals were simply too highly leveraged and priced. The only real question was not *whether* the end would come, but *when*.

LIFE AFTER THE INTERNET BUBBLE: VENTURE CAPITAL

On the venture side, general partners have been looking for life after the Internet. To a large extent, venture firms have been blessed with a chain of innovation that followed the invention of the transistor. The mainframe, personal computer, laptop, and now the netbook have followed. The Internet and telecommunications revolution provided another impetus for expansion. The hardware side has seen the development of the mobile phone, the Blackberry, iPhone, and 3G mobile platforms. The Sony Walkman was precursor to the iPod, and the television to TiVo and X-boxes. The content side has gone from Web 1.0 to 2.0, from Lotus Notes to Excel spreadsheets, from computer gaming to 3D gamer Wii. (We will explore what lies ahead in Chapter Seven.)

Silicon Valley emerged as the hub of innovation and enrichment in the 1980s and 1990s, but as the next chapter suggests, venture capital faces a disconnect between the types of deals the industry has historically financed and those that represent growth areas in the years to come. The dearth of exits, departure of iconic partners, and movement to a global platform add additional hurdles. Venture is looking at much larger capital requirements, longer time frames, and the need for government partnership.

If the United States and EU governments are reluctant to contribute, GSR Ventures managing director Sonny Wu says the Chinese government is not. "In China, the government is playing a big role: electric cars, solar energy, and replacing lamps with solid state lighting are all examples. We are building new lithium phosphate cells for electric cars, and the Chinese banks are willing to finance these. If we invest in big industry verticals, the financing structure must be balanced between the cost of capital and leveraging government support. If you can structure these appropriately, the government will also provide export financing."

WHAT IS THE PURPOSE OF PRIVATE EQUITY?

Now that we have listed the players and described the playing field, there's one final question worth asking: What is the purpose of private equity and venture capital? Why do it? The answer depends on whom you ask. Ask the general partners, the individuals who run private equity and venture funds, and they will generally say it's about incentivizing management and improving corporate performance. It is about funding new technologies and optimizing the American, Asian, or European corporation. It's about building businesses and creating jobs. Success entails buying at the right price, hiring an experienced management team, and financing in appropriate amounts. Good investing requires a solid business plan and the people to execute it.

Ask the limited partners, those who invest in private equity and venture partnerships, and the answer will be considerably more succinct. It's about money—very specifically, cash-on-cash returns. It's about beating the returns of listed markets. The ultimate measure of a true private equity or venture professional is whether or not that person has exited from one or more deals and how many times the initial investment has been returned to the fund's investors. But beware: all of that is far easier said than done.

The best answers to the question, however, comes from those in the industry. Wim Borgdorff, managing partner at AlpInvest Partners, says it's about corporate governance and as an agent of change:

> The reason for private equity's claim to superior returns is that it follows the lines of better governance, creating better companies by true operational improvements, and very good investor alignment. Those are core values, and a return to those is the objective for the next few years. The true contribution to society, for example in Europe, is seen as a way to dynamism and to create competitiveness in markets, which tend to be overregulated and a little static. From that point of view, it's been an agent of change, a financial instrument to do that in a continuous manner.

Peter Cornelius of AlpInvest also highlights the industry's model of corporate governance. "There's a profound demand for private equity. The value proposition of private equity remains intact as a superior governance model. What we can show is that private equity has outperformed public markets over a long period of time." He adds, "It's not about financial leverage, but how you manage a company. Managers could do it without private equity, where you don't have agency problems. But we do have them. And private equity has superior governance. It's a full alignment of investors and owners' interest."

Paul Waller, managing partner of the private equity company 3i, says that creating shareholder value is a key objective. "The focus of private equity is aligning management incentives with experienced owners and managing businesses for shareholder interests. That is, driving value during our ownership phase and generating cash-on-cash returns for our investors. What we sell is shareholder value. At the end of the day, the purpose of private equity is to create shareholder value through ownership typically over five to seven years and to improve and enhance the value of the business." Waller adds, "How do you bring additional value? Smart people do good things. That's probably the origins of our business. Now, we are seeing a more institutionalized approach to our business, ensuring that we systematically improve operational performance in every aspect."

Archer Capital managing partner Peter Wiggs thinks that the industry's ability to quickly respond to market opportunity defines its make. "Private equity combines complete control with shareholder value creation." He notes, "What we have learned is that private equity is a niche product. It's all about having an advantage over the general market in knowledge and speed of transaction. If you are a company that reports to a board in Hong Kong that reports to a board in London, you will lose that advantage."

Waller distinguishes pure private equity from other strategies. "You draw a line where investment strategies move into trading strategies: there's a huge cultural difference. The culture of the teams, once you start moving too far away, is very different, for example, hedge funds have a very different approach. In terms of private equity, you can have a single, integrated strategy. Or you can have a series of buckets that will offer investors different products but the guiding philosophy is that of a principal investor. This is the difference between pure private equity and an asset management model."

Jay Jordan, chairman and managing principal, The Jordan Company, highlights private equity's ability to efficiently allocate resources. "The purpose of private equity is a form of re-intermediation of capital. Private equity can re-intermediate capital to the most efficient use. It is a necessary and very effective component of the capital formation process."

Baring Private Equity Asia managing partner Jean Eric Salata also looks at private equity from the LP's perspective. "Growth capital provides long-term and stable equity financing for business growth. For buyouts, it brings the focus of the owner to the way in which the business is run. From a limited partner perspective, it provides pension funds and endowments with a way of getting long-term asset exposure in markets. There's a lot less volatility. There's a level of due diligence and oversight that is greater than what you get from publicly traded stock. It's a way of enhancing their returns."

The CHAMP Private Equity Group's executive chairman, Bill Ferris, says private equity removes the agency problem and brings accountability back to public corporations. "What is private equity about? Removing the agency problem of public companies—which have lowered the efficiency of public managements—provides better management through more focused resources, and better returns through leverage. In their famous text about the marvels of limited liability companies, Berle and Means claimed that the breakthrough innovation of public companies was the separation of ownership and control. In my view this separation has gone too far, with low-performance consequences. The biggest private equity firms bring ownership and control back together in a better alignment of focus and purpose."

Carl Ferenbach signals private equity's ability to host benefits beyond providing capital:

> Going back 25 years, private equity has been a very effective way of aligning the interest of managers and investors around earning high returns on invested capital. Private capital provided an opportunity for managers to write a check and, if successful, to get a check. Interests were aligned that way. Cash was devoted to paying down debt. Those arguments are equally valid today. In addition, over that period of time, private equity has provided a range of services that management often wouldn't have as a private company: analytics, very efficient financial structures, and a very engaged board. In short, a focused team that has knowledge about the company's operations.

Kevin Fong, special advisor to GSR Ventures in Beijing and former managing director at Mayfield, says that private equity can play a role in resolving the disparate interests of wealthy families. "There is an efficiency of assets model that works well. Private equity is a very sharp scalpel when it comes to how companies are run, whatever their ROE or ROA hurdle rate." He goes on, "In family-run companies, the issues (or opportunities) are with multigenerational families. Look at the Heinz family or the Bancrofts at Dow Jones. They have generations with no interest in the business. They get used to a certain cash flow. It's not just about ownership and management, though there's a place for that."

Limited partners—the investors—take a more focused view. Georges Sudarskis, formerly senior investment controller at ADIA, says that private equity is fundamentally about earning higher returns. "It is very much about temporary ownership of companies when these companies need it: for growth, for restructuring, for redeploying, for reenergizing, and for professionalizing." But, he adds, "What limited partners are also very much concerned about is their cash-on-cash return."

Finally, a study published by the Private Equity Council in Washington reports, "The strategic objective of all private equity transactions and subsequent operations is to raise the value of the acquired company, which normally involves steps to raise its earnings." The report goes on to say, "Private equity buyout funds play two important and distinctive roles in the U.S. economy. In the real, physical economy of factories and offices, their operations facilitate the productive use of existing assets and resources, usually by identifying companies with untapped potential and reorganizing their operations in ways that increase their value, including making additional investments. On the financial side of the economy, private buyout funds operate principally as intermediaries that enable institutional and individual investors to take stakes in leveraged, merger and acquisition transactions and turnaround operations."

If these statements explain the purpose of private equity and venture capital, how does the industry accomplish all this? Certainly, its model of corporate governance is a major contributor. Ultimately, private equity depends on smart, hard-working people. As one general partner puts it, "These are guys who like to do deals." The proof can be found in the fact that few if any partners ever retire until they are carried out of the office. Greycroft Partners founder and pioneer venture capitalist Alan Patricof is 74 at the time of this writing, and his desk is still piled high with offering circulars. KKR founder and managing partner Henry Kravis, 66, was recently heard to comment, "Last I looked, George [Roberts, his cousin and cofounder] and I are still in charge." And Sequoia Capital's founder and valley icon Don Valentine, 76, still answers his own phone on Sand Hill Road. There are many more like them.

That is (in brief) what private equity and venture capital are all about. The next three chapters take an in-depth look at the economy that frames industry activities, its characteristics, and the opportunities and challenges going forward.

CHAPTER 3

2009: A Very Challenging Year

The global economy provides the stage on which private equity and venture capital operate. In retrospect, 2009 turned out to be a challenging year—for everyone. The outlook of GPs and LPs proved largely correct: credit scarcity, depressed corporate earnings, continued deleveraging, and consumers who saved more and spent less. Jobs remained scarce, and housing prices settled at a fraction of their earlier levels. Public markets rebounded in March 2009 and continued to rise during the year, but their marked improvement had minimum carryover to the Main Street economy.

For private equity and venture, the dearth of new deals was equally damaging. In a year in which everyone expected "fabulous deals," sellers insisted on yesterday's prices, and buyers wanted tomorrow's prices. Few if any major transactions closed. Warren Hellman, chairman and cofounder of Hellman & Friedman, says the gap has really hurt deal activity. "In 1987 and 2001, the world was your oyster. There were a lot of good companies with terrible capitalizations. There's a ton of money from private equity firms that hasn't been spent. The auctions are just as competitive. There hasn't been as much of an opportunity to invest as there was in 2002." George Raffini, managing director at HSBC Private Equity (Asia), thinks that the valuation mismatch between buyers and sellers won't be solved overnight. Andrew Liu, CEO, Unitas Capital, also says the gap will take time to close as well. "Like the Thai baht crisis—it took almost a two-year period for the buyers and sellers to come together." Of course, it's not over yet. The capital shortage is real, and market valuations are a term of the moment.

All this macroeconomic distress directly affects the private equity and venture capital worlds. The credit markets shape private equity's ability to finance deals; consumer demand affects the cash flow and earnings of portfolio companies; earnings drive valuations; valuations shape investors' appetite for new issues; and exits underwrite the financial health of the industry, including LPs. All influence the activity of specialized funds, including fund-of-funds, distressed, and secondary as well as real estate and infrastructure. Private equity and venture capital may well be a niche industry, but its scope, success, and failure are very much tied to the global markets. This chapter tells the story: the world economy, the forces that drove it, and their impact on the industry.

A GLOBAL ECONOMY IN 2009

The prospect that "the recession is over" shaped the media's coverage of "turning the economy around" in 2009. Newspaper headlines shared a similar story line: "Jobs, housing, company earnings [pick one] fall, but the decline isn't as bad as we thought." Or "The decline isn't as steep as it has been; recovery is a few months away." Even the chairman of the Federal Reserve jumped in. In August 2009, Ben Bernanke declared that "the prospects for a return to growth in the near term appear good." But the general economy in the West proved far less tractable. The reporting in this book suggests that we are in a multiyear transition period to a new "normalcy," whose eventual outlines are still unclear.

Though no longer on its back, the U.S. economy remained in poor health despite large-scale government intervention. Stephen Roach, Morgan Stanley's Asia chairman and its former chief economist, says, "In the United States, the big driver on the demand side has long been the American consumer. You could see some recovery, but it has been unusually anemic in the past four quarters [ending in mid-2009]. The American consumer needs to save. Does Obama know it? His advisers certainly do."

The banks stabilized. Aside from a handful, many continued to report weak though positive earnings. Since the financial crisis began in 2008, as of mid-November 2009, the FDIC reported 151 bank failures in the United States, with over 123 in 2009 alone. That's still small potatoes compared to the 534 bank and thrift failures in 1989, but greater than those in the 1930s depression.

In Asia, China, India, Japan, and Singapore all reported GDP growth. In Europe, France and Germany reported minimal GDP increases in the third quarter of 2009, while the U.K. and Spain continued to slide.

None of this should matter greatly, as private equity and venture capital are hardy industries. Their forte is finding microeconomic opportunities in an otherwise hostile macroeconomic environment. But it did matter, as their ability to fund, invest in, and exit from deals was hit.

The world—or at least the Western nations—likes to find a bogeyman for what goes wrong. Who "caused" the economic crisis? Was it Wall Street bankers, the credit card companies, the rating agencies, or Fannie Mae and

Freddie Mac? What role did individuals play—President George Bush, Federal Reserve Chairman Alan Greenspan, or executives at Bear Stearns, Citibank, or AIG? Did Treasury Secretary Henry Paulson have an "ethical dilemma," or were his emergency programs the right medicine at the right time? All had a hand in developments that led to the crash, but in the end, they all proved moveable pieces in an unraveling scenario that succumbed to financial reality.

If what happened in the United States provoked the crash, it's hard to ignore what was happening elsewhere. A massive liquidity bubble had enveloped the world, and private equity got swept in. One could equally blame the Chinese central bank, Dubai property developers, or Brazilian commodities dealers. The answer to who or what bears responsibility is "all of the above." The 2007–2009 depression resulted from the catastrophic failure of a system in which people, money, and machinery all played a role. No one, however, truly predicted the depths of the shakeout.

One cause would likely be the extraordinary period of development in China. In 2001, China's GDP was $1.16 trillion, nearly double that of 1990. By the 2008 Olympics, after years of 15 percent annual growth, GDP had leapt to $4.4 trillion, a record of growth unprecedented in world history.

Many factors lie behind this growth, the most important being the willingness of the Chinese people to forgo consumer comforts for investment objectives. Along the way, the artificially low value of the Chinese currency accelerated the government's policy to foster this growth. It worked extremely well. A low currency facilitated selling goods to the United States, while the resulting trade surpluses were invested in U.S. Treasury bonds. In 2000, China owned about $60 billion in U.S. government securities. By February 2008, that figure had grown to $486.9 billion. In February 2009, it was $744.2 billion. In turn, the United States purchased Chinese goods—or more accurately, consumers borrowed money to purchase the Chinese goods. The U.S. trade deficit with China went from –$39.5 billion in 1996 to –$83.8 billion in 2000 to –$266.3 billion in 2008. It was a neat equation.

This growth in China, India, and elsewhere fed a global commodity binge—oil, metals, and other natural resources—that powered this industrial growth. The Middle East benefited, as did resource-rich nations such as Brazil, Russia, and Australia. Banks and debt markets were overwhelmed by cash. Private equity took advantage of the boom and succumbed to excesses in both funds raised and prices paid for investments. Venture had its run-in with extremes from 1995–2000. It had never completely recovered from the 2000–2002 crash, and the industry found itself explaining a lack of returns in a new, global environment.

A GLOBAL STAGE IN 2009

There are larger issues, considerably beyond the scope of this book, that bear on the downturn and recovery. Like the post–World War II reflex to restore the prewar political order, there is a pervasive belief that a largely unchanged economic order can mend the system. The Honorable Paul Keating, former Australian prime minister and treasurer, doesn't think this is so. In March 2009, he said, "The U.S. East Coast political structure and walking dead in Europe will try to keep the current political structure. But the economic center has moved across the Atlantic and the U.S., closer to continental Asia." The result is an economic system out of sync with underlying economic realities. He says that the G8 should be dismantled, the G20 made permanent, and capital surplus states—including China, India, and the Gulf—given their due. The story of China is a story of urbanization, he says. The country will need to change: it is no longer an agrarian economy. Nor is it one in which the financial system is tied to investment rather than consumption. "You can't have a government where resources are allocated by policy instead of the market. In China, public demand doesn't translate into private consumption."

A few months later in July, Keating noted that "a conceit prevailed that the world could be run without reference to the interests of China and India. The G20 meeting in London last April finally nailed that conceit. Now the great surplus states like China sit at the head table, as do the large demographically young states like India and Brazil. The pendulum point of world economic activity has shifted and settled upon East Asia." In fact, at their September 2009 Summit in Pittsburgh, world leaders formally agreed that the G20 will replace the G8.

Since World War II, the United States has been the leader of the free world—and post-1989, the world's self-appointed top gun. The country has a decentralized and powerful private economy, a military to bar none, and an open and democratic culture. But the government is financially broke. The deficit for 2010 is projected to exceed $1.8 trillion or 15 percent of GDP. The (accumulated) national debt stands at $12.1 trillion and climbing, about 90 percent of America's GDP.

As a basis for comparison, in 2008 the European Union deficit to GDP ratio was 1.9 percent, and government debt to GDP was 69 percent on a combined (27 countries) GDP of $18.4 trillion. China's estimated deficit of $139 billion and its national debt of $363 billion represent 3.5 percent and 9.5 percent of its $3.8 trillion GDP in 2009. India's budget deficit is expected to hit 6.3 percent and its national debt 12.4 percent of its $1.2 trillion GDP.

Clearly, America's numbers are staggering both in absolute terms and percentages. This situation has meaning for America's ability to do what it wants socially and economically.

Potentially, it has implications for the U.S. dollar. Though global currency adjustments have occurred, pundits as well as most Americans don't seem to care. Treasury Secretary John Connally's 1971 remark to his European counterparties, "The dollar is our currency but your problem," remains as true as ever. Ironically, as the printing presses roll, the U.S. dollar has remained strong and provided a temporary safe haven. What seems unlikely, though, is that the U.S. government will be able to recoup the dollars it has unleashed. That could be a problem if other currencies rebound and these "Bush bucks" or "Obama bucks" leach back into the economy. Will Americans one day need a Tupperware bowl of greenbacks to buy a loaf of bread or quart of milk? Probably not, but the potential scenario is daunting.

One could reasonably ask whether the economic meltdown was inevitable: just how long could the United States (and certain European countries) maintain their high wages, individual borrowing, and government debt in the face of much lower salaries, higher savings, and government surpluses in Asia? The answer is "longer," but at some point the West would have had to confront reality. Had U.S. financial institutions held the line on leveraged borrowing, thought about principal repayment instead of originating new mortgages, and put an end to securitized lending and other derivatives, the near-systemic breakdown of the financial system in 2008 might not have occurred. Gradual is better than sudden, and it would have given the Western economies time to plan remedial policies. Now the United States (and others) must deal with massive unemployment, the collapse in housing prices, and the credit crisis—all while attempting to implement new social policies at home, fight wars overseas, and weigh global initiatives such as climate change.

One reason for the speed and depth of the downturn was that national economies had slowly melded into one global economy. No single economy was immune, and "delinking"—the belief that national economies can operate separately—swiftly became an unpopular concept. Delinking may prove itself yet, however, as Asian countries come out of the downturn far sooner than the rest of the world. GDP growth was robust across the board in Asia, while still minimal in the United States and Europe during the second quarter of 2009. Says Jeffrey Shafer, vice chairman, Global Banking at Citigroup, "Western economies are still linked, but they are no longer pulling Asia down. It reflects the force of having a region around you that is pushing ahead."

This downturn has been different than those in the past. The most recent crash, in the 2000–2002 recession, was limited to one sector and it reflected corporate rather than consumer cutbacks. Sonny Wu argues that this recession differed from previous ones: "2000–2001 was a technology Internet bubble. It was not an overall economic recession. This is a global, synchronized event. It has impacted on everything from consumer spending to government credit." Whereas corporations account for 30 percent of the U.S. GDP, consumer spending accounts for 70 percent. When consumers stop buying, the impact is felt universally. Kevin Fong, special advisor, GSR Ventures, agrees. "This is much more serious and global. In 2000–2001, the telecom and Internet sectors crashed. But there were other sectors that were healthy. In 2009, all sectors have been impacted."

THE MELTDOWN: A 25-YEAR STORY

Though global economies are already on the mend, the story of the meltdown provides a backdrop for private equity and venture capital today and a lesson for all in the future. Much has already been written, much more will be written. It's an incredible story: no romance, but everything else—money, power, deception, and arrogance. Behind the scenes, though, is a relatively simple story line: beginning in the 1980s, the United States gradually removed regulation from its financial markets. And concerning what regulation remained, those in charge must have been busy elsewhere. This fed the creation of massive debt and derivative securities, while enabling the Madoff and Stanford Ponzi schemes to motor ahead unnoticed. When the bubble burst in 2008, the result was massive wealth destruction followed by systemic deleveraging. Consumer demand dried up and corporate earnings plunged. All of this had severe consequences for private equity, venture capital, and their respective universes.

No Regulation

Though the causes are many, the meltdown began in the United States. Over the past 25 years, successive administrations and Congress have removed the financial governors from the system: from 1994, interstate banking further concentrated the banking system while making it less responsive to local conditions; changes to the Community Reinvestment Act in 1994 opened the floodgates to mortgage lending for marginal and unqualified borrowers; and in 1999, repeal of the Glass-Steagall Act of 1933 made it legal for banks to create bottomless black holes on their balance sheets. Add the unregulated hedge fund market, unfettered short selling, credit derivative swaps, and collateralized debt obligations to this mix, and the result was a turbocharged financial system careening toward an inevitable crash. The question was not *if*, but *when*. William Seidman, former FDIC chairman, put it this way: "We should have the regulation we have in a prize fight, not the regulation we have in a barroom brawl." There is a role for the government in the economy, but the authorities ducked or were simply bought off.

Anil Thadani, chairman, Symphony Capital Partners (Asia) says, "Alan Greenspan thought he would create the first self-regulating market. Instead, he will go down in history as the guy whose policies perhaps contributed to this malaise. You can't remove regulation of an industry where the few manage the money of the many. Greed can make people dishonest, especially if they think they can get away with it. I am not aware of any example in history of a successful, self-regulating market."

YouTube carries a video showing Congressman Henry Waxman questioning Alan Greenspan during Congressional committee hearings. Aimed at eliciting an "I was wrong" confession, the session is a testy standoff. Of course, Greenspan *was* wrong—and not just "partially" as he stated in his testimony.

The post-crash press interviews of Citibank directors Sanford Weill and Robert Rubin sound a common theme—"Don't blame me, blame the market." Each felt he had become merely "a victim of the bad times." But each in his own way gamed the system by pushing it to the limit—and beyond. The system, though, was easy to game. Everyone was in on it, including a few prescient hedge fund managers who made billions. From bankers to congressmen to millions of consumers, they were all happy to participate in a board game that imagined money far faster than the assets behind it.

Warren Hellman offers another explanation for individual behavior. He says,

> Nothing exceeds like excess. We are living in a competitive world. People say to you, "If we don't do this, then Goldman or Morgan Stanley will." These firms are very competitive, whatever you may think. An idea sounds OK, everything sells, and someone comes to you and says, "This product made us $20 million. If we don't want to do it, there are 10 other companies that will do it." There are a bunch of younger guys, who want to compete. Largely, you just kept up in the economic market storm. And then you look back and say, "Why did I do that?" It's very hard to remain objective.

No doubt, Hellman is correct in what he says. But with no rules in place, all bets were off. It just became easier for Greenspan, Weill, Rubin, and the others to do what they wanted.

Massive Debt: Toxic Securities, The Bubble, and Today's Credit Crisis

To begin, all banks—not just Ben Bernanke's Federal Reserve Bank—create money. It's called "the multiplier effect" and is the basis of modern banking. If someone deposits $100, he or she can take that money out tomorrow. But banks know that the depositor won't do that. (Otherwise, why would that person put money in the bank in the first place?) So they keep $8 in the vault to give to the depositor when he or she makes a withdrawal. That's called a "capital adequacy ratio." Your bank then lends the remaining $92 out. The next bank does the same, except they keep $7.36 (8 percent of $92) and lend $84.64. And that keeps happening until the $100 is all gone. In the process, the banks will have lent $1,250. They pay depositors 2 percent and lend it at 7 percent. That's why banking is—or used to be—a very profitable business.

Mortgages are among the loans that banks make. They are good loans because they are secured against a house of greater value and the borrower's promise to pay back the loan out of a monthly salary. So if you don't make your monthly payments, the banks take (foreclose) the house, sell it, and use the proceeds to pay back the loan. But most people have jobs and pay back the mortgage, so everyone stays happy.

Starting in the early 1980s, banking in the United States became a more competitive business. Previously, in most states, banks were allowed to have only one branch and were not allowed to open branches in different states. The main reason for these laws was that it provided jobs for many bankers—though the stated reason, greater familiarity with the local economy, is, in hindsight, not a bad idea either. These laws were changed: many states gradually repealed the "one store, no branches" law. And in 1994, President Clinton signed the Interstate Banking Act, which significantly liberalized the ability of bank holding companies to cross state lines. So banking became a real business. It was no secret that soon there was huge overcapacity—there were way too many banks. So the market began to correct that through a wave of large bank mergers and takeovers.

Once banks began to look at buying other banks, they also started thinking about more creative ways to make money. The U.S. banks cast envious eyes at their European counterparts, who weren't hindered by laws that prohibited geographic expansion nor by the Glass-Steagall Act, passed in 1933 to prohibit what had happened in the 1929 crash—namely, banks getting into the more risky public securities business.

The Federal National Mortgage Association, commonly known as Fannie Mae, was chartered by Congress in 1968. The Federal Home Loan Mortgage Corporation, known as Freddie Mac, was created in 1970. Their intent was pure: to help citizens achieve the American dream of owning their own home.

The process was not complicated: Fannie Mae and Freddie Mac would sell bonds in the market—that is, borrow money from investors—and use those funds to purchase home mortgages from banks. There was an implied (though not an actual) guarantee that the U.S. government stood behind these instruments, thus generating a AAA rating. Those who purchased the bonds would get a yield over U.S. Treasuries (the ultimate no-risk loan). The banks would sell their mortgages to Fannie Mae and Freddie Mac, get back the money they lent to make the mortgage, and then be able to make more home loans. Fannie Mae and Freddie Mac would hold the mortgages until they were repaid and would use the proceeds to pay down the bonds they had sold. Everyone was happy. The only possible issue was that the two agencies had no deposits. So although banks had to keep a reserve on deposit in case someone wanted their money back tomorrow, these two government agencies kept $0 in the vault.

That was still not a problem—not yet. The federal agencies were buying solid loans from banks, so what they sold was backed by solid collateral. But then, through more changes in the Community Reinvestment Act of 1977 under President Clinton, banks were under pressure to guarantee everyone the right to own a home—whether they qualified or not. Says Maarten Ruijs, managing partner and chief investment officer of CVC Asia Pacific, "The mortgage brokers came up with a nonamortization loan. That's why you found people in the United States with a $600,000 loan and an $80,000 income. Then they would call up their friends and say, 'Hey, you should try this.' Their friends did. And these people will have fantastic credit scores, which remained intact because they've refinanced their original loan" as the market value of the house increased. The additional money that the borrowers received was as often as not used to remodel the kitchen or to buy HD TV screens or Lollapalooza concert tickets. In other words, it was consumed, not invested.

Even these loans were slow tinder, though. But Wall Street decided that mortgage-backed bonds offered more profit potential. So they created artificial bonds or "derivatives" that divided these Fannie Mae and Freddie Mac bonds into different categories called "tranches." Effectively, derivatives are synthetic (not the original) securities whose value derives from the underlying (original) obligation. That obligation can be a loan or swap. A loan is a mortgage. A swap is an exchange of money based on a contract. For example, there are interest rate and currency swaps. The amount of money exchanged is set by a defined interest or currency exchange rate. These synthetic assets effectively transfer the risk of nonpayment or default from the original holder to the purchaser of the derivative. In most instances, that was a bank. The reward for assuming this risk is a higher interest payment.

Each tranche (slice) of the derivative bond represented a different risk; that is, the highest tranche had the best rating, and the lowest tranche, the worst rating. Those ratings were determined by the computer models that

Wilbur Ross describes as "financial engineering." The bankers, of course, took fees for creating these artificial securities. So did the rating agencies who took the Wall Street computer models and slapped an "AAA" rating on the bonds. This process generated hundreds of millions of dollars in fees for the investment banks and rating agencies involved.

This concept also provided the foundation for what are called "securitizations." Securitizations were the nonmortgage equivalent of what Wall Street had done for the housing industry; they were bonds backed by actual car loans or home improvement loans that were used to purchase car loans and home improvement loans from the banks so that the banks could lend the money again. According to a 2008 report by the Securities Industry and Financial Markets Association (SIFMA),[1] securitization had evolved from its tentative beginnings in the late 1970s to an estimated outstanding of $10.24 trillion in the United States and $2.25 trillion in Europe as of the second quarter of 2008. In 2007, asset-backed securities issuance amounted to $3.46 trillion in the United States and $652 billion in Europe.

For consumer and auto loans, the securitization market provided most of the funding. This trillion-dollar market has been effectively shut since early 2008. One observer, economist and commentator Peter Schiff, writes,

> [S]ecuritization more than anything else permitted Americans to borrow more than they had ever borrowed before. It permitted loans of all shapes and sizes to be packaged into investment-ready securities. The system worked, fueling unprecedented levels of lending in the home, auto, student, and credit card sectors. But in the last few years, as the collateral underpinning these securities collapsed in value, the trillions of dollars of securitized debt became the toxic sludge at the bottom of our financial pit.
>
> In truth, the only vital function provided by securitization was that it offered foreign savers a pathway to lend directly to American consumers, and Wall Street executives a new asset class to over-leverage for massive profits. With its trillions of dollars of credit injections and stimulus programs, the government hopes to allay this process by force-feeding Americans a diet of more borrowing. They feel that a restored securitization market will help. It won't.[2]

U.S. Treasury Secretary Geithner's Public Private Investment Program (PPIP) is aimed at restoring this market by getting private equity firms to buy into discounted loan tranches. How much pressure will Treasury put on the banks to not overprice the assets? If private equity makes a lot of money, will Congress pass a bill that they will have to share profits? The program has not been well received by the private equity community.

Wilbur Ross says, "The two most dangerous words in the lexicon of Wall Street are 'financial engineering.' Brilliant young mathematicians with elaborate computer programs believed that they could forecast the probability or severity of default on newly created securitizations."

Ross goes on to explain the creation of collateralized debt obligations (CDOs) and credit derivative swaps (CDSs):

> Initially, originators retained the lowest tranches, but as the securitizations grew so rapidly, they began to put too much of their own capital at risk. So they developed a new and extremely toxic product, called a CDO squared. This consisted of taking the lower, unwanted tranches of the initial securitizations, bundling them together into a new CDO, selling the highest tranches of those (which turned out to be most of the whole thing), getting it rated AA and AAA—and then selling it off. What made this occur was the rating agencies acceptance of the banks' black boxes' output. The securities were given an AAA rating. That generous allocation of credit rating is what created the extra trading value, because the AAA and AA tranches could trade at lower yields than the underlying securities.

Turns out, says Ross, "CDOs have not performed well." He describes credit derivative swaps as "another seemingly huge but unclearly defined time bomb . . . in which one party contracts to pay another party in the event that a particular debt instrument defaults. These have been growing amazingly rapidly and now cover an amazing $62 trillion worth notional amount of underlying debt." However, Ross says, "A lot of CDS is duplicative. The real reason that it didn't destroy the world is that it nets out at about 5 percent of the gross amount. For example, I write you GM protection. Then, I buy GM protection, and so forth. CDS has become less of a problem that anyone thought. It was one of the big risk factors."[3]

In a September 2008 Reuters article, Adam Davidson explains why a CDS is so dangerous. He writes:

> [A]t first glance, a credit default swap seems like a perfectly sensible financial tool. Imagine a large bank buys some bonds issued by General Electric. The bank might decide to buy a CDS, a sort of insurance policy. If GE never goes bankrupt, the bank is out whatever premium it paid for the CDS. If GE goes bankrupt and stops paying its bondholders, the bank gets money from whoever sold the CDS. It's easy to see the attraction. Historically, bond issuers almost never go bankrupt. So, many banks and hedge funds figured they could make a fortune by

> selling CDSs, keeping the premium, and almost never having to pay out anything.
>
> In fact, beginning in the late 1990s, CDSs became a great way to make a lot more money than was possible through traditional investment methods. Over the past few years, CDSs helped transform bond trading into a highly leveraged, high-velocity business. Banks and hedge funds found that it was much easier and quicker to just buy and sell CDS contracts rather than buy and sell actual bonds.[4]

Many CDSs were sold as insurance to cover those exotic financial instruments that created and spread the subprime housing crisis. As those mortgage-backed securities and collateralized debt obligations became nearly worthless, suddenly that seemingly remote possibility—an actual bond default—was happening daily. The banks and hedge funds selling CDSs were no longer taking in free cash; they were having to pay out big money.

Writes Davidson, "[M]ost banks, though, were not all that bad off, because they were simultaneously on both sides of the CDS trade" (as Ross says). Everyone that is, except for AIG.

> AIG was on one side of these trades: they only sold CDS. They never bought. Once bonds started defaulting, they had to pay out and nobody was paying them. AIG seems to have thought CDSs were just an extension of the insurance business. But they're not. If you sell enough and price things right, you know that you'll always have more premiums coming in than payments going out. That's because there is low correlation between insurance triggering events. My death doesn't, generally, hasten your death. My house burning down doesn't increase the likelihood of your house burning down. Not so with bonds. Once some bonds start defaulting, other bonds are more likely to default. The risk increases exponentially.

And there was a final component. Had all the banks accounted for these transactions in a transparent manner, alarms might have sounded. But they were all booked in off-balance-sheet entities called "structured investment vehicles" (SIVs). Invented by Citicorp in the late 1980s, SIVs enabled the buyer to borrow money by issuing short-term notes. The borrowed funds would then be used to buy higher-yielding long-term securities, thus generating an implicit profit. Since these entities were all off balance sheet, no one understood the connection—until too late in 2008.

These so-called "toxic assets" provided the accelerant for the collapse of financial institutions. Subprime mortgage activity grew an average 25 percent a year from 1994 to 2003, outpacing the rate of growth for prime mortgages. The industry accounted for about $330 billion, or 9 percent, of U.S. mortgages in 2003, up from $35 billion a decade earlier. By 2007, that number had grown to $1.3 trillion.

William Clinton was elected the forty-second president of the United States in 1992. At the time, the budget stood at $1.1 trillion. The U.S. national debt was $4 trillion. By the time he left office in 2001, the budget had risen to $2 trillion, and the national debt stood at $5.8 trillion.*

By January 2009, when President Bush finished his second term, the national debt had risen to $11 trillion. President Obama sent a $3.5 trillion budget to Congress in 2009, projecting a deficit of $1.75 trillion, further elevating the national debt to over $12 trillion

During the period from 2000 to 2001, the Federal Reserve Board cut interest rates 11 times, from 6.75 percent to 1.75 percent. In 2003, the Fed Funds rate stood at 1 percent, its lowest in 45 years. And then from 2004–2007, the Fed raised rates 17 times, from 1 percent back to 5.25 percent. By August 2009, they were down to 0 percent to 0.25 percent.

In 1980, residential home mortgage loans stood at $958 billion. In 1990, the amount was $1.8 trillion. By Q2 2008, they totaled $11.3 trillion. With the exception of several quarters in 1998–1999, home mortgage origination ranged from $700 to $800 billion annually. In Q2 2001, mortgages to purchase homes began rising, but second mortgages exploded: from about $200 billion in 2000 to $1 trillion in 2001 and 2002; to about $4 trillion each in 2003 and 2004. They remained constant at about $1 trillion in 2005–2007 before collapsing in 4Q 2008.

To everybody's great surprise, the system simply burst at the seams in July 2007. Says Ross, "What all these big failures show is how fragile financial services are, and how quickly they dissolve to nothing once people lose confidence."

By autumn 2009, the financial system had begun to repair itself. Consumer demand picked up, and the home price index had also moved higher, though still down from 2008. Major banks—including JP Morgan, Barclays, and HSBC—reported large profits. AIG reported that they earned money in the second quarter of 2009. The savings rate hit its highest point in 15 years. Unemployment declined, albeit at a slower rate. With the help of government subsidies, even auto sales picked up in the United States.

But the credit markets were still nursing their wounds. The number of bank failures continued to rise, and major financial product markets

*Budgets have surpluses and deficits. The national debt tracks accumulated deficits—the grand total that the United States owes to its creditors. The budget surpluses of Clinton's last three years did little to reduce the ongoing $5.8 trillion national debt.

remained closed. The FRB reported that consumer credit continued to decline in the third quarter of 2009. And as Maarten Ruijs notes, "[A] toxic asset is more than a nonperforming loan. No one knows what the underlying asset is. And you don't know what lies beneath them. The holder can't trade out of them. He just has to watch them run off."

Massive Deleveraging

A direct and necessary consequence of this credit meltdown has been deleveraging. The world could not sustain all this debt without the ability to repay it. Thus banks stop making loans and mortgages, credit lines dry up, and public debt markets grind to a halt until the balance sheet has been fixed by improving equity levels. The financial world went from a period of extreme liquidity to one of extreme illiquidity.

The Federal Reserve Board chairman wrote a book about the role illiquidity played in worsening the 1930s depression. But are generals always fighting the last war? As one *New York Times* online headline stated when the Fed announced it would purchase $1 trillion in securities in March 2009, "The Fed dramatically increased the amount of money it will create out of thin air to thaw frozen credit markets." The massive doses of liquidity provided a boon to the banks and investment banks, but they seem to have done little for the underlying economy (not to mention private equity). All of which is a little odd, as the American taxpayer was the one picking up the bill.

Many private equity GPs saw the debt crisis coming by mid-year 2008 as the banks stopped lending. After the Lehman Brothers bankruptcy, the credit markets seized up, and acquisition financing for buyouts evaporated globally. This was an environment in which not only did the bankers not trust their borrowers, but the banks did not trust each other.

"Fixing the balance sheets of the banks," says Philip Bilden, managing director, HarbourVest Partners, "will be key to the buyout business." What Bilden doesn't seem to have counted on is the banks saying, "Gee, fellas, thanks for the money!" They kept the cash to repair holes on their balance sheets or as working capital to trade securities. But they did not lend it out as working capital or to do acquisition funding. From the standpoint of stabilizing the financial system and not adding to inflation, that reaction was all right. But from the viewpoint of aiding industry or the consumer, it wasn't. Of course, had they handed out the money, banks and consumers would have been back where they started. (That's a problem, too.)

With the banks effectively shut for most of 2008–2009, private equity has been severely impacted. Bilden admits that despite the massive injections of liquidity, credit remained scarce in 2009:

> The credit markets are at the center of the storm. If credit had expanded gradually over the years rather than rapidly ballooning and then imploding, the outlook for the asset class would be much more favorable in the medium term. Today, leverage is scarce for existing portfolio companies and new opportunities. Fund managers raised large funds in a different market environment. Many managers are facing the prospect of not wanting to relinquish capital back to their LPs for fear that they may not get it back in a subsequent fund, even if it is the right thing to do from a performance perspective. This will create the perverse consequence of having fees in some funds exceed capital deployed. LPs will be challenged to exert sufficient influence to impact existing funds; their suboptimal but likely recourse is to not participate in a follow-on fund. The impact on net returns with a steep and elongated J-curve will overshadow these managers and disappoint their LPs.

Ralph Parks, chairman, Oaktree Capital (Hong Kong), says that during the crisis, excess bank debt fueled inflated asset prices. "The value of businesses had been inflated by investment bankers, industry peers, and even hedge funds that were eager to subscribe to pre-IPO convertibles." Parks is referring to a striking multiple expansion on stock prices. Over the previous five years, he explains, private equity had seen a large expansion in the multiples it paid for businesses. By the time 2008 rolled around, these were up from 5x to 6x EBITDA to 9x to 10x EBITDA. Many deals were done on multiples in the low teens. If the banks were willing to lend it, private equity would spend it.

In short, says Maarten Ruijs, risk was fundamentally mispriced. "The banks omitted the pricing of risk as a variable. With their rearview mirror approach, they built an economic model that has a perfect correlation, but had no bearing on reality going forward. What happened yesterday doesn't mean the same thing will happen tomorrow."

Wilbur Ross agrees:

> Instead of operating on the traditional basis of "risk-adjusted returns," many lenders were operating on the basis of "risk-ignored returns." They were seeking returns and not really focusing on the risk component. Historic modeling implicitly assumed that tomorrow would look a lot like yesterday. But the truth is that major credit crises come about when tomorrow turns out very different from yesterday. And in subprime and most other forms of mortgage lending, anyone that did field due diligence would have known that the endemic deterioration of lending standards made it 100-percent certain that tomorrow would

> not look like yesterday, and instead would look far worse. But back then, no one wanted to interrupt the party.

Howard Marks of Oaktree Capital Management says that ultimately debtors have to pay back the money they have borrowed. When they couldn't, because the debt financed either demand that didn't exist or transitory spending, the music stopped. "The credit markets won't be wide open again. Would-be lenders have to get comfortable with risk: no matter how much the government lowers interest rates, you won't lend principal unless you believe that you'll get principal back." Going forward, says Marks, "EBITDA is down and multiples are down. Under current conditions, a lot of maturities will not be met." Marks predicts much of the six-year-deal-related paper issued in 2003, with rising amounts in 2004, 2005, and 2006, will default in 2010–2012.

In the end, banks and investors will take the losses. GDP will shrink. But there are good businesses that need both restructuring and capital. They may now look to private equity for growth and long-term capital. The danger, however, lurks in the large sums borrowed by the global firms to finance the mega-deals. Of course, for the people out of work or without a home because the money has evaporated.

Unparalleled Wealth Destruction

The speed and depth of wealth destruction in late 2008 set records. Anil Thadani says, "No one living today has seen anything like it. What is amazing is both the ferocity and the speed with which the downturn occurred. The speed at which it happened is a consequence of the way in which information is transmitted today. When you get a crisis of confidence it moves like a virus at the speed of light." And, he adds, the numbers argue against a quick recovery. "Going up is always harder. To go from 100 to 50, you're down 50 percent. But to go from 50 back up to 100, that's a 100-percent increase."

A January 2009 *Washington Post* story reported, "The wealth destruction went beyond stocks last year. Jeremy Payne, a senior vice president with market research and analysis firm S&P Capital IQ, estimates that about $10 trillion of wealth disappeared in the global housing market. Add that to the $7 trillion in U.S. stock market losses, another $5 trillion or so in equity losses overseas and the sharp decline in values of more exotic investments such as mortgage securities, and 'we're probably looking at $25 trillion worth of asset price deflation,' Payne said."[5] Over half of the stock market losses were recouped in 2009, but that still left a lot of money that had disappeared.

Stephen Roach, chairman, Morgan Stanley Asia, believes the situation will not change soon. In May 2009, he said, "Though we've begun a bottoming process, it will take a long time to really establish the bottom. The critical issue is to make the leap between a bottoming process and the contours of a recovery. Normally, after a deep recession—and this is the deepest we've seen—it takes a while for recovery to get under way."

Roach cites three key reasons to look for an anemic global recovery. First, "In the aftermath of a major financial crisis, recoveries tend to be really subdued because of lasting damage to credit intermediation: the willingness to lend and the willingness to borrow." Second, "The more synchronous the decline, the longer the recovery. There are a lot of offsets: not all economies are in recession at the same time. This is the most synchronous recession there's been. About 75 percent of world's economies are still contracting now. The norm is about 50 percent." And finally, "The big driver on the demand side is the American consumer. We're moving into a protracted retrenchment. Over the past several years, the consumption growth rate has been 4 percent. It's now likely to be 1 to 1.5 percent over the next three to five years."

Finally, Wilbur Ross believes that we have understated the employment figures and that a rebound is still a way off:

> It will be well into 2010 before anything goes well. In July 2009, housing prices rose from June 2009, but continued to decline from June 2008. And the unemployment figures actually understate the true problem. They show about 15 million unemployed, but there are another seven million who are underemployed or have simply stopped looking. (Those working less than 35 hours per week are not counted in the official statistics.) So we have some 22 million people who effectively don't have jobs. Out of a total workforce of 155 million, that's 14 percent. Unemployment is a lagging economic indicator. It will take a while for that come down.

Moreover, he says, "The savings rate, which had gotten down to zero, hit 6.9 percent in May but fell again in August and September. The increase in the savings rate is generally good, but it takes billions of dollars out of the economy. Housing prices have gone down some $6 trillion since the downturn. Housing is the key because of the effect it has on the consumer. In 2010, once housing prices stabilize, there will be some gradual recovery."

Though housing sales increased dramatically in 2009, the prices paid were considerably lower than the foreclosure prices. One question:

who picks up the tab for the difference? One answer: the government. The consumer's indebtedness has become the Treasury's indebtedness. Says Gary Stead, managing director and cofounder, Shearwater Capital Group, "They are just transferring all this debt onto the government's balance sheet. All the governments are doing this to save their countries. They're all printing money. What are the consequences? No one knows."

Consumer Demand Plunges

"America will change," says Maarten Ruijs, "but will go through a dramatic decline in consumption." The collapse of consumer demand in the fourth quarter of 2008 is known and well documented. One question is, why did it happen then?

One explanation is, that's when the cash taps were turned off. A study by the Federal Reserve Bank of St. Louis reported,

> In the lead-up to the current recession that began in December 2007, credit had expanded strongly in the fourth quarter of 2007. During the current recession, credit expansion contracted sharply from the fourth quarter of 2007 to the first quarter of 2008 while credit contraction began to mildly rise. The picture substantially changes in the fourth quarter of 2008, when our measure of credit contraction becomes larger than credit expansion, a pattern observed only during the 1990–91 recession. Thus, although net credit growth in the commercial banking sector was positive through the third quarter of 2008, even the data on the quantity of commercial banks loans for the fourth quarter show signs of distress in the industry.[6]

The bottom line, says KY Tang, chairman and managing partner, Affinity Equity Partners, is this: "The whole world is paying the price. The Wall Street guy can't sell his house in the Hamptons. So what? But the guy in Minnesota has lost his job, home, and healthcare. Banks are withdrawing working capital from the corporate sector in a major way."

George Raffini suggests a cultural component to the downturn in consumer purchases as well. "There has been structural excess demand out of the United States coupled with structural excess supply from Asia." But, he says, "I don't see it only as bricks and mortar. Even if the decoupling argument has fallen away, I see changes in the social infrastructure. Asia has become somewhat less dependent on the U.S. engine of growth. I look at it from the perspective of the development of local social infrastructure."

Corporate Earnings Falter

With the fall in demand, corporate earnings plunged in 2009 and layoffs became the order of the day. With 10.2 percent unemployment in the United States and 9.6 percent unemployment across Europe, cost-cutters remained in charge.

Asia, however, turned in a somewhat different story. In Australia, for example, though predictions had unemployment peaking at 8 percent by mid 2010, it had reached only 5.7 percent in September 2009. Japanese unemployment rose to 4.8 percent in March 2009 and to 5.3 percent in September 2009, still only about half that in the United States. Statistics are always hard to come by in China, but the *People's Daily* reported that unemployment remained steady at 4.3 percent in the second quarter of 2009. Approximately 24 million were looking for jobs. In Singapore, the jobless rate climbed to 3.4 percent in the third quarter of 2009. Despite a drop in exports, the region seems to be experiencing a considerably milder downturn than the United States or Europe.

The world's markets tend to key off U.S. corporate earnings, which have declined along with the U.S. employment figures. Reuters reported that the blended earnings growth rate for the S&P 500 dropped 35.5 percent for Q1 2009 but rebounded to a 18 percent decline for Q3 2009 versus 2008 figures. But corporate Q3 earnings throughout the European and Asian countries remained remarkably solid. Though large GDP contractions were forecast at the macro level, corporate results were generally positive in both regions.

Large Government Intervention

Against this precarious backdrop, Western governments announced "stimulus programs" aimed at injecting liquidity into the economy. Leading the league has been the United States, with Britain and the European Union next. The U.S. bailout has been an ongoing story. Depending on how you count, the total amount seems to be between \$3 and \$4 trillion, though estimates as high as \$11.6 trillion and \$23 trillion have been made. All other countries pale in comparison. Take Germany and China. Germany has announced stimulus programs of close to \$100 billion and China's is set at \$586 billion. Germany is focusing on tax breaks and public works investment. China's program is across the board and aimed at stimulating bank lending and creating new jobs through public works spending. There was a call for a \$140 billion stimulus program in the U.K., which most critics considered too high. Again, all of these pale against the U.S. numbers.

The U.S. government is nominally solving both problems through a host of programs, including Troubled Assets Relief Program (TARP), Term

Asset-Backed Securities Loan Facility (TALF), and the Fed's $1.25 trillion program to purchase mortgage-backed securities. European and Asian governments have announced their own programs, though they are far less generous than the U.S. solutions. While all these programs will be helpful, the jury is still out on whether these actions will undo the massive deleveraging that has hamstrung consumer demand. Carl Ferenbach of Berkshire Partners doesn't think so. "The government provides a useful and necessary regulatory role in how our economy works, but it hasn't been good at creating economic value."

Why is the U.S. stimulus program so high? On the one hand, the United States is still the world's largest economy. With a GDP of $13 to $14 trillion, it's close to three times Japan's and China's and four times Germany's. It is also one of the countries—some think the only country in the world—where an independent judiciary respects property and enforces the rule of law. The Russians called a conference in Moscow in June 2009 to advance an alternative to the debt-heavy and deficit-ridden American dollar. Sitting in Abu Dhabi or Zurich or Singapore with surplus funds, investors have to decide whose treasury bills they will purchase: Brazil's? Russia's? India's? China's? The continuing strength of the dollar in perilous times is not hard to understand. The question is, how long can it last?

Economics is an uncertain science, but the implications are certain: until the structural deleveraging has worked its way through the economy, corporations may return to profitability at a lower cost basis on pre-crisis revenues, but unemployment will remain high and credit tight. Overall consumer demand will decrease. Whether those who have money will spend it or bow to financial reality is unknown. Most governments seem to be at the end of their financial stimulus programs. Seemingly, the United States can't go any further, but then it does. Asia and Europe have room for more, but their inclination to spend has dwindled.

All this will impact private equity in terms of structuring and pricing deals: debt will be down, but so will the acquisition multiples. Pricing remains a tug of war, but my guess is that the private equity buyers will win—they have the cash. And, to the extent that general partners are looking for growth to finance earnings expansion, they will most likely find it in Asia.

The Banks

One of the key ingredients shaping the industry will be the role that commercial banks now play. Nowhere was U.S. and European government intervention more evident than in the banks and financial services. At *AVCJ*'s Sydney conference in March 2007, Gerard Noonan, the investment committee chairman with JUST Super superannuation fund, was discussing his thoughts on the private equity market. He noted emphatically, "We're not really talking about private equity. We're talking about private debt!" How right he was.

If real estate agents enshrine "location, location, and location," and venture capitalists have their "management, management, and management," today's mantra in private equity would have to be, "banks, banks, and banks." During the first half of 2009, banks all but disappeared. Those that were active were financing large mergers whose parties had impeccable balance sheets. As the world's economy remained mired in recession, private equity GPs were seeing good deals flow but didn't have the funds to close the transaction. If a borrower could get a loan at all, it was at 1x to 2x EBITDA, with 50 percent down.

Initially, Western governments seemed uncertain as to what to fix first. Certainly the banks were high up on that list. Citicorp flirted with a dollar per share, RBS sold a majority interest to the U.K. government, and HSBC issued stock rights for one-fifth of the stock's high of less than two years earlier. The banks stopped lending, putting more than just the banking sector in jeopardy.

Even in countries whose banks are relatively free of toxic assets, the situation seemed pretty much the same. Andrew Liu of Unitas Capital underscores the difficulty in getting loans. "On the acquisition side, we have a couple of headwinds. First, in spite of the public markets, sellers still have unrealistic expectations. Equally significant, getting any kind of leveraged finance is difficult. But the leverage we were given in one particular instance is one turn of EBITDA. So we've been forced to front most of the purchase price as equity, at least for the next two to three years."

President Barack Obama courageously nailed his colors to the mast on healthcare, financial reform, and energy while the economy imploded beneath him. Rather than staying focused on programs that would stimulate real demand, he sought to keep his social agenda intact. His list of initiatives is long—worthy of a country with low national debt, a strong currency, and solid corporate earnings. Unfortunately, the situation in today's United States could hardly be more different from that ideal scenario.

The plight of the U.K. banks is well known. The Continental European banks are equally in trouble. Dr. Ernst von Fischer, senior adviser to Sal. Oppenheim Private Equity Partners in Beijing, says the Europeans just followed their American counterparts. "Europeans made the mistake of believing the bankers. The problem started in the United States, but Europeans have just fallen into the trap."

Asian banks face a different situation. The Indian and Chinese banks were largely free from toxic assets. But the Indian banks developed what Anil Thadani calls a "sympathy syndrome." Says Thadani, "They created their own crisis in India—all by themselves. It was an extraordinary phenomenon. They said, everyone else is not making loans, so we won't either."

Tim Sims, founder and managing director at Pacific Equity Partners (PEP), thinks a big part of the problem has been structural. He says, "In 1979, I was studying deregulation at the Kennedy School at Harvard. As I remember, in the U.S. it was not until 1976 that the first bank went interstate, State Bank of Maine. The U.S. has tolerated one of the most fragmented and underdeveloped retail banking systems in the world, and this has been allowed to underpin the world's most complex and demanding economy. This has been a very dangerous and unsustainable anomaly."

To encourage housing loans, he says the U.S. government built two financial organizations divorced from the basic business of banking. Over time, their practices gave way to political expediency rather than financial prudence. Says Sims,

> The U.S. built two massive quasi-government structures: Fannie Mae and Freddie Mac. They grew to finance 70 percent of domestic housing. They purchased loans with perceived government backing, securitized them, and sold them at sovereign ratings. Predictably, over time these agencies came under serious political pressure to lend to disadvantaged borrowers. This is a unique structure in the U.S., where the main mortgage provider has none of the responsibility and experience of a commercial deposit-taking institution. It is easy to overlook these disconnects when faced with the overwhelming reputation of the U.S. economy as the world's most advanced capital power.

At the beginning of the crisis, William Seidman was cautious if not worried: "The situation today is more complicated than it was in 1989. There are more big banks in trouble, the crisis is international in scope, and while we had a recession then, there's a depression now."

He explained, "The banks that are in trouble are limited to three choices: they can raise capital in the private sector, shrink the size of the bank, or, change the accounting rules. Banks can't raise capital in the private sector, though I think they can if they are willing to pay the price. HSBC did just that through a discounted rights issue. They can choose to make capital adequacy ratios by shrinking the bank's balance sheet. That will result in less loans. And they are trying to change the accounting rules. We'll see how they all come out."

David Coulter, Warburg Pincus managing director and former Bank of America CEO, highlights two issues: earnings power and solvency. The large banks have the ability to generate earnings, but the stability of their balance sheets is what's at issue. The regional U.S. banks don't have the same problem of toxic securities, he says, but they have lent to local businesses. As the economy sours, those loans also come into question. But Coulter reminds us, "Banks have the earnings power to work through a range of problems over time." And further: "There is also an important confidence issue. The signals sent by Washington are crucial."

In May 2009, the *Wall Street Journal* reported that the federal government projected that 19 of the nation's biggest banks could suffer losses of up to $599 billion through the end of 2010 if the economy performs worse than expected, and it ordered 10 of them to raise a combined $74.6 billion in capital to cushion themselves. These numbers are pretty big. But the bank's share prices rose, because investors were expecting worse, and they were able to raise the additional capital in the public markets.[7]

David Coulter believes that the banks are in better shape than the headlines suggest. "Much of the U.S. banking system is in reasonable shape. Unfortunately, press commentary in the first half of 2009 was not balanced, and solutions were pushed while there was still significant confusion about the cause of our problems." Coulter's optimism proved correct. In June 2009, 10 major banks repaid $68 billion of the $238 billion that the government lent them in TARP funds. The U.S. government, however, still had $90 billion in loan guarantees out to these financial institutions, which enabled them to raise capital at favorable rates.

New Sources of Debt?

What remains unclear is when the banks will start lending again and on what terms. David Rubenstein says the banks must start to lend again. "When the buyout world started, the reason debt was used was in part because there wasn't much equity around. But buyouts were not a real profit center for banks. As the buyout industry grew, buyout lending became very profitable for the banks. The bankers will come back in part because of the potential profitability. Remember, banks will lend because that's their basic business."

Peter Wiggs of Archer Capital agrees that, in mid-2009, "The credit markets are now pretty closed. It will come back because banks have to write business. The great thing about write-offs is that for every $1 the banks write off, they have to generate $100 of business. So they go back in."

However, Steve Pagliuca, Bain Capital managing director, emphasizes that the issues will not be solved overnight. "The key issue we're seeing is a massive deleveraging in the world. It has been caused by the previous 10 years of overspending by consumers and overlending by the banks. The magnitude of real estate losses [home mortgages] and the swiftness in downfall of consumer demand took everyone by surprise. Losses on sliced and diced packages of subprime mortgages created a huge hole in the system."

Pagliuca also underscores the structural problem. "Ten years ago, 75 percent of lending was done by banks, 25 percent done by nontraditional sources. Over last five years, 75 percent has been done by nonbank institutions. There's been a massive shift from regulated banks to nonbank institutions. Even nonbank entities that had some regulation, such as AIG, set up subsidiary units that were subject to very little regulation and also had very little transparency of financial information."

The role of the banks will be revisited, if not reduced, by private equity. The GPs will write larger checks, and sellers will need to contribute to the pot. However, Georges Sudarskis of ADIA says the importance of borrowing in the industry is overstated. "We accepted as a theorem that private equity was equivalent to leveraged buyouts. It's an absolute misnomer. Private equity are 'deals with temporary ownership of companies when they need it.' Debt may be a facilitator. Debt in venture and growth capital is unknown. It's only in controlled buyouts that debt was used to make it work."

Bill Ferris of CHAMP says that making do with existing—and restructured—debt may become necessary. "There are many companies out there which have more than enough debt on board already. So we won't necessarily be looking to raise debt to make new deals work; rather, we will be bringing fresh equity to the table and negotiating sensible terms and covenants with existing lenders."

Going forward, says David Rubenstein, private equity may also need to look elsewhere for leverage. "Banks will restrict themselves to the more senior part of the debt. However, because the CLOs and hedge funds will not be as involved in providing the junior debt, these portions of the debt will likely come from SWFs, state pension funds, high networth individuals, and seller financing. Creativity will keep almost everything on the table. One example: when Merrill Lynch sold Bloomberg, Merrill provided most of the purchase price through seller debt." Merrill was not alone. In September 2009, eBay included $125 million in seller financing and kept a 35 percent stake when it sold Skype to Silver Lake Partners and others for $1.9 billion.

Peter Wiggs is summarily direct: "We all like buoyant markets. But the reason that private equity has blown up is not because of the collapse of the world economic order. We all made dumb investment decisions over the past four to five years. You can't borrow 9x EBITDA."

Limited Partners: When Access Is No Longer Enough

Institutional investors are the source of equity capital for private equity and venture capital partnerships. Much of how they see the world depends on where you sit on the LP continuum: pension plan, endowment, or sovereign wealth fund. In general, though, LPs have been hit with declining portfolio values, borrowing or selling other securities to meet cash needs, and requests for exemption from cash calls. There is also an increasing clamor for another look at "alignment of interests."

Over the past 10 years, limited partners were more concerned about "access" to successful general partners than they were about many of the issues bothering them today. That is, it took years to give your money to top fund managers. It's unknown whether that will change in the future—and to what extent.

Lindel Eakman, director at UTIMCO (University of Texas Investment Management Company), goes back to the basics: "Why do you invest in private equity? To seek higher returns and to get paid for the illiquidity. We have the capacity to deploy capital that is illiquid, and we want to get paid for that. The two points of view are not incompatible—they are co-dependent. The benefit of long-term capital is that it allows you to generate higher returns."

At the heart of the issue for LPs are fees, returns, and valuations. At *AVCJ*'s Beijing February 2009 Roundtable, Philip Bilden commented, "At 2 percent of $100 million on committed capital, we're paying a reasonable fee for a small venture fund. Paying similar fees on billion dollar-plus funds distorts the original intent of venture and private equity fund economics." On which Eakman notes, "The 200 basis points is beside the point. That it hasn't come down to 50 basis points is what concerns me."

The fact is, as Gary Rieschel of Qiming Venture Partners points out, the basic model governing GP-LP relationships hasn't changed much if at all in the past 25 years. Whether the manager is in the top decibel or the lower quartile, the fund gets 2 percent for management fees. There's a 20-percent carry after the LPs' money has been returned. All the other transaction, monitoring, and management fees go to the general partner. There are differences between the European model and the U.S. model in terms of when and how the money is paid out. But as markets rose and fell, the basic structure remained the same.

Bilden points out, "Fund pricing is a function of supply and demand of capital." If a GP is consistently returning 30 percent IRRs (internal rates of return), few if any LPs are likely to question the fee structure. But in the current downturn, that's simply not the case. LPs are asking many questions about fees, investments, and returns.

Georges Sudarskis says that the average *realized* multiple for the past 10 years has been1.7 to 2.2 times invested capital. Of course, his figures represent only the average. Those who have been fortunate to invest and participate in the top quartile or top decile funds have made more than that. With portfolio markdowns of 20 to 30 percent at 2008 FYE, meaningful distributions far in the future, and capital calls looming on the horizon, is it any wonder that LPs are starting to complain?

Martin Day, vice-chair of the Institutional Limited Partners Association and managing director at OMERS Private Equity, a Toronto-based pension fund, reports that after an LP meeting in March 2009, the mindset of LPs is best described as "grumpy." He continues, "It's not that GPs aren't going through their own issues. This is a problem that they got us all into. People believe this is a self-made problem."

Steve Byrom, head of private equity at Australia's Future Fund, notes that LPs' options are limited. "LPs have been 'an angry group,' particularly within the United States. They've been trying to use the secondary market to help them out, but so far the market hasn't cooperated. North of $60 billion were put into the secondary markets last year. So far in 2009, the amount is in excess of $30 billion. What is getting priced and transacted is a small fraction of this amount."

A case in point is Harvard Management Company (HMC). Having reported a decline of 22 percent through October 31, 2008, by the time the dust settled in June 2009 the endowment had recorded a 27.3-percent drop. HMC put $1.5 billion in private equity limited partnership interests up for sale. Despite bids estimated at 50 percent of the face value, recent reports suggest that only $300 to $400 million has been sold.

Distributing "Excess Returns"

Limited partnership agreements are complicated documents. Peter Cornelius says that at the center of the storm lies the task of dividing up the enormous amount of money that has flowed into fund managers' hands over the past five to 10 years. "We can show that private equity has outperformed over a long period of time. There is an issue, though, in terms of distributing excess returns."

The starting point is simple economics. First, says Dr. Ernst von Fischer, are the losses: "People have lost a tremendous amount of money, up to 50 percent. In our lifetime, this is wealth destruction without precedent. No one has experienced anything like this in their lives." The losses are pretty much global, whether investors are in the United States, Germany, or China.

KKR announced a 32-percent drop in the value of its publicly traded fund. Other private equity funds have reported similar results. Private equity purchases, including the $26 billion Hilton deal (Blackstone), the $30.7 billion Harrah's purchase (Apollo and TPG), and the $4.7 billion EMI sale (Terra Firma) are all in trouble—the list goes on and on. Cerebus's $7.4-billion Chrysler rescue package has already been marked down to an estimated $1.4 billion value in late 2009.

The result, says Day, is that many GPs are surrounded by write-downs. "Clearly some GPs are in dire straits. Every GP has problems—some just happen to be more headline companies. Every portfolio has a number of write-offs." With a number of private equity GPs landing on the Forbes' billionaires list, it's not hard to understand why LPs are beginning to question who benefits from their money.

So how are these "excess returns" being distributed? Says Day, "Management fees and transaction fees are very much a hot button. Most LPs will believe that this whole area was significantly abused in the past couple of years." In particular, he says, "GPs should stop charging all monitoring and management fees back to these portfolio companies. If these companies are in dire straits, stop taking out the equity."

Transaction Fees

One sovereign wealth fund says the burning question is this: "How do they use my management fees? The LPs are just up in arms this year. There's a real backlash developing against GPs that have creamed money out of transaction fees and monitoring fees."

In the early days, private equity funds *took* money in the form of their 2-percent management fees, but generally *made* their money on the carry—gains made by listing or selling the company. Fund sizes were also a lot smaller. Then after the stock market crash of 2001–2002, the larger private equity funds began charging for various aspects of the transaction in which they were involved. These include advisory fees, management fees, and straight dividends. On a $100 million fund, the management fee is $2 million. On $88 billion worth of funds, total fees can well exceed $1 billion. At that level, say LPs, why come to work in the morning?

Day thinks it's time to put LPs on the disbursement list. "We want a 100-percent offset on transaction fees." Eakman adds, "There needs to be more governance, certainly more transparency. The total amount of fees that come out of the portfolio companies is pretty amazing. Those fees need to come back to the LPs."

Betty Sheets, senior investment manager, Private Investments at IBM, is equally unhappy. "For starters, there won't be any transaction fees in 2009 because there won't be any deals. But that doesn't mean GPs can't get fees from portfolio companies. They wrote documents that allowed them to do it."

Howard Marks argues that the rewards should follow the returns and not be charged as a matter of right. "Forty years ago, no one I knew got a percentage of profits. That should only be available to exceptional money managers. In the future, managers won't routinely be able to get 2 percent plus 20 percent or 1 percent plus 20 percent. Only the best managers—those who protected their clients during this crisis—should get a piece of the profits." He adds, "As Warren Buffett said, 'When the tide goes out, we find out who has been swimming without a bathing suit.' A small percentage of alternative investment managers will cheer. The rest are likely to have a tougher time raising funds."

Sheets says there are more complications:

> Another issue is, how do you get funding for weak deals in the prior funds? A lot of GPs invested quickly, raised new funds, and now don't have much dry powder [uninvested funds] in the prior fund. A lot of LPs don't want to increase their commitments. There is no good solution. Possibilities could involve GPs having a successor fund invest in the previous fund. Or raising an annex fund or getting a debt facility. Or it could involve recalling prior distributions or having a subset of LPs do the follow-ons. All create issues, especially around valuations.
>
> Then there's the whole issue of clawback liabilities. The GPs did these leveraged recaps. They bought the deal at 6x EBITDA and borrowed 4x. Then the value increased to 8x. So they did a recap and increased the debt to 6x, declared a profit, took 20 percent of it, and send it out. Now, the deal is only worth 4x. But the GP has taken carry that he isn't entitled to in this market and the original cost basis is impaired. They didn't treat it as a return of capital, but as a dividend. Generally, the clawback is only due at the final liquidation of the fund, which is generally long after the termination date. LPs won't want to wait possibly years until the fund is fully liquidated to recoup those dollars.
>
> As GP organizations start falling apart, people who are on the hook are leaving the firms. Will they honor their liabilities? Will LPs even be able to find them? Accountants don't always disclose whether a fund has a clawback liability. Also, most clawbacks are after tax. The

> government has already taken a big chunk in taxes, and it's hard to get it back from them.

Of course, there are those who take a different view. One senior institutional investor said in private, "The fees are egregious, but they occur mostly in the mega-funds. I was never fee-centric. If you're investing, whether the fee is between 1.5 and 2 percent isn't going to make a difference if they return 30 percent. Whether the hurdle is 6 percent, 7 percent, or 8 percent, that's not going to make a difference." But he admits, "Our fund had a strategy of avoiding the mega-funds."

The Denominator Problem

Many LPs find themselves a victim of what the industry has termed "the denominator effect." An institutional investor gives private equity an allocation of funds as a percentage of overall funds available in the institution's bank account. The LP's total assets are the denominator, and different asset classes (including private equity and venture capital) are the numerator. With the denominator shrinking because of the downturn in the public markets and mark-to-market in the private equity portfolio, many LPs found that the numerator had grown too large for specific asset classes; that is, they were overallocated to private equity.

This approach was made popular by David Swensen, chief investment officer at Yale, in his 2000 book *Pioneering Portfolio Investment*. Unfortunately, the public portion of many portfolios declined by 30 to 40 percent, leaving private equity in a disproportionately large position. The fact that private equity and venture portfolios have also fallen, thereby reducing the numerator, hasn't helped much: as many institutions count on their endowments for operating cash, these investments are illiquid. Hence the need to sell private equity assets or go to the debt markets to borrow. By definition, LPs will have less to go around to GPs.

Where Are the LPs in All of This?

With all these issues hanging in the air, one might think the LPs are ready to strike. The answer, though, is "Maybe yes, maybe no." They are, they have, but . . . For starters, LPs are a disparate group. They generally don't talk with one another except at a fund's annual meeting. They come from different countries and different time zones and have different investment profiles. For those who have won access to top GPs' funds—access that may have taken years to achieve—the last thing they want is a fight with the GP.

As Sheryl Schwartz, managing director, Alternative Investments at TIAA-CREF, says, LPs have different strategies and priorities. "LPs have always tried to address these issues. However, everyone has different issues that are important to them. One institution may be focused on fees, another on co-investments, and another on reducing the carry. LPs have different priorities, which limits their ability to get together. Every negotiation is a trade-off."

Schwartz believes that private equity "is a permanent part of the landscape and capital structure. A lot of LPs are having liquidity issues, because they assumed certain things in their models that didn't happen. For most LPs, the duration of their assets and liabilities must match. Therefore, I think that, for most LPs, having an allocation of 40 percent to illiquid assets won't work."

Dr. von Fischer concedes that most likely the LPs will be reluctant to act. "There are certainly more concerns, yes. Will we be more vocal? I don't know." He says that in China, for example, "because things were better than elsewhere, so far questions are less existential."

The CEO at Harald Quandt Holding, Fritz Becker, agrees: "There's more public speech than action. There will be pressure in the near term, but LPs are willing to pay high fees if there are returns." The problem, he says, is that "a lot of fees are charged with no results."

Joncarlo Mark, senior portfolio manager at the California Public Employees' Retirement System (CalPERS), feels that LPs will become more active as GPs invest in different types of deals.

> Over the last few years, a number of buyout firms have raised significant amounts of capital—much more than ever before. Given the dislocation in the market and the absence of leverage, there are questions on how this capital will be invested. We are already seeing GPs doing all-equity deals, including the purchase of public equity or quasi-public equity (PIPEs). In addition, many firms have opportunistically purchased debt securities, where the risk/reward characteristics met private equity return expectations or where the GP was able to take control of the company through debt purchases in the secondary market. It is unclear how all these deals will work out, but institutional investors will have to decide whether to limit such nontraditional deals or let the GPs be more opportunistic.

Dr. von Fischer observes that GPs have become more solicitous of their LPs: "All our questions are answered more fully now, and in a much friendlier manner." Walden International founder and chairman Lip-Bu Tan notes that GPs are truly working quite hard: "On our side, we're very focused on operations, cash flow, and monitoring our companies very tightly."

The question remains, how patient should LPs be in what looks to be a very difficult environment? Pennsylvania State Employee Retirement System's director of alternative investments, Bruce Feldman, says that going forward, if limited partners are smart, "they will try to negotiate more LP friendly terms in partnership agreements and side-letters."

Betty Sheets, who attended the March 2009 International Limited Partner Association (ILPA) conference, believes that "some LPs are saying something about terms. My sense is that they will live with the terms they negotiated unless GPs come back for changes. If GPs come back for relief on other terms, LPs will be pressing to make changes."

Wim Borgdorff of AlpInvest Partners asks,

> Will anything change? We've seen grumpiness before with investors, but when push comes to shove, at the end of the day, private equity is a capital-intensive activity. So funding is an important part of value chain, but it is subject to supply and demand. Short term, we are in a phase where there's disappointment, discontent, a level of disbelief of what people thought they were into and what they did get delivered for outcome. People are looking at a portfolio: under-invested in good times, overinvested in bad times. 2006 and 2007 will prove historically very low-performing vintages. That will trigger a lot of questions on the whole governance of limited partnership arrangement. Current arrangements have been very much, "You give us the money at inception, and we give it back to you when we're done." People will start investigating how to be more involved and protected along the way.
>
> Another area is compensation. I think that core values center around creating better companies, operationally improving their businesses, and creating better alignment between investor and management. There's sentiment that this alignment should get a little stronger, while compensation mechanisms, when returns are real, still generate substantial wealth. We think fees should be there to take care of realistic expense so that people are able to cover basic cost of operating.
>
> But we've seen this supply-demand dynamic before. You could see the economy reboot very quickly, and then this negative sentiment could dissipate quickly. But we expect a very slow environment, in which an economy will go sideways. There will be more time to discuss these issues.

Ultimately, the LPs are masters of their own fate. Martin Day concludes, "Smart investors have overextended themselves, and others have way overextended themselves; that won't stop LPs from investing." Today's buzzwords are "distressed" and "secondaries." The pension funds have money and are still looking to invest. Asian-focused funds have been particularly successful, but U.S. and European funds also raised new money in 2009.

"Most LPs don't see major changes, but the environment is clearly different," says Day. "I believe that LPs will recover and continue to support the industry. I don't think there will be dramatic decreases in allocations."

Fritz Becker says that those who haven't performed will not be able to raise their next fund. "I don't think there will be a major change. But a lot of teams won't be able to raise new funds."

Lindel Eakman thinks the new environment could improve the industry. "GPs and LPs will have deeper relationships. GPs want to know that their investors are good for the capital and understand the risks of the asset class." He adds, "LPs will still make commitments and put money to work."

What is certain, though, is that LPs were shocked by the downdraft. Daniel Mintz, founding managing director of Olympus Capital, thinks that LPs "are getting more real about understanding GPs business models, and focusing on where they are aligned with their GPs, and where there are misalignments in the incentives and fee structures. Now, investors are asking, why am I in this asset class? What metrics do I use to ensure I am achieving my objectives and getting paid adequately for making a long-term, illiquid commitment? How do I match the nature of capital with the nature of the investment opportunities?"

One institutional investor, who prefers to remain anonymous, notes, "Funds were really demand driven, and that whole relationship and equation has to change. Now, LPs are more willing to go to GPs to mitigate stresses; for example, capital calls and management fees. LPs will be a lot more demanding, and it's in the interest of GPs to see how they can accommodate the LPs."

Lip-Bu Tan also calls for better relationships between the parties. "The GPs and LPs have to work much more closely in this difficult economic environment. This is a time when LPs have to have more patience and continue to support GPs."

One senior institutional investor, speaking privately, is more cynical and sees little change. "We lived through the 2001, 2002, and 2003 meltdown. All of the LPs said that we are going to cut fees, cut carry, and be on a level field. That never happened. They will just raise less money. The LPs will be their own worst enemies. The GPs will cut the size of their funds to create scarcity—or the illusion of scarcity—and hold terms. The S&P recovered dramatically in 2003, and private equity went with it."

Philip Bilden thinks that private equity fundraising for mega-funds has probably peaked out. "Industry professionals often overlook the fact that private equity and venture capital have a market structure that cannot be divorced from the laws of economics—notably supply and demand. Like other mature industries, we now have overcapacity in a trillion-dollar asset class. Suboptimal players across the whole food chain—advisers, consultants, fund-of-funds, fund managers, service providers, conference organizers, and intermediaries—will need to fight for survival and relevance in a bloated industry structure."

In any event, says Richard Slocum, director of private investments at the Robert Wood Johnson Foundation, LPs are watching their money more carefully. "With their cash commitments, some large foundations, endowments, and pensions are borrowing money now and are being very careful in managing their liquidity positions."

Venture Capital: Waiting for a "Netscape Moment"?

With fundraising stymied, exit gates shut, and distributions to limited partners virtually nonexistent, the venture world is asking, "What's next?" As Dick Kramlich, general partner and cofounder of New Enterprise Associates (NEA), puts it, "How do we get out of this morass? It will take a 'Netscape moment': an emerging company with a technology that is so arresting, that has been proven, and is in an early phase of growth. Then an underwriter who says, 'This will be a big company.'" But Kramlich and others also say that although the future looks promising, there are more than a few clouds on the horizon.

WHAT'S DIFFERENT NOW

Why will venture change? Simply put, the industry faces a new investment landscape and a number of challenges that require different answers from those in the past.

Sutter Hill Ventures managing director Len Baker says conditions were right in the 1970s for venture capital's growth. "I started in venture in 1973, when the business was still in the process of developing structurally. It was adapted for a particular set of conditions in Silicon Valley: capital was plentiful, and it was fairly cheap to start companies. Technology was moving very fast, but it was susceptible to venture financing. Then we had a big bull market beginning in 1983."

Gary Rieschel also makes an important point: "Another reason for the VC success is that in the early days, the partners were all investing in what they were good at before they got into venture. That has changed, with green tech and alternative energy now the center of attention."

But then the industry looked up, and voila—there was the dot-com explosion. Fortunes were made, but it was also the beginning of the end. One reason, says Len Baker, is that investment was driven by fund allocations, not industry needs. "The 'Yale model' of asset allocation generated capital flows that were driven by asset allocation theory, not investment opportunities. The result was that too much capital got directed toward 'alternative assets': hedge funds, real estate, private equity, and venture capital. Of these asset classes, the one least equipped to absorb excess capital is venture capital. The excess capital flows into venture capital were bailed out by the bubble and the fact that technology was permanently overvalued in the bull markets between 1983 and 2007."

In fact, Baker's thesis is supported by a paper that Paul Kedrosky wrote for the Kauffmann Foundation in June 2009.[8] Kedrosky writes, "The venture industry's current returns are already challenged and set to become considerably worse. In 2003, the five-year trailing performance of the venture industry was more than 20 percent, and it had never been negative back to 1990. That changed, however, in 2004, as the dot-com collapse caused five-year venture capital performance to dip below zero, touching –2.4 percent and –6.7 percent in 2004 and 2005 respectively."

Why the change? Kedrosky explains,

> There are at least three possible reasons, all interrelated. There could be too much capital allocated to venture, the effect being higher valuations and lower exit multiples. The second explanation might be shrinking exit markets, with, for example, the decline in IPOs preventing venture investors from earning the same returns as they have historically. Finally, it is possible that the venture business might be structurally flawed.
>
> With its core information-technology area maturing and becoming less capital-intensive due to declining costs and overseas manufacturing, and with exit markets less willing to take on young and unprofitable companies, it becomes clear that the real question for venture is one of capital. . . . A five-fold increase in venture capital commitments by limited partners led to a collapse in performance from which the sector has never recovered.

The results have not been good, says Baker. "Returns for the asset class—even the top quartile—have all been single digits. Some of the best firms had funds that were bailed out by a single deal." (That, incidentally, was the Google IPO in 2004.) NEA managing director Peter Barris agrees that venture capital "never recovered from the 2001–2002 market crash. The single largest issue for the venture industry since the Internet boom and bust is that we haven't returned a lot of capital. The macro distributions have been small. There are a lot of questions about the anemic IPO industry. We were starting to come out of it, when the IPO door slammed shut in early 2008. Then it became sealed in the third quarter."

One conclusion is a strategic shift in how the industry sees itself—or should see itself. Structurally, the industry was built to deliver semiconductor, then computer, then Internet technology. That it did, but then it went overboard in the dot-com bubble. Gary Bridge, managing director of Horsley Bridge Partners, says the dot-com era spending was ultimately the death knell for the industry:

> What happened in 2000 was more of an "internal to the VC industry" phenomenon. The people in our industry had too much money, and as a result they went on a huge spending binge, fueled by LPs flush with money to be put to work. In retrospect, professionals were investing in many ideas with no hope of real success. The Internet sector was the first area to feel the pain from this binge. There were some good companies formed during this period, but they were overwhelmed by too many me-too companies that couldn't get revenue traction. Soon after that, the telecommunications bubble burst. This sector had only a handful of giant companies able to buy or integrate the entire product being developed by hundreds of new companies being formed to serve them. As the market retrenched, these giants cut spending meaningfully, and the smaller companies went out of business very quickly.
>
> I don't think we'll see acceptable returns as an industry for another five years. That means we won't have had acceptable returns for 14 years. Investors have already become skeptical about the return parameters of this industry and that skepticism will become even more pronounced. A minority of the VC firms will be able to earn positive returns, some earning very acceptable returns. Where will these companies formed in the last nine years go? Some will be able to go public; some will cease to exist, be acquired cheaply, or become the "living dead." I am afraid that the positive outcomes won't carry enough weight to provide the industry as a whole with acceptable returns.

By the time venture began to recover from the 2001–2002 crash, the world had changed. The original *Red Herring*, the Valley's must-read magazine, closed its doors in March 2003. China and India were on the rise, and venture's old saw about "never doing a deal more than 50 miles from the office" no longer worked as the Valley beat a hasty path to Asia.

Exits are also different. Alan Patricof says, "Our exit strategy is sale to another company. We don't invest any longer with the idea of taking a company public. It helps to condition yourself to realistic exits. Our exits will be strategic. I can't say that others have accepted that. There just isn't a public market today." Of course, the dearth of IPO exits could be temporary, a function of today's economy.

Other factors have also played a role, says Patricof. "The underwriters that took us public are gone. All the small market makers and research people are gone. We've had a fundamental change in the way our business is operating now. We're in a private market. We will sell our companies through M&A transactions."

Never say never, but Patricof is simply stating a fact. Len Baker agrees: "The IPO market as we know and love it will not come back."

Without exits, and with constraints on working capital, portfolio companies are hunkering down. Lip-Bu Tan says, "It's important to be capital efficient. Most venture guys are focused on their portfolio. We used to see valuation markups of 2x to 2.5x from prior rounds. Nowadays, it is not easy to get a markup in subsequent financing rounds in this market. But if the portfolio company is solid, you can still close a Series B round at a markup from the Series A valuation." He continues, "We are now going through a phase, 'doing better with less.' It's very important to be patient. A lot of industries will go through consolidation. In addition, providing value-add to portfolio companies is important. It's crucial to stay focused on quality, hands-on management."

Tan has taken his own advice. He was recently named CEO of Cadence Design Systems, where he can more closely focus on the company's products for fabless semiconductor companies.

Strategic Investors

At the same time, strategic corporate investors with large cash reserves have grown in importance. Says Intel Capital's president, Arvind Sodhani, "Corporates who invest from their balance sheets don't have the dynamics of the LP situation. We are investing globally and supporting companies in their needs. Remember that most of the GPs in China and India raised their capital from U.S. and European LPs. There are plenty of LPs who have made it known, 'Don't come to us for funding.' Those portfolio companies will come to us because we are able to finance. Everything in the economic environment suggests that it won't change much for the rest of the year."

Sodhani emphasizes, "If we are making an investment, we are doing it for strategic reasons. We have a very strict financial filter to make sure that that the portfolio company we're investing in will be a financially successful and viable company."

He says the company's strategy is "to promote technology innovation and entrepreneurship around the world so that more people will use bigger and faster microprocessors and other Intel products. Going forward, I don't see much change in our investment style. We are investing in all of the big, important countries. We tend to be local investors. We have a hundred investment professionals in 26 countries, and half of our investments are outside the United States."

Fewer, Smaller Firms

Gary Bridge agrees that the changes will affect the industry's professionals. He says, "The old-guard GPs are transitioning out, and many of the continuing professionals have never tasted success. Even a GP with 10 years of experience may not have had real success yet. That must be discouraging to some. One wonders if some VCs will be prepared to stay in the industry and mentor their younger professionals."

Many funds will disappear, and they will be fewer and smaller in size. Says Patricof,

> There will also be a trend toward smaller funds that can make good money, not in absolute returns, but the IRRs may be better. Holding periods may be shorter. The grand slam will be rare, but we can see ourselves doing doubles and triples.
>
> I envision a world going forward with more, smaller funds. Even though the multiple will be greater, the absolute number of dollars from any one fund will be less than we have seen in the past. For example, if a $150 million fund goes up four times, the profit is $450 million. If a $500 million fund doubles, it produces a profit of $500 million. At the same time, I believe there will be smaller, more frequent realizations in shorter time periods. So the IRRs will do better.

Given the downturn, Ted Schlein, managing partner, Kleiner Perkins Caufield & Byers, warns, "You want your portfolio companies to be managed carefully. A lot of these CEOs were around in 2000–2001. They get it. They have to be prudent: cash is king, so make sure you have enough money to get through."

A New Investment Profile

How will the industry adapt to this new environment? Says Len Baker, "What does venture do? It shrinks." Beyond that, Dr. Ta-lin Hsu, founder and chairman of H&Q Asia Pacific, speaks humorously but says the industry must develop new skill sets. "U.S. venture capitalists are becoming more like Chinese venture capitalists. If you are a VC doing business in China, you can't just focus on your technology. You have to find out from the government what land is available and what the tax rate is. You need to meet the mayors or governors. If you don't know the government's position on the issues with which you are concerned, you're in trouble. In the United States, technology ventures relating to clean energy and climate control require knowledge of government policy. That has fundamentally changed venture capital."

The industry also should look at new investment areas. Clean tech and alternative energy have gained traction. Ted Schlein says that 45 percent of the firm's investments are in the green tech area. "We have 40 to 45 different green tech investments: new types of fuels, new energy-generating efficiencies. There's a very good alternative energy environment. The policy in Washington is supportive. The culture and climate are on."

Others are more cautious. Says one general partner, "John Doerr has gone wild on alternative energy. But does he have his politics mixed up with his investing?" Doerr is a pretty savvy investor, so maybe he's on to something. Kleiner Perkins is currently raising several annex funds to support investments in previously closed funds.

Joncarlo Mark thinks that areas such as alternative energy, mobile platforms, and the life sciences will see great innovations ahead. "Venture is about investing in innovation. Take clean tech. The political willpower is there to push for new types of energy, new materials, recycling, and better resource management. So if there's some new technology, that's something for venture to do." In a *New York Times* interview, Vinod Khosla, founder of Khosla Ventures, points out: "Clean-tech companies taking large amounts of money—that's project finance, not technical risk. That's a differentiation most people have lost."

Len Baker, however, argues the other side: "The nature of investment opportunities in clean tech doesn't fit the venture model. They tend to be capital-intensive, require long-term financing, and depend on government subsidies or government rule-setting. So the question is, can you imagine the best type of institution to make these investments?"

Gary Bridge also questions many of today's investments. "Nobody knows what the next big thing will be. Some clean-tech, green-tech companies will be big companies. Solar seems to be an overplayed area. In the

Internet space, I'd say no to Web 2.0. It is hard to see what hasn't been invested in during the last two to three years. The bottom line, though, is you never know what will come along to bolster the industry returns."

Fundamentally, though, the business model has changed. Says Gary Reischel, "Where venture succeeds is, can something be done to a reasonable milestone with a reasonable amount of money? Can we get to a prototype, first silicon for $5 million? If you need much more than $10 million, it's a problem. For clean tech, there's nothing that you can prove for under $40 to $50 million. There's an awful lot of companies that have raised $5 or $10 million, but can't raise the additional capital.

"The software license model used to be a good package for VCs," he says. "You get some money up front and build the company. But software as a service model is a much harder model to fund as a venture capitalist. You don't get that license model revenue. VCs really thrive when you can get a technology into the market and then build the hell out of it."

In the chapters ahead, this book will look further into new investment ideas as well as Asian and European venture capital.

IN CLOSING

The private equity and venture capital worlds of 2009 were tough ones for just about everyone. Despite large-scale government action, the U.S. and European economies wallowed in a widening trough, while Asian economies moved forward, albeit at a slower pace. Though certain indices improved, structural issues in the U.S. banking industry, LP-funded venture capital, and consumer spending were barely addressed. Dedicated cost cutting meant continued unemployment. Banks reported earnings but remained reluctant to lend. Private equity was cashed up, but there was no credit and deal prices remained elusive. LPs finally had to face a number of issues, from low returns to overreaching on fees. Says Dick Kramlich, "One of the misconceptions is that venture is a lifestyle business. It's not. It's a very intense and difficult industry."

What does 2010 look like? The next chapter tells the tale.

CHAPTER 4

2010: Private Equity and Venture League Tables and Niches

Teo Ming Kian, formerly chairman of Singapore's Economic Development Board and permanent secretary at Singapore's Ministry of Finance at the time of this writing, says, "Globally, the private equity industry is confronted with several challenges during this global financial crisis. These include the lack of credit, downward pressure on returns, battered equity markets, and difficult fundraising environment. Given the challenges, limited partners may also struggle or fail to meet capital calls, limiting the ability of private equity firms to make investments. As leverage disappears, there is also a reversion to classical private equity where there is a greater focus on operational value-add rather than financial engineering skills."

He adds, "The future of private equity is not completely depressing. The poorer economic conditions have significantly brought down market valuations creating many attractive investment opportunities, including in Asia. While mega deals have for now disappeared from the scene as a result of the credit constraints, deals in the mid-sized and growth area are still possible. Despite the challenging environment, we must also remember that the private equity asset class has consistently outperformed public markets in the last two decades." Mr. Teo sums up today's financial world nicely.

THE 2010 ECONOMY (BRIEFLY)

Anil Thadani says,

> The first signal of recovery will come from the United States. The problem was created in the U.S., by a combination of innovation and

> greed—greed that energized the creativity. There was no value being created, but it was like a game of musical chairs. However, having created the problem, the U.S. is best at facing up to it and wiping the slate clean. Europeans and Asians are hung up by a sense of history. The U.S. is best at saying, 'Let's wipe the slate clean, and let's start over.' Others see China leading the way, with much milder versions of the downturn in Australia and the Asian countries also creating opportunity there.

Indeed, the U.S. numbers had begun to turn around during summer 2009, including home sales, some credit markets, and the manufacturing index. But Asian figures had already turned positive, and European statistics also indicated a bounce back. "The consensus view is that we will see a very gradual recovery," says Peter Cornelius.

Steve Byrom, however, thinks that the economy is in for a long recovery period. "The risk is that we're looking at a structural deleveraging cycle that may take years to play out. The forecast deleveraging required in 2011–2014 makes 2008 look like a minnow in the pond." He continues, "This recession may be quite different from the previous recessions, as the consumer doesn't seem to have a strong position this time around. The consumer seems to be losing a lot of wealth here, getting hit hard."

Scott Sandell, general partner at NEA, is equally cautious. "The economy, both in the United States and globally, is enjoying an unprecedented amount of government-funded stimulus. This stimulus will eventually diminish, and when it does, the economy may not return to growth. Much depends on whether the massive amount of debt currently held by governments, businesses, and households is written down to levels that can be supported by a smaller economy. If it is not, it will hamper the economy going forward, much like what happened in Japan during the 1990s."

The world's economies will need time to recalibrate from the widespread write-downs, plunge in orders, and credit contraction. As Stephen Roach has observed, ultimately the Main Street economy is a function of consumer demand in the United States. As consumers cut back on spending amid rising unemployment, businesses reduce their inventories to compensate for falling revenues. Rebuilding these inventories will create jobs. But judging when and to what extent that will happen is not clear.

With high unemployment, the shift in spending habits may be permanent, at least for the next several years. According to the Bureau of Economic Analysis, the personal savings rate as a percentage of disposable income increased to 6.9 percent in May before falling back to 3.3 percent in September. That was an improvement from the previous year, when the rate was near zero. The *New York Times* reported, "This happens in most recessions, but this time it could be different." Why? Because the easy credit terms of the past seem to be gone. Americans have also lost a large amount of the value of their savings in retirement plans as well. Add those savings to the eventual end of the stimulus programs, and the impact on the economy will be large.

In Europe, the story is not much different. France and Germany reported slight increases (0.3 percent) in GDP growth in the second quarter of 2009, though still well below the prior year's levels. Other European countries including England, Spain, and Italy still reported negative GDP growth. Asia, however, seems to be in much better shape, with countries reporting positive GDP growth in the third quarter 2009: China 8.9 percent, Japan 4.8 percent, and India 5.3 percent.

Harjit Bhatia, managing partner and head of Credit Suisse Private Equity Asia, thinks consumer demand in India will continue for such basic industries as housing and food, but says the luxury segment will face a difficult time. "India doesn't have adequate roads, but they're selling high-end Mercedes and Audis. You can expect limited demand."

THE PRIVATE EQUITY AND VENTURE CAPITAL WORLDS TODAY

As markets find a new equilibrium in the post-recovery world, private equity and venture capital will inhabit a large space. This can be categorized by size, focus, and location. Additionally, the limited partners can also be divided into groups depending on the source of funds: pension funds, endowments, and sovereign wealth funds. Finally, there are the debt providers, namely the banks and mezzanine funds.

This book discusses the private equity and venture worlds using league tables, which rank and compare the firms by dollar fund size. These tables are a useful if not definitive statement of how firms are doing within each category. That is, if a firm has raised more money, presumably that occurs because investors have applauded their past performance and reinvested. This is not always the case, though, particularly in 2007–2009. During that period, fund managers quickly raised follow-on funds based on what the market would bear, not necessarily on realized returns. Depending on the funds' success over the next several years, this gap may well come back to haunt the general partners.

In the tables throughout this chapter, "AUM" stands for "assets under management." Many of the firms actually manage more assets; for example, The Carlyle Group has $86.1 billion and KKR has $50.8 billion total assets under management (respectively) as of summer 2009. These figures refer only to private equity funds.

TABLE 4.1 The 10 Largest U.S. Private Equity Firms

Rank	Firm Name	Region	AUM (USD billions)
1	TPG	U.S.	39.6
2	The Carlyle Group	U.S.	33.6
3	Kohlberg Kravis & Roberts	U.S.	32.6
4	Blackstone Group	U.S.	32.1
5	Warburg	U.S.	29.1
6	Goldman Sachs	U.S.	26.1
7	Apollo Management	U.S.	23.8
8	Bain Capital	U.S.	21.3
9	Advent International	U.S.	17
10	Providence	U.S.	12.6

Source: Preqin (December 2008).

Private Equity Firms

The global firms shown in Table 4.1 are the ones that the press likes to cover and people like to talk about. David Rubenstein was featured in the book *The Iron Triangle: Inside the Secret World of the Carlyle Group*; Henry Kravis was the involuntary star of the indy movie *The War on Greed, Starring the Homes of Henry Kravis*; Steve Schwarzman, whose 60th birthday party at New York City's Armory, "now enters the short list of hot blowouts of New York history" (Liz Smith); and David Bonderman, whose own 60th birthday party featured the Rolling Stones and carried a bigger price tag than Schwarzman's—he just held it out of town (in Las Vegas). Yet they and other GPs work hard and are successful. They are charitable. Rubenstein paid $21.3 million for a copy of the Magna Carta and then gave it to the National Archives; Kravis gives to a long list of urban charities, Bonderman to an outdoors group; and Schwarzman, who will have his name sandblasted into the New York Public Library's main entrance, gave $100 million to the institution.

The European buyout houses (see Table 4.2) are virtually all in London, with exceptions in Stockholm and Paris. Less flamboyant than their American counterparts, they have done major deals across the continent. Peter Cornelius says that the European firms have made great strides at home. "Prior to the crisis, U.S. private equity firms were very successful in penetrating foreign markets. Conversely, European private equity firms have yet to show that they can compete successfully outside of their home market. That said, European firms have been playing catch-up in their home market, where they have been expanding rapidly over the past two decades."

TABLE 4.2 The 11 Largest European Private Equity Firms

Rank	Firm Name	Region	AUM (USD billions)
1	CVC Capital Partners	U.K.	28.3
2	Apax Partners	U.K.	16.9
3	Bridgepoint Capital	U.K.	10.7
4	Permira	U.K.	10.7
5	PAI partners	France	9.9
6	Charterhouse Capital Partners	U.K.	8.9
7	BC Partners	U.K.	8.8
8	Cinven	U.K.	7.6
9	EQT Partners	Sweden	7.5
10	Nordic Capital	Sweden	7.5
11	3i	U.K.	6.2

Source: Preqin (December 2008).

Joncarlo Mark says that the middle market firms (see Table 4.3) occupy an important place in the market. "There will always be a need for smaller, middle market firms, focused on sub-$1 billion deals. The market is competitive, but financing is more available. It is less subject to the ebbs and flows of the overall financial markets. It's also a necessary component of these markets. Entrepreneurs need capital for growth. Other sources of capital may not be viable for family businesses, where succession is important."

Carl Ferenbach lists his criteria for a successful investment: "What we would define as a good company is one with a capable, focused management team, that has real barriers to entry, has limited exposure to disruptive technology or events, and which has balanced relationships with those that supply and demand." These criteria for a successful middle market deal sound similar to those of the mega firms.

TABLE 4.3 The 5 Largest U.S. Private Equity "Middle Market" Firms

Rank	Firm Name	Region	AUM (USD billions)
1	Hellman & Friedman	U.S.	16.4
2	Thomas H. Lee Partners	U.S.	12
3	Madison Dearborn Partners	U.S.	11.9
4	Silver Lake	U.S.	11.5
5	TA Associates	U.S.	8.8

Source: Preqin (December 2008).

TABLE 4.4 The 15 Largest Asian/Australian Private Equity Firms

Rank	Firm Name	Region	AUM (USD millions)
1	Carlyle Asia	U.S.	9,270.50
2	Kohlberg Kravis Roberts & Co.	U.S.	8,000.00
3	CVC Asia Pacific	U.K.	6,924.00
4	TPG Capital	U.S.	6,866.00
5	Pacific Equity Partners	Australia	4,654.20
6	Cerberus Capital	U.S.	4,562.00
7	Unitas Capital	U.S.	3,890.00
8	AIG Investment Corporation	U.S.	3,799.00
9	Avenue Capital	U.S.	3,728.00
10	Affinity Equity Partners	Hong Kong	3,500.00
11	Goldman Sachs	U.S.	3,300.00
12	Hopu Investment	China (PRC)	3,231.40
13	Advantage Partners	Japan	2,946.10
14	Hony Capital	China (PRC)	2,859.30
15	CDH Investments Management	Hong Kong	2,744.70

Note: This list excludes real estate and global funds with a focus on Asia.

Source: AVCJ Group, Ltd., as of June 30, 2009.

The Asian private equity community is increasingly broad and diverse (see Table 4.4). It comprises the global funds that have come to Asia as well as GPs spread across the continent. Maarten Ruijs says, "The scale of the issues is a lot smaller than elsewhere. Also, there's a lot more diversity here: you have many different markets that are in different stages of development. In general, companies are less geared [have borrowed less money]. Performance should be slightly better."

Jean Salata also observes that most Asian deals are not highly leveraged. "The good thing about Asian private equity is that relatively small amounts of debt have been involved here." But KY Tang notes that this hasn't made the banks any more generous. "Today, banks have the liquidity, but they don't have the appetite for risk. You can't get approval from the credit committees because they are working out their existing non-performing loans."

Andrew Liu says his investment focus is on consumer demand. "If we invest in China, Australia, or anywhere, eventually the export market will return. In the meantime, we're focusing on companies that cater to domestic consumption. If you look at statistics, they are still in favor of Asia." But the losses, he feels, will be less: "The countries, populations, the banks themselves are in better shape. A few years ago, one of the titans was predicting the demise of the local firms. In fact, now we are seeing a retrenchment of the global firms. They are pulling back to focus on their home markets."

According to AVCJ Group, Ltd., there were some 486 private equity and venture firms in China as of June 1, 2009. Total assets under management as of the same date were $38.6 billion. One of the biggest stories is the development of *renminbi* (RMB) funds: funds denominated by restricted local Chinese currency. (*Renminbi* literally translates as "the people's money.") Initially, the government supported two funds, CDH and Hony. Sources in China indicate that another four to six venture funds are also under consideration for government funding, including CITIC Capital, IDG, and New Horizons. "RMB funds are one of the irreversible trends," says Tina Ju, founding managing partner of KPCB China. "They are new but permanent."

AVCJ reports that India has 198 private equity funds with $26.1 billion in assets under management. There are also a number of venture funds, though they are not large. Ashish Dhawan, managing director at ChrysCapital, says the policies of the newly elected (2009) government will tell the tale. "India is capital-starved and needs technology. My sense is that we will have a government that looks well on private capital. It's friendly capital. India won't have any blowups or bankruptcies during the downturn. I think it will be viewed in friendly terms."

Hong Kong, which does most of its business in China, reported $54.4 billion in assets under management. Singapore is home to a number of hedge funds, but leading private equity investors include the government-linked GIC and Temasek. Singapore reported $13.5 billion in assets under management. Its government has been very proactive. (Read on for more about this.)

Even Malaysia has responded to the downturn. In July 2009, the country's prime minister announced new reforms to spur investment. A change in the *bumiputra* laws, which required ethnic Malay investors to hold a combined 30-percent stake in listed companies, reduced that requirement to 12.5 percent. The government reduced the powers of the Foreign Investment Committee, which has been blamed for the lengthy approval process required for foreign investments. Said Prime Minister Razak, "The world is changing quickly and we must be ready to change with it or risk being left behind."

Japan had $38.6 billion in assets under management, and Taiwan, $5.6 billion in assets.

Venture Capital Firms

The U.S. venture capital community is split between the East Coast and West Coast, with not a lot in between (see Table 4.5). These are the largest groups in the U.S., though there are many others who are active and

TABLE 4.5 The 10 Largest U.S. Venture Capital Firms

Rank	Firm Name	Fund Size (USD Millions)	Location
1	Warburg Pincus LLC	7,670.0	New York
2	Technology Crossover Ventures (aka: TCV)	7,420.9	Palo Alto, CA
3	New Enterprise Associates	7,404.7	Menlo Park, CA
4	Oak Investment Partners	7,315.0	Menlo Park, CA
5	Sequoia Capital	5,673.0	Menlo Park, CA
6	Accel Partners	4,884.2	Menlo Park, CA
7	VantagePoint Venture Partners	4,059.2	San Bruno, CA
8	The Carlyle Group	3,852.2	New York
9	J.H. Whitney & Co. LLC	3,796.8	New York
10	Kleiner Perkins Caufield & Byers	3,750.2	Menlo Park, CA

Source: National Venture Capital Association and Thomson Reuters (2008).

investing. Venture capital in the U.S. has been discussed in the previous chapter and throughout the book. European and Asian venture capital are discussed separately in the following sections.

Europe remains a difficult place for venture capital (see Table 4.6). In her 2003 book, *Smarter Ventures*, Katherine Campbell lays out several reasons for this, many cultural. William Stevens, formerly secretary general at EVCA and now celebrating 10 years as CEO at Europe Unlimited, believes the limited potential for success rather than the risk of failure is the reason. "In terms of the culture, it's not so much risk taking, but the chance for winning. Raising 200 million euros on the stock exchange is very difficult. If you don't have this success potential, why would you want to become one of the sleeping dead in a portfolio company? The problem is less cultural, more structural. For example, biotech seems better. There are many more top university professors who are willing to become a CTO of a biotech company. In those markets, where there have been IPOs, you see it happening. You can also see it happening in clean tech: it's in the U.S., but also in Europe."

As the numbers suggest, Asian venture capital is a very modest industry—its greatest potential lies ahead (see Table 4.7). The industry has been hurt by the financial crisis, but less so than others have been. Until 10 years ago, the term "Asian venture capital" was largely a misnomer—it did not really exist. The Asian market was dominated by minority investing through private equity firms. This was changed by the growth of software programming in India and the replication of U.S. ventures successes in China. Japan has been a leader in well-designed and manufactured consumer electronics, Korea has built the standard for flat-screen technology,

TABLE 4.6 The 12 Largest European Venture Capital Firms

Rank	Firm Name	Fund Size (USD Millions)	Location
1	PAI partners	6,400.60	Paris
2	Apax Partners Worldwide	4,183.20	London
3	Terra Firma Capital Partners, Ltd.	2,685.50	London
4	MacQuarie's Infrastructure and Specialised Funds Division	2,535.00	Australia
5	Index Ventures Management SA	2,096.40	London
6	Henderson Equity Partners (aka: Henderson Private Capital)	1,732.70	London
7	Park Square Capital, LLP	1,681.90	London
8	Benchmark Capital	1,425.00	U.S.
9	Inventages Venture Capital S.A.	1,342.20	Switzerland
10	SGAM Private Equity (aka: Societe Generale Asset Management)	1,308.20	Paris
11	Sofinnova Partners	1,267.20	Paris
12	Edmond de Rothschild Investment Partners	1,243.20	Paris

Source: National Venture Capital Association and Thomson Reuters (2008).

TABLE 4.7 The 16 Largest Asian/Australian Venture Capital Firms

Rank	Company Name	Nationality	Total Capital under Management (USD millions)
1	JAFCO	Japan	5,875.00
2	Sequoia Capital	United States	3,061.30
3	SBI Investment	Japan	2,457.20
4	H&Q Asia Pacific	United States	2,197.40
5	Daiwa SMBC Capital Asia	Japan	2,038.00
6	IDG Ventures	United States	1,930.00
7	KTB Securities	South Korea	1,312.00
8	JAIC Asia	Japan	1,299.00
9	VinaCapital	Vietnam	909.10
10	Suzhou Ventures Group	China (PRC)	731.40
11	Matrix Partners	United States	725.00
12	ORIX Capital	Japan	714.90
13	Kotak Investment Advisors	India	705.00
14	GSR Ventures	China (PRC)	700.00
15	Tokio Marine Capital	Japan	683.00
16	Legend Capital	China (PRC)	683.00

Note: List excludes real estate and global funds with a focus on Asia.

Source: AVCJ Group, Ltd., as of June 30, 2009.

and Taiwan has been a leader in chip manufacturing. Online gaming and SMS messaging have proven successful throughout all of North Asia. In time, no doubt, innovative solutions to technology problems will also emerge as the industry matures and continues to build its own "Silicon Valley" infrastructure.

Tina Ju says that in the near term, China's ability to bounce back after the downturn will be most important. "I am very optimistic about the long-term prospects for the private equity and venture capital industry in China. In the near term, however, a lot depends on the sustainability of the recovery into the second half of 2009. Until we see that the recovery is sustainable, I will remain cautiously optimistic."

Middle East

The Middle East is home to a nascent private equity and venture industry (see Table 4.8). Middle East private equity fund managers raised a record $6.4 billion in 2008, up more than 10 percent over 2007 and more than double the amount raised in 2005, according to the Gulf Venture Capital Association's (GVCA) 2008 annual report. Large funds are primarily responsible for this growth, with the average fund size in 2008 being $258 million, compared with $213 million in 2007 and just $177 million in 2006. This trend is driven by the need for more flexibility in structuring deals and the past success of large buyout transactions. Three regional funds have crossed the $1 billion mark, and, as the report notes, the current

TABLE 4.8 The 10 Largest Middle East Funds

Rank	Firm Name	Fund Size (USD Billions)	Location
1	Abraaj Capital	5.03	Dubai
2	Global Capital Management Limited	2.17	Bahrain
3	Investcorp	1.10	Abu Dhabi
4	Swicorp	1.01	Dubai
5	Emerging Markets Partnership (Bahrain)	0.98	Bahrain
6	Gulf Capital	0.81	Abu Dhabi
7	Amwal Al Khaleej	0.53	Riyadh
8	Carlyle	0.50	Dubai
9	Ithmar Capital	0.32	Dubai
*	Citadel Capital	NA	Cairo

*This firm invests directly, so figures are not available.

Source: Zawya Private Equity Monitor (March 2009).

economic downturn may make it more difficult for all but the most established fund managers to secure the successful closure of these larger funds.

The report found that over the past four years, Egypt, Saudi Arabia, and the United Arab Emirates were the largest recipients of private equity funds, at 33 percent, 15 percent, and 14 percent, respectively. The majority of funds are focused in the Middle East and North Africa (MENA), with Turkey sometimes included as part of that region.

Real Estate Private Equity

Real estate private equity is a large component of the private equity industry (see Table 4.9). It is fund-based, which distinguishes the sector from everyday real estate investment and development

Michael Pralle, former global CEO, GE Real Estate Investing and Lending, describes the real estate private equity industry as one in the midst of a crisis—not surprisingly. "Everyone has their hands full, unless they didn't invest in 2006 and 2007. It's a real weakness in the private equity model. Economics drives you to seek out riskier and riskier investments. If you tell someone that you will give them an 18-percent return on overall funds invested, then you must target deal level returns in the high 20s. There's about a 10-percent deduction from gross to net with all the fees most private equity firms require. So you keep adding riskier deals to your portfolio."

TABLE 4.9 The Top 10 Real Estate Private Equity Firms in 2008

Rank	Name	USD Billions (Raised)	Location
1	The Blackstone Group	19.75	New York
2	Morgan Stanley Real Estate	16.77	New York
3	Tishman Speyer	11.36	New York
4	Goldman Sachs Real Estate PIA	11.19	New York
5	Colony Capital	10.95	Los Angeles
6	The Carlyle Group	9.6	Washington, DC
7	ProLogis	8.8	Denver, CO
8	Beacon Capital Partners	8.08	Boston
9	LaSalle Investment Management	6.69	Chicago, IL
10	Macquarie Global Property Advisors (MGPA)	6.56	London

Source: Private Equity Real Estate magazine (Lehman Brothers omitted at No. 6).

Pralle describes three major developments in real estate private equity. "The most important change in the industry is that it's gone from an era where the funds could charge significant non-performance-related fees to one where that is no longer possible. Investors want closer alignment between performance and returns." He adds, "The fees are essentially the same as for standard private equity fees: the preferred hurdle rates, asset management fees, and equity fees to cover overheads."

A second trend is globalization. "There was a time when there were very few global investors: Morgan Stanley, GE Capital, and ING Clarion. Today, there are many firms—Macquarie, Goldman, Allianz, AIG, Apollo, and other big insurers and institutions—who had investments in the U.S., Europe, or Asia but are now global."

Finally, he says, there's been a significant repricing in the industry.

> From 2000–2007, cap rates compressed from 8 percent to 10 percent down to 4 percent to 6 percent. This allowed the model to work, as investors were willing to pay more and more each year per unit of cash flow. When the market turned, the model no longer worked. Cap rates are now reverting as investors are unwilling to pay as much as previously per unit of cash flow. Also, in 2008–2009, there's been a dramatic repricing of real estate as a result of less leverage and the higher cost of cash. It drives you to a lower price for the building.

Pralle says that investors paid the price for their excessive enthusiasm.

> People demanded very little equity premium that they earned on real estate. The prime real estate in London was yielding 4 to 4.5 percent. Risk-free U.S. Treasury rates were about the same. Cap rates in London and the U.S. for prime property have moved out at least 200 basis points. People bought properties in expectation of price appreciation. But they have changed their expectations. They also demand a higher return on equity for real estate investing, as they now demand for nearly all asset classes. From September 2008 to March 31, 2009, there have been write-downs of 40 to 60 percent. Everybody is in the doghouse together.

Looking at Asia, Grant Kelley, founder and CEO of Holdfast Capital, observes, "The China real estate market is looking a little overheated. The best opportunities can be found in secondary markets such as the Bohai Peninsula where valuations are more realistic." In Korea, he says, "The Korean banks and corporations are better capitalized today, but the stock market has been hit hard and the credit markets have also been impacted. Real estate has been abandoned by the capital markets, and there is room for distressed investment." In Japan, "real estate fundamentals are weakening: vacancies are rising, land prices falling, and debt maturities looming. According to the IMF, Japan's economy will contract 6.2 percent in 2009."

In sum, says Pralle, there will be great deals, but not everyone will benefit. "Looking forward, it's like a self-correcting mechanism. With deteriorating cash flow, there will be some tremendous deals. Real estate will attract new capital, there will be new funds raised, and an enormous amount of money will be made." He adds, "Success or failure seems to be more market- than intelligence-driven. It's hard to make money if you invested in 2006 or 2007, regardless of how smart you were. It will be like the RTC days: if you could get the money, you made money. But it may be challenging to raise the capital in the current environment." (RTC is the Resolution Trust Company, created by Congress in 1989 to liquidate insolvent savings-and-loan associations in the wake of the 1980s S&L crisis. The causes have a familiar ring: imprudent real estate lending.)

Fund-of-Funds

As mentioned in Chapter Two, fund-of-funds invest in other funds not in the underlying portfolio company securities. It has been an enormous growth sector over the past decade (see Table 4.10). HarbourVest Partners, for example, has committed $31.6 billion as of September 2009 since this table was completed.

TABLE 4.10 The 10 Largest Fund-of-Funds Firms

Rank	Name	USD Billions Committed	Location
1	AlpInvest Partners	42.3	Amsterdam
2	AXA Private Equity	34.9	Paris
3	AIG Investments	24.6	New York
4	Goldman Sachs	24.0	New York
5	Pantheon Ventures	22.6	London
6	Pathway Capital Management	20.6	Irvine, CA
7	Capital Dynamics	20.0	Zug, Switzerland
8	Partners Group	19.6	Baar-Zug, Switzerland
9	Lehman Brothers	19.0	New York
10	HarbourVest Partners	17.8	Boston, MA

Source: Preqin (2006).

Philip Bilden says the field has become competitive, and many new funds will not survive. "There are now over 200 fund-of-funds globally, with over 40 Asian fund-of-funds or advisors that have emerged just in the past few years. Many of the new entrants in Asia rode the wave of escalating capital flows to the region as investors wanted Asian exposure. Many of these newly formed niche fund-of-funds will have a difficult time getting refinanced, given the difficulty of showing performance in the recent cycle and high valuation period from 2005-2008. They will need differentiation and reasons for their LPs to continue in a more capital constrained environment."

Distressed Funds

Distressed funds invest in companies whose debt exceeds their ability to service it (see Table 4.11). As Richard Slocum notes, "Equity may well have bought a good company but at the wrong price." He explains that where a fund comes into a company through the capital structure makes a very big difference in its returns. As bankruptcies happen, it will become more obvious that coming in through debt can be a lot easier than through equity.

Initially, there was a belief that the industry would clean up in 2009 by buying the debt of companies that were overextended. That has been only partially realized, for two reasons. The main reason is that most private equity firms aren't designed to do that. Howard Marks says that in the early days of the crisis, several firms bought debt at what they thought were good prices, only to see the discounts plunge even further. "If I

TABLE 4.11 The 10 Largest Distressed Funds

Rank	Firm Name	Region	AUM (USD billions)
1	Oaktree Capital Management	U.S.	20.5
2	Avenue Capital Group	U.S.	9.5
3	Cerberus Capital Management	U.S.	8.4
4	MatlinPatterson Global Advisors	U.S.	6
5	WL Ross & Co	U.S.	5
6	Sankaty Advisors	U.S.	3.7
7	Angelo, Gordon & Co	U.S.	3.6
8	Bayside Capital	U.S.	3.3
9	Crestview	U.S.	3.1
10	MHR Fund Management	U.S.	3.1

Source: Preqin (December 2008).

were a private equity investor and my manager was buying a portfolio of debt, I would want to know what makes that right for him. The combination of not having much to do and having cash on hand will lead managers into the field. Many of them will venture into it and will lose money. Some very large private equity firms did some big transactions in 2008 and lost everything."

The second reason is that only portions of debt were offered at attractive discounts, but there wasn't as much available at those prices as many funds initially thought. Going in to work out situations requires skill sets that aren't as readily available to funds whose expertise is building companies based on leverage and operational expertise. The funds certainly have the money to hire the expertise, but, as Marks suggests, will LPs trust a name that has been in the business for only six months? By mid-2009, many of the discounts on distress debt had been considerably reduced.

Secondary Funds

As private equity limited partners undo their investment positions, secondary fund GPs will play an important role in the next several years (see Table 4.12). In general, secondary funds have benefited from the downturn.

Jeremy Coller, CEO and CIO, Coller Capital and one of the early pioneers in the market, offers a broader perspective on secondary transactions. "What is the private equity secondary market?" he asks. "*Public* equities really took off in the late 1960s. Today, nearly 100 percent of turnover in public markets is secondary trading. *Private* equity took

TABLE 4.12 The 10 Largest Secondary Fund Firms

Rank	Firm Name	Region	AUM (USD billions)
1	Goldman Sachs	U.S.	10
2	AXA Private Equity	France	4.8
3	Coller Capital	U.K.	4.8
4	Lexington Partners	U.S.	4.3
5	HarbourVest Partners	U.S.	3.4
6	Pantheon Ventures	U.K.	3
7	Paul Capital Partners	U.S.	3
8	AlpInvest Partners	Netherlands	2.7
9	NB Alternatives	U.S.	2.6
10	Pomona Capital	U.S.	2.1

Source: Preqin (2008).

Note: Figures correct at the time of writing; 2009 data unavailable.

off in the 1990s. In the same way, there is huge growth still to come in its secondary market. Having said that, the secondary market in private equity will never represent the proportion of total activity that it does in public equities because private equity funds are self-liquidating. The owners of positions in private equity funds don't have to sell—they can just let the funds liquidate."

Coller thinks that limited partners should take a more active role in managing their investments. "In the old days, appreciating that private equity was a long-term investment, investors held to maturity. But the world is changing incredibly fast today. What was a sensible investment decision in 1990, or in 1999, or in 2005 doesn't necessarily make sense today. It's the same for private equity as for other asset classes: as an investor, you need to be actively involved in the shape of your portfolio.

That said, Coller thinks there is currently a fundamental disconnect between the expectations of buyers and sellers. "The bid-offer scenario wasn't working. Private equity valuations lag those in public markets, and when public markets are volatile this adds up to a big difference. In effect, buyers look forward and sellers look backward—in mid-2009, at very outdated valuations. This forced potential buyers to offer much larger discounts than would have been required if valuations had been more realistic, in effect, stifling the market. How could an investment manager tell his CIO or trustees he was proposing to accept a 60-percent or 70-percent discount?"

LIMITED PARTNERS

Limited partners invest the capital that the general partners use to buy assets. The "limiteds" (as they are known) are large institutional investors including pension funds, endowments, and high-net-worth individuals. They are a wealthy lot, but, as the discussion in the previous chapter suggests, one whose relationship with the funds has yet to be fully defined.

Pension Funds

Assets at the world's 300 largest pension funds grew 14.2 percent in 2007 to almost $12 trillion, according to an annual survey conducted by *Pensions & Investments* and Watson Wyatt Worldwide. In 2008, however, they declined 12.6 percent to $10.4 trillion. The decline—only the second in 20 years—is the largest drop since *P&I* ran the first ranking in 1989 (see Table 4.13).

TABLE 4.13 The Largest Global Limited Partners Pension Funds

Rank	Fund	Country	Total assets USD Millions
1	Government Pension Investment[1]	Japan	1,284,612
2	Government Pension Fund	Norway	339,149
3	ABP	Netherlands	243,071
4	California Public Employees	U.S.	214,556
5	Federal Retirement Thrift	U.S.	210,609
6	National Pension	Korea	190,352
7	Local Government Officials[2]	Japan	176,397
8	Postal Savings Fund	Taiwan	154,160
9	California State Teachers	U.S.	147,185
10	New York State Common	U.S.	138,425
11	Pension Fund Association[2]	Japan	129,542
12	Florida State Board	U.S.	118,673
13	General Motors	U.S.	110,334
14	ATP	Denmark	110,202
15	New York City Retirement	U.S.	107,304
16	Central Provident Fund	Singapore	105,338
17	PFZW	Netherlands	99,532
18	Employees Provident Fund	Malaysia	98,844
19	National Public Service[2]	Japan	98,045
20	Texas Teachers	U.S.	95,982
21	AT&T	U.S.	89,563

Note: Ranked by total assets, in millions of U.S. dollars. U.S. fund data are from the P&I 1,000, published January 26, 2009; unless otherwise noted, Japan fund data are as of March 31, 2009, Australia fund data are as of June 30, 2008, and all other fund data are as of December 31, 2008.

Source: Pensions & Investments/Watson Wyatt Worldwide.

Pension funds have been major investors in private equity, with some (CalPERS) taking a position in the management company (Carlyle and Apollo). Looking at the market, Joncarlo Mark feels that large leveraged buyouts (LBOs) will be few and far between for the next year or two. First, he says, "It's tricky because of the lack of leverage. Next, there's uncertainty about true macroeconomic conditions. Last, the first half 2009 strength in the equity markets have set some unrealistic pricing expectations, creating a large bid-ask spread. However, there's a lot of dry powder out there. These funds will need to invest."

In June, the CalPERS board moved to increase its private equity allocation to 14 percent. "CalPERS is underfunded relative to our liabilities, and our board sees the alternative asset class as a key component to getting out of this hole. Many other pension funds may follow." He adds, "We're seeing returns flattening. Q1 wasn't as bad as we thought it would be. We hope that by year end we will have positive returns."

CalPERS is making a bet here. A July 2009 *New York Times* article[1] listed the numbers the pension plan confronts. The fund just posted a loss of 23 percent, which leaves it 66-percent funded. In other words, it has only $66 on hand for every $100 in benefits promised to California's state workers. CalPERS' real estate portfolio has tumbled 35 percent, and its private equity holdings dropped 31 percent in 2008. This loss, of course, represents a mark-to-market valuation, which may be less than it appears. John Dear, CalPERS' chief investment officer, believes that private investments earn 3 percent higher than public markets. Over a $180 billion fund, this can make a difference in enabling CalPERS to achieve its targeted 7.75-percent annual return.

Going forward, Mark also thinks that private equity will have to look at other types of deals. He says, "There seems to be too much money and not enough attractive deals that clear the bar from a return standpoint. If the buying market doesn't get better, GPs may have to either cut their fund size back or broaden their investment horizon. You may see private equity players become pure opportunistic players. That may mean doing PIPEs or debt deals, for example. But that will require the LPs to get comfortable with this strategy. Private equity may well do the types of deals the hedge funds used to do—this time with more long-term capital."

Limited partners will not abandon the asset class, but as Carl Ferenbach observes, many LPs will have fewer assets to allocate. "They have lost 25 percent of their portfolio value. They like private equity, so they won't give it up. If they're going to keep up their allocations to it, then each of the GPs they support will get a smaller amount. It grew at a remarkable pace. There will now likely be a step back—not into the dark ages, but a step back. With that step, there will also likely be some triage of managers."

Private Endowments

Endowments are small by public pension standards, but, as the list in Table 4.14 indicates, still significant. They generally represent (large) gifts by families to fund a specific interest or for a designated purpose. Endowments have different aims, reflecting the interests and philanthropies of their founders. The Ford Foundation was founded by Edsel Ford in 1936 "to advance human welfare." The Gates Foundation was started by Bill and Melinda Gates in 2000 "to enhance healthcare and

TABLE 4.14 The Largest Endowments

Rank	Name (state)	Assets USD	As of Fiscal Year End Date
1	Bill & Melinda Gates Foundation (WA)	38,921,022,000	12/31/2007
2	J. Paul Getty Trust (CA)	11,187,006,719	06/30/2007
3	The Ford Foundation (NY)	11,045,128,000	09/30/2008
4	The Robert Wood Johnson Foundation (NJ)	10,722,296,000	12/31/2007
5	The William and Flora Hewlett Foundation (CA)	9,284,917,000	12/31/2007
6	W. K. Kellogg Foundation (MI)	8,058,127,639	08/31/2008
7	Lilly Endowment Inc. (IN)	7,734,860,156	12/31/2007
8	John D. and Catherine T. MacArthur Foundation (IL)	7,052,165,312	12/31/2007
9	The David and Lucile Packard Foundation (CA)	6,594,540,283	12/31/2007
10	The Andrew W. Mellon Foundation (NY)	6,539,865,000	12/31/2007
11	Gordon and Betty Moore Foundation (CA)	6,409,252,816	12/31/2007

Source: Foundation Center.

reduce extreme poverty, and to expand educational opportunities." The William and Flora Hewlett Foundation was established in 1966 by Bill and Flora Hewlett "to support education, culture, and the performing arts, and to address serious social and environmental problems facing society." The J. Paul Getty Trust was started by J. Paul Getty in 1953 and "is committed to advancing the understanding and preservation of the visual arts locally and throughout the world."

Kevin Fong observes, "Endowments are hurting. Their portfolio balances are down, and their ability to generate liquidity is a problem. They have capital calls coming up. They are supposed to pay out a certain amount for operations. Foundations have to generate 5 percent liquidity to meet structural obligations." Fong's observation seems correct. In Bill Gates's first annual letter in 2009, he says his foundation's "assets decreased in value by about 20 percent in 2008," but "it is better than most endowments." In fact, the William and Flora Hewlett Foundation saw its assets decline by 32 percent in 2008 from the previous year. As of March 2009, the Getty endowment had declined about 27 percent from July 2008. Nonetheless, these endowments remain committed to their goals and have continued their charitable giving and grants.

TABLE 4.15 The 11 Largest University Endowments

Rank	Institution	2008 Endowment
1	Harvard University	36,556,284,000
2	Yale University	22,869,700,000
3	Stanford University	17,200,000,000
4	Princeton University	16,349,329,000
5	University of Texas System	16,111,184,000
6	Massachusetts Institute of Technology	10,068,800,000
7	University of Michigan	7,571,904,000
8	Northwestern University	7,243,948,000
9	Columbia University	7,146,806,000
10	Texas A&M System	6,659,352,000
11	University of Chicago	6,632,311,000

Source: National Association of College and University Business Officers (NACUBO).

It's no secret that university endowments have fallen significantly since the numbers in Table 4.15 were compiled. For example, at June 30, 2009, Harvard's endowment stood at $26 billion and Yale's endowment had dropped to $16.3 billion. A January 2009 *New York Times* article reports, "The value of university endowments fell about 23 percent on average in the five months ended November 30, 2008. The steep declines are forcing colleges and universities across the country to contemplate wage freezes, layoffs and a halt to construction projects."[2] At best, the decline will mean smaller allocations to fewer private equity funds. On the positive side, though, it may also mean that limited partners begin to take their investments more seriously, a positive trend for all concerned. This issue is one that will be explored in the next chapter on industry issues.

Sovereign Wealth Funds

Table 4.16 shows the world's 16 largest sovereign wealth funds. The total assets under management for all sovereign wealth funds as of April 2009 was $3.62 trillion.

ADIA The largest sovereign wealth fund is the Abu Dhabi Investment Authority (ADIA). In April 2008, then ADIA investment professional Georges Sudarskis shared his views and knowledge on "the dynamics and inner workings of a professional investment team within a sovereign fund." In sum, he said, "A sovereign fund's attitude towards private equity investments is no different than that of any other institutional investor." He

TABLE 4.16 Sovereign Wealth Funds

Rank	Country	Fund Name	Assets USD Billions	Inception	Origin
1	UAE - Abu Dhabi	Abu Dhabi Investment Authority	627	1976	Oil
2	Saudi Arabia	SAMA Foreign Holdings	431	n/a	Oil
3	China	SAFE Investment Company	347.1	n/a	Non-Commodity
4	Norway	Government Pension Fund—Global	326	1990	Oil
5	Singapore	Government of Singapore Investment Corporation	247.5	1981	Non-Commodity
6	Russia	National Welfare Fund	219.9	2008	Oil
7	Kuwait	Kuwait Investment Authority	202.8	1953	Oil
8	China - Hong Kong	Hong Kong Monetary Authority Investment Portfolio	193.4	1998	Non-Commodity
9	China	China Investment Corporation	190	2007	Non-Commodity
10	Singapore	Temasek Holdings	85	1974	Non-Commodity
11	UAE - Dubai	Investment Corporation of Dubai	82	2006	Oil
12	China	National Social Security Fund	77.9	2000	Non-Commodity
13	Libya	Libyan Investment Authority	65	2006	Oil
14	Qatar	Qatar Investment Authority	62	2003	Oil
15	Algeria	Revenue Regulation Fund	47	2000	Oil
16	Australia	Australian Future Fund	42.2	2004	Non-Commodity

Source: Pensions & Investments/Watson Wyatt Worldwide (as of April 30, 2009).

added that the ingredients of success include "diversification, patience, hard work, and a long-term perspective."

ADIA was formed in 1976 by Sheikh Zayed bin Sultan Al Nahyan to invest and diversify the Abu Dhabi government's cash surpluses. Since then, ADIA's assets have grown substantially. As of this writing, according to London-based IFSL, ADIA manages over $627 billion in assets—over twice that of the next largest state fund, the Government Pension Fund of Norway.

Said Sudarskis in April 2008, "Listed stocks as well as private equity have had a long ride up. Housing prices have had a long ride up. It would be fair to say that both these rides were largely fueled by massive leveraging of the financial economy."

The abundance of cheap debt from 2002–2006 aside, Sudarskis said that private equity owes its success to a number of factors—all of which are available to sovereign funds. Among them are investing in institutional private equity (the fund-of-funds route), superior means and effort directed at the validation of the investment thesis (due diligence), superior structuring and purchase terms negotiation, good governance, incentivizing both management and alignment of interest with shareholders, and the tension of the limited holding period.

One of the real drivers of ADIA's success is well known in the financial world—compounding. The longer the period and the higher the return, the greater will be the end result. For example, at a 4-percent-per-annum return, an initial investment will be worth 2x its original value in 20 years (see Figure 4.1); at an 8 percent return, the original stake will multiply five times in value. But over a 50-year time horizon, these returns leap to seven times and 47 times the value of the original stake, respectively (see

FIGURE 4.1 Wealth Differential After 20 Years

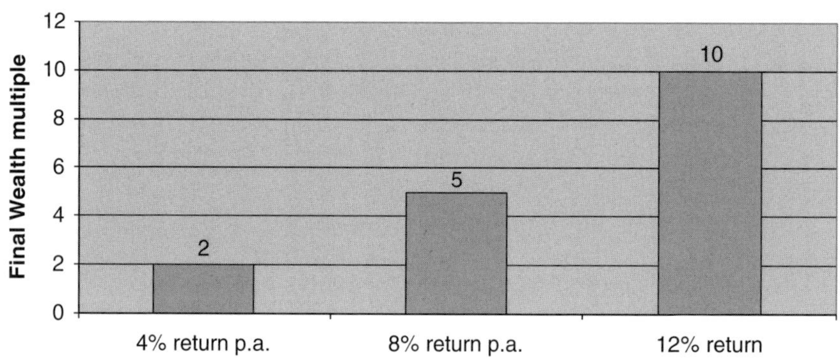

FIGURE 4.2 Wealth Differential After 50 Years

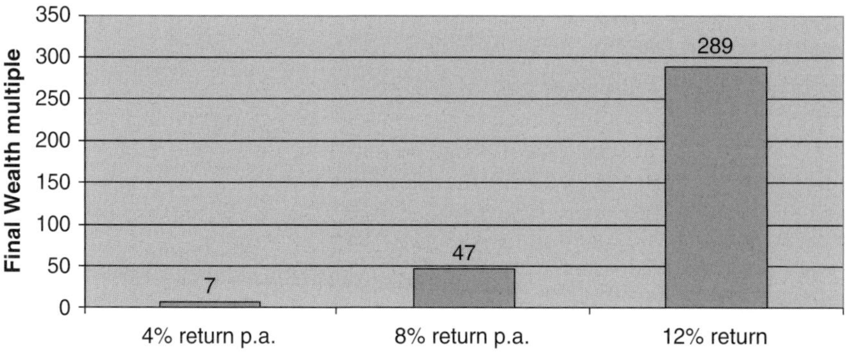

Figure 4.2). And if the annual return is 12 percent (not an unreasonable return expectation for private equity investments), then the multiple jumps to almost 300 times the original investment.

Sudarskis stressed that ADIA's returns were equally due to hard work and analysis: understanding companies better, "focusing on management teams and business strategies rather than Excel spreadsheets." He cited other factors as well: planning and thinking ahead, governance, diversification, patience, the willingness to take a contrarian view, and the search for value. Finally, he said that allocation among asset classes and identifying and investing in top quartile funds were vital to realizing high returns.

"Private equity is about patient capital. If an investor is eager for quick returns, then private equity isn't for him. One is never diversified enough. For example, we have 3,500 portfolio companies across all industry sectors, growth stages, and regions of the world. On average, our managers buy and sell two companies each day."

ADIA has done exceedingly well. By its own calculations, at the end of 2007, it earned $3.30 for every $1 invested during the 10-year period between 1997 and 2007. That compares to the Morgan Stanley Capital Index of $1.97 and the S&P 500 Index of $1.77.

Control Positions Exaggerated

Sudarskis also suggested that the role of state funds in control buyouts had been greatly exaggerated. "The SWF attitude toward private equity investments is just like any other institutional investor on the planet, whether it is pension funds or endowments. I think that what we do is standard operating procedure, what we follow is a robust method for diversification, what we try to execute upon is based on thoughtful planning, and that this philosophy should be followed by any institutional investor. Do you know many deals where SWFs attempted to wrestle control?"

Wilbur Ross agrees, saying, "With limited exceptions, I don't see SWFs as much different than state pension funds. For the most part, they act as investors, not as politicians. Even big state pension funds have agendas."

Sudarskis concludes, "If you fast forward to today, we didn't see the credit crunch coming, though all the signs were here: cheap financing, lax credit terms, soft covenants, bigger and bigger deals. Wasn't this obvious that in 2006–07 something like this would occur?" He believes that "the credit crunch will take some time to pass. Fundraising will be more difficult, deals will be harder to come by. Deals will require more work from the fund managers. It will have to be more inventive, involve more creative financing. On the other hand, the quality of deals will improve."

Other SWFs

Most SWFs are not as constrained as U.S. pension funds or endowments in terms of liquidity. They will continue to look at good deals including distress—debt or equity, acquiring secondary interests in funds, investing in growth markets such as India and China, and finally, in infrastructure.

DEBT PROVIDERS

Debt providers fall into two broad categories: senior debt, which is mostly provided by the banks; and mezzanine or subordinated debt, provided by insurance companies, other financial groups, and special mezzanine debt funds. Needless to say, the financial crisis has changed the amounts and terms that debt providers are willing to extend to private equity funds.

The Banks

KY Tang feels the banks won't be turning on the spigots anytime soon. "The credit markets seized up in 2008. We're beginning to see some early signs of improvement, but they are still fairly frozen." The major Western banks have all sold stakes to governments, with several U.K. banks now controlled by the U.K. Treasury. U.S. banks are shedding their TARP money, though the government remains a guarantor on their debt.

It's likely the banks will slowly begin to lend again. But, says David Coulter, the demand for credit has also slowed. "Many commentators keep saying that 'Banks have to start lending.' There are two sides to the equation: not only the supply of credit, but demand for credit. In this type of economy, demand for credit goes down."

Mezzanine Finance

Matthew Chanin of Prudential says that after the junk bond era of the 1980s and recession of the early 1990s, "Mezzanine reemerged in the mid-1990s. We decided that middle market leveraged debt fit our strategy. For us, the middle markets are companies in the $25 to $500 million revenue range. The transaction size varies from $10 to $100 million."

During the bubble, says Chanin, the market reminded him of where it was 30 years ago. "The period of 2003–2007 wasn't that different from the way it felt in the mid-1980s. But the amount of money that was pumped into levered deals was much larger. It had the same kind of feel. It produced the same result."

In the interim, he says, it had its ups and downs, but once again seems attractive. "That was a period in which not much money was chasing deals, so we could put money to good work. Then, as things got hot, there was an incredible number of CDOs that wanted to do leveraged financing, second lien financing by hedge funds, and money flowing into private equity. All that blew up. We're now where terms for mezzanine providers are once again attractive."

And what are those terms? Chanin elaborates:

> In the U.S., the typical mezz structure is a 12-percent coupon, another 1 to 2 percent that would be in the form of payment-in-kind (PIK), and equity participation. Gross returns have been about 18 to 19 percent, and cash-on-cash about 1.7x. Net returns after fees and carry are then at the 12- to 14-percent level. We try to maintain a current cash return of about 8 percent. The rest comes in the form of gains on the sale of investments.
>
> Our market never got as overblown as the big deal market. Deal multiples and leverage never got as high. It's certainly come down, but not as much. Institutions can get a deal done. The senior leverage is 1.75x to 2x EBITDA. Total leverage is 2.75x to 3x, depending upon the resilience of the credit.

He adds, "The banks have really tightened quite a bit. We have seen signs of improvements in the bond market, but the bank loan market has not really improved. I saw a deal last week for a very stable company in the food processing industry: it took five institutions to put together a $115 million credit."

In sum, says Chanin, "It will be a while before banks are willing to be aggressive again. But the banks were really in this business to make fees—originating loans, securitizing or selling to CDOs, providing M&A advice, and everything but putting the loans on their books. Now, they have to rethink that strategy."

That strategy is one among many that the banks and the industry will need to rethink. The next chapter explores the many issues confronting private equity and venture capital across the world's markets.

CHAPTER 5

Private Equity and Venture Capital in Markets Around the World

Private equity and venture capital have gone global. The industry was born in the United States, and that country remains, to a great extent, its principal hub. But reflecting the industry's strengths and returns, the rest of the world has caught on. The road ahead can only grow in size and reach: the industry now extends to Europe, Asia, and the Middle East; South America and Africa will follow. Its parameters reflect a number of fundamentals as well as different economic and financial conditions around the world.

UNITED STATES

An economic forecast is a cauldron of many factors: financial, regulatory, corporate, and political. The general consensus is that the American economy will go sideways. The major concern, says Wim Borgdorff, is systemic. "What worries us in the U.S. is that there are quite a few structural issues to be resolved. There are fundamental issues around the financial and regulatory system, for example, which need to be resolved."

Lip-Bu Tan also points to the need for basic changes in America's infrastructure. He notes, "The recovery will be slow. The infrastructure needs to be changed. Some industries, like automotive and banking, will be restructured with U.S. government support. Hopefully we will see some improvement in the second half of 2010." On a micro level, Leonard Harlan of Castle Harlan comments, "There are a lot of broken balance sheets, but not broken companies." That is to say, the businesses remain sound, though their capital structure has too much debt. Potentially, private equity has a role to play in remaking these companies.

The industry's prospects have been discussed in the previous chapters. These will continue to play out in 2010 and 2011. The coming years are likely to be transition years for both the economy and the industry in the United States. In many respects, the banks will hold the keys for home mortgages and corporate lending, whereas the disappearance of previously vast securitization markets will shape consumer credit. Those companies with strong balance sheets as well as funds with dry powder will have the ability to borrow money and to make deals.

For LPs, Sheryl Schwartz suggests that for those committed to the asset class, taking a long-term view is important. "I think there will be fewer players, both GPs and LPs. But, when I'm making investments, I'm investing for a five- to ten-year period. My thoughts on where we will be in the next six to twelve months are irrelevant. We are opportunistic, but, overall, when we're formulating our alternatives' strategy, we're looking five to ten years out."

CHINA

In the world to come, China will play a far more important role than it has in the past several decades. Regardless of one's opinion of Mao Tse-tung's accomplishments and failures, history will look back at his leadership as a mere 50-year blip on China's 5,000-year-old past.

China's greatest asset has long been its people. The human price paid for what Mao Tse-tung accomplished was staggering: few if any other nations would have paid it. But the end result was to create order out of chaos. The post-Mao period was marked by a period of hesitancy, but beginning in the early 1990s, there was an accelerating trend to bring China into the twenty-first century. The Chinese economy is not without its problems, and its political culture is at odds with American democracy. But what the Chinese people have accomplished is undeniable. The question is, of course, what lies ahead?

To begin with, China is not a monolithic entity. Much like the United States or Europe, there are many constituencies that come together in Beijing but nonetheless exist outside of it. Those centrifugal forces lie at the heart of the central government's domestic political agenda: how to contain them while promoting its other social and economic objectives.

China is also four times the size of the United States and about three times the size of a combined Europe (excluding Russia). That means internal competition, internal demand, and internal needs are (at least) three to four times as great. It is also a country with a very strong central government that places a huge premium on policy. Its legal institutions are beginning to grow, but "the policy" is well established. Politics trumps the law, not the other way around as in the United States and European nations.

As a country, China is oriented toward the union, not the individual. Although Chinese culture places enormous emphasis on individual education and achievement, "face"—one's standing in the union—is of greatest importance. Leonard Harlan recounts a conversation that he had with a Chinese fund manager. "There's no real law in China. So how do you keep people honest? Face. If the fund is operating in a town or a region or in Silicon Valley where GPs are known, it's part of their face network. If you're in their union, they will deal responsibly with you."

The other side of that coin is China's place in the union of nations. Some would call China's international "face" nationalism; others, pride in what the country has achieved.

It is also a country that for millenniums has been more interested in keeping others out rather than in conquering them. The Great Wall, built over a 2,000 year period, is as good a symbol of this as any. No Mainland Chinese leader will countenance an independent Taiwan nor a separate Tibet. Within those parameters, however, there is considerable latitude. The People's Liberation Army (PLA) made a big show of marching into Hong Kong at one second after midnight on July 1, 1997. Since then, a curious observer would be hard-pressed to spot a PLA soldier, even at their Prince of Wales HQ Building.

Finally, China continues—and will continue—to grow. The Pacific seaboard is home to many twenty-first-century cities. The rest of the country is not. Kevin Fong thinks that "Beijing, Shanghai, and Shenzhen are a veneer. The risk is that China is asking to be treated as a global power, but they have the other 800 million people that they need to bring up to global standards." Yet, the Chinese government is doing just that. The entire country is a construction site.

China is a very complex and idiosyncratic country, one that will be a strong international competitor. It also means that many of China's needs are compatible with those of other nations, and it will be a great friend. Many people understand this dichotomy; others should.

Says former Australian prime minister the Honorable Paul Keating, "China was slated to win the big economic race because China had five times the population of the largest economy, the United States. But the big picture told me that the rise of China was inevitable and that China's unity owed as much to its own sense of civilization as it did to its modern statehood. So this great state, with its profound sense of self and the wherewithal to make a better life for its citizens, has eased itself into a major role in world affairs."

Looking at the economic crunch, Yichen Zhang, CEO of CITIC Capital Holdings, notes that China has the means to accomplish its goals. "In terms of short-term ability to cushion the impact of the crisis, China probably has more resources than anyone else. One thing's for sure: the government is willing to use those resources."

Tom Quinn, managing principal, The Jordan Company, L.P., agrees that the Chinese stimulus program will be largely effective. "I see the China stimulus program working: it will be targeted and will get out there. They want people to get back to work. They are building roads, bridges, and infrastructure that they need. As opposed to the U.S. program that will take a long time to get through, in China, when they decide they want to do something, they do it. There's a lot more credit available over there. I think it will bear fruit."

Dixon Doll, cofounder and general partner of the early-stage venture capital firm DCM, uses the phrase "last in, first out" to describe the country's recovery. He says, "They have targeted stimulus programs and continue to build up their infrastructure and boost domestic consumption in order to offset weaker external consumer demands. A lot of people have used the term 'last in, first out' to describe the country's bounce back from the recession. We also expect to see increased Chinese IPO activity fairly soon."

Gary Bridge thinks that China's immediate response to the downturn has been forced on them by years of double-digit growth; that response is "putting its people to work on a permanent basis, ASAP. Many of the people who came from the countryside to work in the cities have gone back to the countryside because of the slide in export business. People can't go back to living in a cardboard shack. China needs to put these people to work; for example, building roads and infrastructure. The export business will pick up again, but it won't drive growth as it had in the past. The consumer economy has arrived."

Zhang notes that the Chinese government is very much aware of the structural issues as it plans ahead. "My personal concern is really on the longer-term structural changes that China has to make. Those will be difficult and painful. On the one hand, the premier is very confident and upbeat that the country will be able to face this challenge. At the same time, he is realistic. He is constantly emphasizing that to make these long-term adjustments, we need to carry on and continue the reforms. The key is execution. In the short term, China can put money to work and instruct banks to lend. The longer-term reforms will be a lot more difficult."

He also emphasizes that China's financial system is not an issue. He says, "During the National Congress in March 2009, one economist said, 'There is no financial crisis in China.' The impact of the global financial crisis is not on China's financial system, but has hit the real economy directly. The financial system is fine."

Finally, Dr. von Fischer points out, "China's banking system is OK. I don't think they have a debt problem. Two to three years ago, people didn't think the Chinese banks could go public. Now they are the largest banks in the world by market cap."

China's Currency and Capital Markets

Another important development is China's goal of making the *yuan* a global currency and internationalizing its capital markets. For private equity and venture capital, that means domestic *renminbi* (RMB) funds will become increasingly prevalent.

Renminbi funds launched about two years ago as a means for the Chinese to put their capital to work locally. There are currently a number of restrictions on the funds, and the government is still in the process of formulating regulations. It seems likely that these requirements will lessen over time as the funds grow in importance. Says Zhang, "The leadership realizes that the current global exchange system is untenable. It wasn't as clear then as now that China is trying to promote an alternative global currency. They are trying to push the RMB to become more of a global currency."

Of course, the *yuan* will not be a global currency until it becomes freely tradeable. Some economists see that as unlikely in the near future. Others are less pessimistic.

In a June 2009 interview with Reuters, Guo Shuqing—chairman of state-controlled China Construction Bank (CCB), the world's second-biggest bank by market value—said, "I think the U.S. government and the World Bank can consider the possibility of issuing *renminbi* bonds in the Hong Kong market and the Shanghai market." Guo said it was in American interests to see the *yuan* become a currency that is traded around the globe, largely because of the symbiotic relationship between U.S. purchases of Chinese goods and China's purchases of U.S. assets with the proceeds. He said that China is likely to continue to progressively ease controls on the convertibility of the *yuan*, with cross-border direct investments one of the next targets.

Dick Kramlich of NEA has no illusions about China's ambitions for its currency and capital markets. He says, "China is taking direct aim at the U.S. capital markets. If you look at relative markets, the U.S. markets have lost a lot of leadership. China has an opportunity to make strides in the capital markets."

Len Baker of Sutter Hill Ventures is concerned about the wider consequences of this happening. "As those develop," he says, "they will need foreign expertise less and less. There's a big question mark: how will economic liberalism resolve itself? Will this crash and failure of Western capitalism lend legitimacy to those voices in Chinese government that argue that government ownership is better than private ownership?"

Zhang also suggested, "Wen Jia Bao's comment, worrying about the dollar, was mostly aimed at a domestic audience. This premier works very hard, likes to let people know that he is on top of the issues. It was a little off-the-cuff and was picked up by the Western press." Off-the-cuff or not, the Chinese authorities are taking U.S. deficits and debt seriously.

On private equity, Zhang says, "The government is increasingly realizing the importance of the private equity and venture capital industry." But he notes, "China cannot have a private equity and venture capital industry that is dependent upon foreign funding. I have advocated policies to channel domestic savings into the domestic private equity and venture capital industry. The government is taking that well."

Just how well is evidenced by China Development Bank's September 2009 announcement that it would launch a $5.1-billion private equity group to support government-backed acquisitions and infrastructure projects.

China will need to build up its institutional capital. Otherwise, says Zhang, the country will face a chronic shortage of capital. "A company can either go IPO or get a loan, but there's no systematic way to build up a business. The corporate pension funds and insurance companies are not big enough. The National Social Security Fund (NSSF) is the only one big enough to invest."

And the NSSF is investing. Biao Xing, who heads the NSSF's local private equity division team, says "We have three people in our division and there is no more than 10 percent of the total AUM (about $8 billion) to invest. We have more and more connections from local and foreign GPs, but so far we are permitted by our regulators to invest only in NDRC (National Development and Reform Commission)-approved RMB funds." In April 2009, Reuters reported that the NSSF is looking to invest in private equity funds to help it manage part of its RMB563 billion ($82 billion) portfolio. "We will pick at least three to five private equity firms this year, focusing on investing in small and medium businesses and the service industry," said its chairman, Dai Xianglong.

Another large Chinese institutional investor is the China Investment Corporation (CIC). CIC has made billion-dollar investments in Blackstone and Morgan Stanley as well as putting $100 million in Visa's IPO in March 2009. However, one source close to the group believes they "are pretty disorganized internally." To that end, in July 2009 the group appointed a board of advisers (which includes several foreigners) to assist with changing that.

One concern for Dr. von Fischer, however, is the role the Chinese government will play in local RMB funds. "I have seen increased government involvement in the RMB funds. I have seen how market forces can turn an economy around, but how can government resist investing private equity in companies?"

Zhang shares that concern. "I am also concerned that all of the small private equity funds popping up invariably have government backing behind it. A number of funds are being started by local levels of government. At least, local governments are not trying to manage the funds themselves. These days, they go through a process to pick a professional investment team. There are clearly issues there to be concerned about, but they are not just installing a government official. That is an encouraging first step."

Zhang says the process will take time. "Generally, there's still a lack of understanding on the general and limited partner structure. The entire partnership company law has only been in force for about a year. There are still issues for taxation and registering as an entity that can hold securities. Hopefully, over time a lot of the wrinkles will get worked out."

Private Equity in China

Foreign direct investment (FDI) has been significant in China for over a decade. Private equity looked like it would follow suit. In 2004, Newbridge bought a controlling interest in Shenzhen Development Bank, and in 2006 Carlyle bid to acquire Xugong Construction Machinery Co. China's focus quickly evolved from watching others invest to helping its own industry grow. That has included the *renminbi* funds and other industry activity.

Zhang notes a few other trends that impact the industry. "The only trend in China that is similar to others is back-to-basics. Given that you have to add value, private equity will have to get involved more on the operational front. A second trend is that control type deals will increase. SOEs are difficult to buy. Only a few players with government backing can do that. Although many first generation owners have been unwilling to give up control until now, they will soon face generational transition issues. They may be more willing to give up." The future looks bright though, says Zhang. "In the U.S., people are saying that private activity accounts for 4 percent of GDP. In China, it's less than 1 percent."

For foreign capital, the challenges of investing in China are significant. Competition is tough and the government is omnipresent. Andrew Liu warns about picking the right company. "Only 20 percent of investment in China generates 80 percent of the profit. The reason is that you really have to dive into a Chinese company. The typical model of buying control and dropping in operational improvement is still unproven in China. So, you better be happy with the existing quality of the management team. If your idea is to change the management team, then don't make the investment. A lot of China is picking the right industry, right company, and that you're comfortable with the existing management."

Strategic investors will be allowed full control, but with the government's focus on domestic firms, overseas financial investors will have a tough road to hoe. As David Rubenstein remarked on Carlyle's bid for Xugong, "I've been over to China for four closings already, and the deal still isn't done." In fact, the transaction never got done, with Xugong abandoning plans to sell a stake despite three years of negotiations. For Carlyle's part, the Chinese government had not come to a policy decision on the sale of majority stakes to overseas financial buyers when they announced the deal. By the time the deal collapsed, they had.

In the third quarter 2009, China's GDP grew at 8.9 percent. According to data from the Ministry of Commerce, FDI in July fell 35.7 percent year-on-year, to US$5.4 billion. Analysts said that falling FDI may be more related to strained liquidity for multinational firms rather than weakness within the Chinese economy. They added that the drop in FDI would have little effect on China's overall economic growth.

Venture Capital in China

If overseas private equity has been stalled in China, venture capital is zipping along. Beijing and Shanghai are the leading financial centers, with Beijing probably a nudge ahead, given its proximity to the central government's offices.

China will benefit from changing market dynamics. If venture was born in the United States and blossomed in Silicon Valley in the 1980s and 1990s, it has since grown global. Sonny Wu thinks that China is an ideal proving ground for the next generation of venture capital. "The Valley is different now than five, 10, or 15 years ago. A lot of innovation is becoming more dispersed." Wu adds, "The credit market isn't as tough in China. It's largely government directed and still spending increasingly more than before."

Ted Schlein of Kleiner Perkins also sees opportunities in China. "There are different opportunities in Asia. The market place is at different levels of maturities. In China, there are the life sciences. A lot of current businesses that we're doing in the U.S. can be brought to China."

Gary Bridge of Horsley Bridge Partners disagrees; he feels that venture capital in China still has a way to go. "There's still a disconnect between the universities and the venture capital industry. And the technology isn't as raw. In the early-stage area, there is more 'me-too' technology currently. This will change, but it will take time."

Kevin Fong agrees with Bridge. "I definitely wouldn't say that the technology is better in China. That comparison is different in different sectors. The big difference in China is that there's a lower cost basis. The markets are growing quicker, people are embracing change, and their companies get to profitability quicker. There's still a feeling of optimism and growth."

Fong also thinks China's cost advantage will gradually erode. "China's impact on the tech world will only increase its importance. Although its rise to importance during slow economic periods will happen more quickly, at the same time it will also lessen some of their advantages as costs decline elsewhere." For example, he says, "The decade of the new millennium is about lower operating costs. Whether it's done through currency devaluation or deflation, where you had a 10:1 or 3:1 advantage in China, it will disappear more quickly."

In terms of valuations, Tina Ju notes that the bid-ask spread that exists in other markets also exists in China. "There are two significant trends in today's China private equity sector. First, there is still a gap between buyers and sellers, which has had a dampening effect on the number of deals that are being done. Second, we are seeing renewed interest in innovation—a number of venture capital firms are willing to invest in more early stage and pre-revenue ventures."

If you can't beat them, join them, says Len Baker. Sutter Hill was "the original investor in Chingwei and has an advisory relationship with them. What are the types of investments? The Chinese version of YouTube, Youku.com, and BabyCare.cn." Says Baker, "SHV has never defined ourselves as backing 'technology.' We think of ourselves as backing change-intensive businesses." Many others would like to feel the same way.

Adds Sonny Wu, "China has a greater chance of coming back, partly because it's still small but the expertise is still with the U.S. and European firms. It's not realistic to think that GSR and others will dominate, but we will continue to gain traction." For the next lap, though, China has seemingly moved to the pole position. The Chinese government will use their reserves to good advantage. The U.S. government will be running on running on reserve.

JAPAN

A Chinese friend recently asked an acquaintance from Japan what the Japanese thought about China. The Japanese person paused and then replied, "There are two houses, two families. They are neighbors and live next to each other. In one house, the family has many sons. They are well educated and always behave themselves. The family in the other house also has many sons. But they are always fighting, and there are many problems. Then, suddenly, they get rich. No one knows why."

As Japan looks across the sea to China and confronts a new government at home, it remains an enigma to many on the outside. Yet I believe the country is very comprehensible to those who live there. If China is a nation of families, always fighting and competing, Japan is a feudal domain in which everyone has their place. Responsibilities and obligations are prescribed by society. This social order is both a blessing and a curse. It is one reason Japan was able to rebuild itself so effectively after World War II. It is also, as Jeffrey Shafer observes, one reason why "there's a lot of complacency in the society and unwillingness to change."

Yoshito Hori, founder and managing partner, Globis Capital in Tokyo, as well as dean and founder, Globis University, says that Japan's culture has taken its toll. "I feel a bit pessimistic about the GDP growth of Japanese economy. The biggest problem for Japan is the declining and aging population. It is gradually influencing the growth potential of Japan. Japanese strength in manufacturing can't produce any more employment because Japanese manufacturing is shifting overseas. The key to survival is the advanced end of technology. That is the exciting challenge to overcome for Japanese companies."

He feels, though, that Japan's financial markets are in relatively good shape.

> Japanese banks aren't much affected by subprime or derivatives because they didn't buy too much of it. They have not been nationalized this time like European or American counterparts. Due to the downturn in the economy and the stock markets, they may have to write down assets allocated to equity stocks. Also, there could be the problem of NPLs [nonperforming loans]. I don't think the equity market will go much further down, but real economy will continue to decline for a little while until 2010. The speed of the downturn in early 2009 was so fast that people were freaking out, but things are settling down gradually.

In terms of how overseas VC firms will fare in Japan, Hori notes that their problems were of their own making. "During the Internet bubble, quite a few firms came into Japan. Most of them left because of their poor management in Japan and deteriorating financial health in their home country. They blamed the Japanese economy for their exit, but the real reason they left was not because of the economy but because of the fact that they could not afford to be in any other countries. Now they are looking to India and China. It could be interesting to see how they manage in the emerging markets."

One of Japan's biggest problems is the lack of political leadership. Prior to the August 2009 elections, London's *Independent* wrote,

> The sun appears to be about to set on a long political era in Japanese politics. After a resounding defeat for his Liberal Democrat Party (LDP) in local elections in Tokyo, the Japanese prime minister, Taro Aso, has given in to pressure and called early general elections for next month. Opinion polls point to a decisive victory for the opposition Democratic Party of Japan (DJP). The LDP, which has been in office more or less continuously for half a century, seems to be finally on its way out . . . .
>
> The DJP has promised less bureaucracy, more decisiveness on policy and a push to reform the welfare system but, in truth, it is no radical force. It leaders, like those of the LDP, are drawn from the political caste that has ruled Japan since the end of the American occupation. Some suggest that it is little more than a glorified faction of the LDP. And while voters are weary of Mr. Aso and his colleagues, they remain unenthused by the DJP and its uncharismatic leader, Yukio Hatoyama. Yet it is hard to regard the prospect of a change of government in a country as politically and economically stagnant as Japan as anything but a breath of fresh air. A new administration might not be the solution in itself to the country's problems, but it could be the first step.[1]

In the August 30 elections, the Democratic Party won in a landslide, taking 302 of the 480 seats in the powerful lower house. About 70 percent of Japan's voters took part, which many saw as a rejection of the ruling Liberal Democrats rather than an embrace of the victors. Nonetheless, the future remains promising, if unclear, as a country in need of change hopefully awaits the new government.

The macro opportunity for private equity and venture capital "continues to be big in Japan," says Joe Bae of KKR Asia. "For us, Japan is an option on a large economy. Dedicated and consistent relationship building is important. We want to position ourselves at the table when the market begins to open. We're not chasing small-cap deals, but trying to stay focused on the type of deals we like: large, industry-leading companies with sustainable competitive advantages." He adds, "I see Japanese banks continuing to support their clients in their home markets. For the right deal in Japan, we can still raise capital."

Hori describes a good exit his firm had from Globis's portfolio company, Gree. "It's like MySpace, with a strong monetizing model," he says. "When we invested in July 2005, revenue was only $280,000. We invested $1 million for over a 10 percent stake. In 2009, it was making $110 million in revenue, $60 million in pre-tax, $40 million in net profit. The company went public with over $1 billion in market cap in December 2008, which is incredible considering the timing of the IPO, which was right after the Lehman shock. We exited on and after the IPO with roughly 100 times return."

Gree's strategy? "The company started out as a PC SNS provider, and then shifted to mobile SNS by tying up with KDDI. Then they started to provide mobile games and became number one. The advertising model didn't work well, so they began selling items and avatars that are used in the game. Most revenue is actual revenue, selling virtual merchandise."

George Raffini of HSBC Private Equity believes that Japan is playing or should play an integral role in Asia's economy. "Intraregional trade in Asia and the decoupling argument are valid, but that logic would be made easier if Japan were growing. Many people are focused on America, but the slowdown in Japan is material to Asia. I think that the country can propel the rest of Asia. It's easy to underestimate how important Japan is to the rest of Asia."

Nonetheless, Japan has remained a difficult place to invest for overseas private equity. For the world's second largest economy, the number of private equity investors is very small. The number of successful deals has been even smaller. Daniel Mintz (whose firm, Olympus Capital, has exited successfully in Japan), says that the cultural barriers remain high. "Japan was never headed toward the U.S. model. It's about companies and their boards who are made up of inside management. You have a whole generation that grew up with a zero cost of capital. Their expectations for return on capital are just very low, so you've really got to work to create differentiated deals—they don't fall into your lap."

Japan's economy grew at an annual rate of 4.8 percent in the third quarter, ending its worst slump since World War II. The data suggested that the increase was due to factors other than a rise in demand (inventory restocking and exports), which may stymie further growth in the future.

In the 45 years after World War II, Japan built an extraordinary manufacturing plant and financial capacity. In the 20 years since 1990, that capability has drifted as the country suffered through the aftermath of the 1980s liquidity binge. Whether the new government harbingers a change or more of the same is a question that Japan—and the world—is asking. Given the right sentiment, the private equity and venture capital industry has a role to play in transitioning the economy to a new era.

KOREA

Jae Woo Lee, founding partner at Vogo Investment in Seoul, feels good about the Korean economy. He says, "The current state of the economy looks quite OK. Korea is posting a healthy trade surplus thanks to a few globally competitive large conglomerates." He is also optimistic that two signs of a healthy economy, a stable capital market and exchange rate, are doing well.

Lee also says the financial crisis of 1997 was different from today's downturn. This time, the country was better prepared. Lee explains,

> In the Asian financial crisis of 1997–1998, there was no organized equity capital to support restructuring in Korea. Both the financial sector and the corporate sector were required to restructure their high leverage by external forces, such as the IMF. Since there was not even the concept of private equity in Korea, the nationwide fire sale naturally opened a wide window of opportunity to the foreign funds.
>
> Today, the Korean economy is in need of restructuring, but the nature looks to be quite different. The average debt/equity ratio is dramatically improved from what it was in 1997: it was 424 percent then, while the current average is 92.5 percent. The Korean banks are relatively healthy due to stricter supervision compared to other developed economies. After their bad experience of overleverage 10 years ago, Korean corporates became much less dependent on banks' financing. So even though the government and the banks would like to see more active restructuring, there's no real urgency for Korean companies to sell their assets.

He is cautiously optimistic on private equity.

> You will see more deal opportunities. But you may not see the valuations that you saw 10 years ago. On the other hand, you won't see the ridiculously high valuations that occurred over the past couple of years, either. There is a clear hangover from the aggressive acquisitions done by large chaebols [conglomerate family-controlled firms]. For example, Kumho Group is trying to sell back DaeWoo E&C. Banks are not as active as before in providing acquisition financing. This will provide more investment opportunities to private equity firms. There will be selling of noncore businesses by financially weak conglomerates and privatization of state-owned companies. The new government hasn't changed their view that the

> privatization is the only way to ensure operational efficiency, which will eventually benefit the Korean economy.
>
> However, except for MBK, who has a broad international LP base, Korean private equity firms have clear limitations in size due to shallow local long-term capital sources. One exception is NPS [National Pension Service], which has strategically decided to increase its exposure in [the] alternative asset class. This could result in more deal opportunities for large established global private equity firms. You already saw KKR buying OB Beer Company and Blackstone going into a JV investment agreement with NPS. Even so, PE firms may have to be ready to pay fair market price for the reasons I already mentioned.

Also, it's important that private equity prove it can add value to the companies it invests in, says Lee. "In general, there is still a stigma attached to foreign firms. Many Koreans believe that Newbridge and Lone Star were punters. It is a task for all private equity firms, regardless of whether it's foreign or local, to change the perception [of them] as value creators. You should prove your investment will ensure better governance, more transparency, and operational efficiency. I believe many foreign PEs have a lot to talk about their track record in this perspective."

"Korea will provide significantly more investment opportunities compared to the last few years, but they may not be cheap," Lee concludes. "But where else can you find sizable buyout deals in Asia other than Korea and Japan? If you believe you can build value on the right platform, Korea will be the place."

Lee is circumspect about Lone Star's controversial bid to sell Korea Exchange Bank. He says,

> Lone Star was absolutely correct: they had a deal. However, you saw that Newbridge sold Korea First Bank very smoothly, on the surface, even though the original deal had a controversial put option provided by the Korean government. Many people didn't even notice when Koram Bank was sold to global banking giant Citi by the Carlyle guys. On the other hand, the KEB sale attempt was quite noisy. I personally believe Carlyle and Newbridge had a better understanding of the local sentiment and handled the situation with much more finesse, utilizing their own senior managers who were on the ground. The key for successful investment may be the kind of local platform you have built in that market place.

In South Korea, there are certainly opportunities, but Korea is justifiably known as a highly nationalistic place. Before the 1997 financial crisis, foreign investment was simply not allowed. Today, says Daniel Mintz, "If you are looking at a must-own asset for big *chaebols*, stay away—they'll pay whatever it takes to win."

George Raffini notes that Korea really hit a bump in the road in 2008. "The currency fell, and there was a slowdown in domestic economic activity. I think there will be more market buyout activity. For Korea, we like industrial and engineering. Korean companies are very driven." He adds, "Korea really differentiates itself in manufacturing products that have longer product cycles, such as engineering and more capital-intensive products. Examples include companies that make products for petrochemical, engineering and construction projects such as heat exchangers. They are leveraging off their engineering skills."

HONG KONG

Hong Kong has long been a gateway to China. It is now part of China, though the Basic Law has another 38 years to run before the territory formally reverts to the PRC. Figures released by Hong Kong's financial secretary, John Tsang, indicated that in the first quarter 2009, the economy shrank by 7.8 percent. For the three months ending June 30, however, Hong Kong's GDP rebounded, increasing 3.3 percent. Nonetheless, the second quarter figures were still down 3.8 percent from the comparable quarter in 2008. Helping the second quarter figures were China's aggressive stimulus measures and an increase in exports. The government also said it expects the economy to contract by 3.5 to 4.5 percent for the entire year, a more optimistic outlook than the 5.5 to 6.5 percent forecast in May.

Hong Kong's recovery reflects Asia's overall recovery. Hong Kong has also weathered many an economic storm in its history. The territory remains a leading center for Chinese business, over 80 percent of its GDP is service income, and its foreign currency reserves had climbed to US$208.2 billion by July 2009. As former chief secretary Anson Chan liked to say, "No one ever made any money betting against Hong Kong."

SINGAPORE

Singapore is one of Asia's financial hubs as well as one of its wealthier nations. An August 2005 article in *Der Spiegel* referred to the country as the "Lee Family Enterprise,"[2] reflecting the influence its founding father and his sons and daughter-in-law have had on the government. The minister mentor, Lee Kuan Yew, has built a prosperous state, which continues to reflect his core politics and beliefs.

Singapore is home to several private equity and venture funds as well as affiliates of international groups. But the current economic crisis has hit Singapore hard. Teo Ming Kian, who was the permanent secretary (Finance) for Singapore at the time of writing, has this to say:

> Singapore cannot escape unscathed from the global financial crisis. As an open economy with a very small domestic market relying on exports, we are greatly affected by the sharp drop in global demands. We expect the Singapore economy to contract by 4 to 6 percent for all of 2009. Unemployment has also increased. Interestingly, while the manufacturing and services sectors of our economy that rely on global markets have been declining, the construction sector has actually been doing well, because both the public and private sectors are confident of and are continuing to build for the future.
>
> Singapore banks entered the crisis from positions of strength with strong capital buffers and low non-performing loans. They do not have significant exposures to toxic assets. Singapore banks have a large and stable deposit base and thus do not have to rely on wholesale funding. Asset quality concern will remain a risk for the Singapore banks as economic conditions deteriorate but we expect them to be able to ride through the crisis fairly well.
>
> The Government's FY 2009 Budget introduced a "Resilience Package" of S$20.5 billion [US$14 billion] that cost us a basic budget deficit of 6 percent of GDP—very big by historical standards. Unlike other countries, we did not need to borrow for this extraordinary expenditure as we had been living within our means and had been saving for such a rainy day. With the additional resource, the Government was able to among others, introduce a Jobs Credit scheme that provides a grant equivalent to 9 percent of the wage cost of hiring resident workers to all businesses. And a Special Risk-sharing Initiative shares 80 percent of any loan defaults with financial institutions, hence encouraging these financial institutions to lend to businesses.
>
> Singapore will intensify our push into R&D, enhance efforts to commercialize research output, and make innovation more pervasive across the economy. We have a light tax regime with no capital gains tax. We recently initiated a S$200 million (US$137 million) program to encourage companies to use Singapore as a test-bed for new products and services. Several strategic research programs in clean water and energy, interactive digital media and translational and clinical research in biomedicine have started and have already yielded some good

> results. Several large and small enterprises have set up here to participate in the program.
>
> But more importantly, to move decisively towards a knowledge-based innovation-driven economy, Singapore will establish itself as a compelling "marketplace" for talent to congregate to generate ideas, create new knowledge and apply them for societal and economic benefits. In this regard, Singapore is developing into a hub of research centers of universities from around the world with the likes of MIT, Technion and other European universities concentrated in the Campus for Research Excellence And Technological Enterprise (CREATE). In turn, this serves as a magnet for talent with diverse nationalities, cultures and background. This virtuous cycle should bring about a vibrant environment that is attractive for enterprises, big and small, to start up and grow.

These measures seem to be paying off. In August 2009, the Trade and Industry Ministry announced that Singapore's GDP grew 20.7 percent in the second quarter, compared with a 12.2-percent slide in the first quarter. The ministry said, "This improvement was largely driven by the spike in output from the volatile biomedical manufacturing cluster and inventory re-stocking."

INDIA

India has long been its own neighborhood. Since independence in 1947, its economy has been driven by a commitment to self-sufficiency and regulated by a meddlesome bureaucracy. Those are reasons the country was generally ignored by Western investors until five years ago. In fact, India has been changing since 1991, when prohibitions against monopolies and licensing were phased out by the government.

India entered the modern era about the time of the Y2K bug, the computer virus that experts feared could grind the world to a halt on January 1, 2000. The bug proved largely illusory, but it kick-started India's software outsourcing industry. Although foreigners eagerly took advantage of the country's cheap programming skills, the sector was largely overlooked by India's otherwise ever-present regulators. The rest, as they say, is economic history.

Ashish Dhawan of ChrysCapital says the country is in good shape. "India is not the epicenter of the crisis. The banking system is quite clean: loans to GDP are about 55 percent. China is twice that. Other western countries are at 100 to 200 percent." He adds, "In countries like India, household savings are 22 to 23 percent. In the U.S., the consumer needs to save. There's not much room for the Indian consumer to save more. Income growth will slow down, but the Indian consumer is largely unlevered. The downturn will be much more muted."

Harjit Bhatia of Credit Suisse Private Equity Asia agrees that the Indian economy will remain steady. "In India, unemployment is rising, but it's not as bad as elsewhere. There's impact in the software and consumer finance areas. Institutions have realized that delinquencies will increase."

Bhatia adds, "I think that the Indian stimulus package will be relatively small compared to some other Asian economies. The Indian government will try to boost the economy primarily through monetary rather than fiscal measures. The deficit is already high. In the short to medium term, the Indian economy will be impacted adversely by the slow down of incoming portfolio investments from foreign investors, though those related to infrastructure buildup will continue. A lot of projects like airports and roads are already funded. That will keep the economy going for the next 12 to 24 months."

And he notes, "One of India's engines of growth is coming from rural areas, not just big cities. Rural income has improved in recent years. Look at consumer products company Hindustan Unilever. Its major growth is coming from rural areas. In the context of a billion people, 200 million lifts up the whole."

India has other anomalies as well. As TPG managing partner Dan Carroll points out, "It's the only major country in the world whose annual GDP depends upon the weather forecast." Bhatia concurs: "A normal monsoon in 2009 will help the country grow at 5.5 to 6 percent. That's down from 8 percent, but still solid." In addition to all the official numbers that exist, "There's a huge thriving parallel economy as well, which depends upon unrecorded cash transactions. That's important. When secondary real estate sales happen, people often pay a substantial portion of transactions in cash." Thus the actual size and growth of Indian economy may be larger than the published numbers.

Dhawan expects a hit to industrial production and exports. More important, he says, "Credit does not impact private equity in India. Borrowing only impacts 8 to 10 percent of deals that are buyouts. Most funds were levering up to 2x to 3x EBITDA. The impact is more on GDP than on deals."

Overall, he says, investment will fall, but in the process, wring out the excesses. "In bull market years, we had $18 billion of investing. About one-third of investment was in real estate: it was speculative in nature and won't happen going forward. Of the remaining $12 billion, valuations are down 50 to 60 percent. The size of that $12 billion is going to be $5 billion.

I see volume shrinking dramatically: valuations are down, so are deal sizes. In 2009 and 2010, there will be about \$5 to \$7 billion of investment." He continues, "In our space, there are 10 serious global players that are here to stay. There are four or five Indian players who can compete for the \$100-million deal. Investors will do fewer deals as they try to stretch out their funds."

Although Dhawan feels that deal volumes will not return to pre-crisis levels, what will change is the ability of private equity to influence their portfolio companies. "Private equity really kicked off in 2002–2003. In the current phase, entrepreneurs are much more humble, willing to accept private equity as a partner. Private equity has matured. It's more of an operating mix within teams that has evolved."

Gulpreet Kohli, one of Dhawan's partners, agrees that less investment will prove beneficial. "The good thing in India is that leverage is a lot less than in other countries. Growth will be at the general partner and portfolio company level. It's difficult if you're export oriented, but the silver lining is that the Indian banking system is clean. Because India is very insular, it's highly regulated." Indians surprised everyone and voted in a solid Congress Party coalition in May 2009. The expectation is that reform will continue for the next five years.

Luis Miranda, president and CEO, IDFC Private Equity, is more positive yet still cautious about private equity's prospects. "India will be the center of the universe for some time: there's growth happening here. Not that there will be champagne with it." He admits that exports are feeling the pain, as well as some infrastructure companies. "But there is both GDP growth and a demographic story. We have a large working class component, which will continue to grow for the next 10 years. That will also fuel growth, because India has a high savings rate."

His own experience with the government's announcement that \$500 billion is required for infrastructure has been muted. "That created a lot of excitement, but there's been more talk than action," he says. Why? "Partners to the previous government were the communists, who were against opening infrastructure to the private sector. Second, regulatory frameworks were not in existence. Investor appetite has also changed. In airports, the last big privatizations were the Delhi and Mumbai airports. That was three years ago." Of course, that may change with the Indian government newly elected in May 2009.

Moreover, he adds, "Roads were the big story of the previous administration. A lot of plans that were announced haven't taken off. Look at power: \$150 billion was announced. The actual spend has been much lower. The government has focused on big power plants as power continues to be a source of constraint on growth."

In sum, says Dhawan, India will stay the course. It "will be unlike the U.S. and Europe, where the landscape will change dramatically. We have seen it in financial services and the ownership of large institutions. I don't see that much happening in India."

However, Kohli points out, "India will continue to grow, because India is less export dependent—only 15 percent is export driven. I think that 2010 will be a consolidation year. The export sector will suffer, but Indians won't stop buying consumer goods, medicines or eating out."

The Center for Monitoring Indian Economy Pvt. Ltd., or CMIE, estimated GDP growth at 4.7 percent in the June 2009 quarter, compared to 5.8 percent in the preceding quarter and 7.8 percent a year ago. A bad monsoon was one reason.

MIDDLE EAST

The Middle East spans three subregions: the Gulf, the Levant (the eastern Mediterranean), and North Africa. The countries in the Gulf have proved the most vibrant. Specifically, these are the United Arab Emirates and Saudi Arabia. Dr. Karim El Solh, the CEO of Gulf Capital, says, "The myth that the Middle East is uncorrelated with the rest of world has been debunked. Abu Dhabi and Saudi were down more than 50 percent in 2008. Dubai's stock market was down 72 percent in that year, but has rebounded 40 percent in 2009." He continues, "Some Middle East banks have been affected, because they invested in CDOs, high-yield issues, and so-called capital guaranteed structures linked to Lehman, Bear Stearns, or AIG credits. A lot of the regional banks depended upon international capital markets to fund themselves through MTN programs and bond issues, so their borrowing spreads grew dramatically in line with the rest of the global market."

Dr. El Solh is nonetheless optimistic about the prospects for private equity.

> Although we have closed control acquisitions and acquired sometimes 100 percent of companies, the Middle East private equity scene historically was all about minority investments and growth capital. One benefit for private equity is that in 2008, sellers were forced to compromise and come back to reality. Control stakes are becoming increasingly available and valuations are becoming more realistic. In the past, our competitors were the debt markets and IPO market. A family that owned a business would rather borrow to the maximum extent before getting diluted. Our other competitor was the IPO market since business owners would frequently bypass private equity funding and take

> their companies public directly without private growth capital. Now, business owners will have to come back to us to finance their business. The lending and IPO markets are virtually shut down for the time being.

His own firm, Gulf Capital, "is a very hands-on private equity firm with strong operational control. In today's turbulent environment, we spend the majority of our time monitoring and managing our portfolio companies. We're spending about twice the time that we did before in 2006–2007. Though our companies are solid, it is getting harder and harder to get bank financing. This is our major bottleneck today."

Looking ahead, Dr. El Solh's fund, GC Equity Partners II, is focusing on "healthcare, education, food, utilities (power and water), and oil and gas. It's a play on the growth of the population and the government spending on infrastructure. We now have one of the youngest and fastest-growing populations in the world." He says, "The next phase of growth will be led by the GCC governments. We're counting on the government's largesse to keep investing in infrastructure, which will inevitably trickle down to the private sector. In 2010, I think the private sector in the GCC will be back on its feet."

He also feels that Dubai is misunderstood by many outside the region and that it will inevitably recover,

> given that it has one of the best infrastructures in the region and remains a prime tourist and business destination. Dubai perhaps was affected in the last year more than other Emirates and countries, as it has always been an open economy, and is more likely to go up and down in tandem with global markets. By definition, when you're that open and depend significantly on global trade and tourism, you're bound to be linked to the global economy. The UAE federal government bought $10 billion of Dubai Government bonds in February (2009). It was a strong message of endorsement from the federal UAE government.

Georges Sudarskis, however, has a different view:

> While Dubai had the right mindset—entrepreneurship, global ambitions, and the fight against corruption—all of a sudden, the bubble burst. The impression that a miracle could be made out of sand—this myth has largely faded. We're only in the first and second inning. Abu Dhabi, by design, is the pillar of strength, the safety barrier, and the lender of last resort for the whole of the UAE. This may also mean there could be a profound, durable transformation in the UAE power structure. You are very likely to see a change in methods and in speed

> of execution. As Dubai developers fall into default, Dubai runs the risk of losing some of its luster. Kuwait, Qatar are all having similar issues—problems arising out of accelerated, unchecked real estate growth.

Dr. Adnan Soufi, managing director, Financial Investments Group, at the Saudi Economic and Development Company (SEDCO) in Jeddah, is cautious yet optimistic about private equity in the region:

> The region is quite positive on the asset class. We can see China and the Middle East as prime areas of investment. It is a matter of timing. The business cycle is slow here. The region has a strong potential in energy, energy services, and infrastructure and business services.
>
> Oil is both a blessing and a curse. Though everyone has been impacted by the financial downturn, MENA is one of the more resilient regions. The Middle East (ME) and GCC are among the world's fastest growing regions. Significant steps have been made, but further reform will be essential to seize a broader role in the global economy. We see a great opportunity for the ME and GCC to play a pivotal role in the China-India-ME play. Economic dynamism is obvious throughout the region, but both government and business leaders must take advantage of the opportunity to build a vibrant private sector focused on creating value and play an important role in the global value chain.

Going forward, Dr. Soufi says, SEDCO's private equity efforts are concentrated on "*Sharia*-compliant, growth capital with the right companies and the right business models. We are focused more on Asia because we expect more growth opportunities in Asia. In Europe, growth capital investment opportunities are rare. In the U.S., it's more limited. We think China, and to some extent India are interesting. And we also like growth capital in Australia."

In sum, he says, "The best opportunities will be in this crisis. Per capita income and local demand are still growing, despite the crisis. There's a huge demand for housing and the middle class is expanding."

CHIME

One of the more intriguing opportunities for the Middle East and Asia is what *AVCJ* calls "CHIME": China-India-Middle East. It stands in contrast to the better known though less robust "BRIC" (Brazil-Russia-India-China) advanced by a former Wall Street investment bank. In fact, the CHIME concept had its origins in the days of the old Silk Road, which ran from Persia (Iran) and Arabia through Central Asia and India to China. It presents a natural ecosystem of trade and ideas linking the economies and people of Western and Eastern Asia: the capital surpluses and infrastructure needs of the oil-exporting Middle East with the industrial capacity and consumer markets of India and China. The development of these interrelationships will be an important trend to watch over the next decade.

CHIME's future is illustrated by the financial firm First Eastern Investment Group. Their investment banking license from Dubai made the firm the first Chinese investment bank to be licensed by the Dubai International Financial Centre. Victor Chu, the Group's chairman and CEO, told CNN in a November 2007 interview, "When I first went to the UAE 15 years ago there were only a few thousand Chinese residents. Today the number is 200,000."[3] He also believes that China could invest as much as $20 billion annually in the Middle East. In sum, he said, "Historically, for Gulf investors the Far East stopped in Singapore. It's only really in the last 10 years that Middle Eastern capital has found China." Going to Asia, Dubai's Istithmar World Capital opened its first office in Shanghai in 2007. Istithmar is directly owned by the government of Dubai.

AUSTRALIA

The Honorable Paul Keating thinks that Australia will weather the storm and emerge reasonably unscathed in a new world economic order. He feels the country has a number of advantages: it is better integrated with North Asia; the banks have monetary room—the overnight cash rate has been steady at 3 percent (rising to 3.5 percent in November 2009); the banks have no exposure to CDS, and there's no sub-prime housing stock; commercial banks aren't invested in the investment banking industry; and the country's superannuation funds will have A$4 trillion (US$3 trillion) by 2020.

The Australian private equity market ramped up from 2004–2006, peaked in 2007, and has cooled down since. Bill Ferris observes that the country has a different buyout model than others. "One of the aberrations of 2005–2007 was that private equity privatized public companies that weren't broken at a 25-percent premium. Leverage made the numbers look possible." He adds, "Is the private equity model broken? No, it's not broken. It never really depended upon excess leverage ratios, though it does depend on some leverage to improve economic performance."

But Grant Kelley of Holdfast Capital says that Australia is feeling the times as much as other markets are. "Australian banks are well capitalized. They are renewing corporate lines, though on tougher terms. They are in only very few cases doing fresh originations for new clients or big ticket acquisitions." As a result, says Kelley, "No one is doing even a 3x cash deal. The reason multiples are low is because there's no leverage."

Another factor, the exit market, will also remain tough, says Ferris's partner, Joe Skrzynski, a managing director at CHAMP Private Equity. "There are some trade buyers who are well cashed up, and some listed companies who will look to consolidate their industries. There will be creative markets with more vendor financings. The vendor will take the risk that prices will come back up. Our biggest competition was always strong trade buyers."

Skrzynski adds that the downturn will encourage good managers to think more seriously about the private equity sector. "The big thing that will change is the availability of good management. Prior to 2003–2004, nobody at level top 200 companies in Australia wanted to work for private equity. With further steps of regulation, and executive salary reduction, all of those things will impact the willingness of public company executives to take a private equity job. The distraction level of complying with regulation will also increase the value of private equity. Private equity will become the solution to companies that can't get debt and equity."

Ferris sums up the outlook for Australia: "I think the companies that will come through best will not be the ones who just cut costs blindly across the board, but [those] who strategically reconfigure their companies to operate more strategically. That may involve capital expenditures. One of the biggest victims will be the sacred cows of the past."

EUROPEAN UNION

The European Union (EU) has come a long way from the Treaty of Rome, which the six original member states signed in 1957. But European issues are complex. The surface veneer that covers 27 individual countries runs an uphill gauntlet of interests, needs, and priorities. Beyond the multiplicity of member states, each country has its own divisions and politics: Italy has long been more a confederation of municipalities than a single state; Spain has Catalonia in the north and Andalusia in the south; Germany, its *Länder* (federal states), with Bavaria and Hamburg as good examples. Belgium is split between the (French) Walloons and the (Dutch) Flemish. Even Holland divides between the Protestant north and Catholic south. Great Britain is made up of four countries—and so forth across the continent.

The June 2009 G8 meeting in Italy showed that agreement is not easy. A *New York Times* article on the European Parliamentary elections in June 2009 reports that, "Europeans across 27 countries voted between Thursday and Saturday for the 736 seats in the European Parliament, an institution with growing powers but still a low profile. Such votes are often seen more as barometers of support for individual national governments than as indicators of power shifts." The article continues, "But with political parties conducting largely national campaigns, the elections may have appeared irrelevant to many voters who know that their votes could not change the makeup of any national government."[4]

Then there is the question of Russia. Sooner or later, if the EU is to succeed, Moscow will have to relate to the EU as an equal partner. Its citizens have increasingly become part of the EU's commercial activities both as businessmen and consumers. Integrating Russia into the EU will be a long but necessary process. What will Europe look like in 200 years? By and large, Europeans look to their governments to take care of them, more so than the United States and Asia. That, of course, raises the question of how the social welfare systems erected by these countries can be sustained once the current generation begins to retire. Some Europeans happily admit that the continent will succeed as a tourist destination, selling luxury goods and a high standard of living to wealthy tourists from emerging countries. They point out that Europe is a design center and a services center for its own populations. It has room to expand as the poorer countries of Eastern Europe become members. Whether that is enough to succeed in a competitive world remains an open question.

The EU is a start. If Brussels has become a logistics and administrative hub, it has begun to develop a cadre of pan-European rather than national officials. There is a common currency that everyone likes, and, indeed, border crossings are a relic of the past. The EU is building a common approach in new areas such as anti-competition and the environment.

European economies have rebounded slowly. France and Germany reported 0.3 percent and 0.7 percent GDP growth respectively in the third quarter 2009, improving upon their second quarter performance. The economies of the U.K. and Spain continued to decline.

All of this, of course, sets the stage for private equity and venture capital. As William Stevens points out, it's tough to operate in this kaleidoscope of laws, markets, and consumers. Although generally well understood in London, building private pools of capital to restructure businesses and fund technological start-ups is the exception rather than the rule. Says one general partner, "Europe is a pretty mature market. It has less flexibility to restructure. Capital is a lot less available, and valuations are low."

Wim Borgdorff believes that Europe has become part of the world economy but maintains its own priorities. "The whole continent has become much more part of a global system. They move in tandem. Because of the structure of its economy and the involvement of government as a major component of GDP, Europe is of a somewhat different order. The depth of the downturn will be dampened, but it will take longer to pick up."

He believes that fund raising will reflect market realities. It "will be slow, as slow as it has ever been. There are a couple of reasons. First, managers raised huge funds in the last couple of years, so they don't need the money. Second, investment activity will be slow, as anyone who has an asset won't sell in a down market. This market will be driven by people who have to sell."

Will Schmidt, managing partner, Advent International, says Central Europe could potentially become a problem. "Central Europe entered a downturn after EU accession. Most of the region's debt was in euros, and the Pole and Czech consumers even borrowed in Swiss francs because interest rates were lower. Then there were big local currency devaluations relative to the euro, which came as a surprise to everyone because they thought the currencies were inextricably linked. Everyone got caught off guard. However, the situation is stabilizing and in fact improving because the currencies have come back and the economic decline has slowed."

RUSSIA

Russia remains an ever-changing part of the European mix. According to the Federal Statistics Service, its economy fell 8.9 percent in the third quarter compared to a year earlier, but was up 13.9 percent over the second quarter 2009. Patricia M. Cloherty is the chairman and CEO of Delta Private Equity Partners, whose present fund invests in Russia. She says that Russia has its own profile. The statistics aside, Cloherty offers this view: "The crisis may pass more quickly in Russia. The economy is in its infancy, and rebuilding is necessary. In Russia, companies that were privatized are now being nationalized, and probably will be reprivatized through either IPOs or private deals. I have a fair amount of confidence that both President Medvedev and Prime Minister Putin seek a strong private economy. They may get there in a uniquely Russian way."

"Pre-crisis," Cloherty says, "many useful bills were backed up in the Duma. Post-crisis, the government needs to pay more attention to infrastructure. Much was spent in supporting the ruble, but there's some $385 billion left and no debt. The Russian government also has moved to assist the major banks." She says, "The interesting thing in Russia is that there's a shock absorber: it's called 'money in the mattress.'"

She cautions, though, that "the amount of borrowing from international banks revealed the fragility of Russia's 10-year-old economy. There were only a handful of hydrocarbon companies that had any liquidity, and the banking system is also not yet broad and deep. For the past 10 years, the financial infrastructure wasn't attended to because people were making a lot of money without it."

Looking to the future, Cloherty continues to see opportunities in the consumer-related markets, including financial services, TMT (technology, media, telecommunications), and consumer products and services. Entertainment always is a big space, and the Internet is just beginning. But she is concerned about how the country treats smaller businesses: "One thing that concerns me in Russia is that the large businesses dominate relative to SMEs [small and medium enterprises], given the huge natural resources base of the country. The diversification of the economy through SMEs is slow, even though a country may rest on its having a broad base of smaller growing businesses."

Cloherty also notes, "There is general nervousness with all emerging markets at this time, including Russia. These countries must take steps to welcome investors before overseas investors become comfortable again. When you invest in private equity and venture capital, normal risks are compounded unless a country tries to mitigate risk in every way possible. Investors always tend to gravitate toward lower risk, especially in these hazardous times."

Private equity and venture capital firms operate around the globe. The changes brought about by the economic downturn in 2008 and subsequent rebound in 2009 will shape the industry. But they will also face a number of regulatory, tax, and internal issues. The next chapter discusses these challenges and how the industry is likely to respond in a changed world.

CHAPTER 6

Industry Issues

As the world faces new financial realities, private equity and venture capital have been caught in the remedial politics that have swept Washington, Brussels, and London. (Asian governments have shown themselves less interested in clamping down on the industry.) As a result, GPs and interest groups are responding to several regulatory and tax initiatives in the United States and Europe. These measures are designed to improve transparency, while reining in the excesses of lending and risk taking that initially brought the financial services to the government's door.

Private equity and venture capital also face a number of internal issues. Among them: no credit, a large bid-ask spread on deal pricing, succession, appropriate business model, fund raising, capital calls, adapting to globalization, fund structure, going public, "the public face of private equity," and pushback from LPs. As the industry prepares to welcome its next generation of leaders, there is certainly a lot on its plate.

UNITED STATES

Congress and the regulatory agencies were caught flat-footed by the 2008–2009 financial implosion. The Senate and the House didn't seem to understand how or why it happened; they just don't want it to happen again. Regulators, such as the Securities and Exchange Commission (SEC), have been criticized for not doing their job. And private industry executives have been the object of recriminations by both Congress and the media. Primary targets seem to be the banks, hedge funds, and derivatives markets. In the round-up of usual suspects, though, the authorities want to put private equity and venture capital on the regulatory radar screen.

In the United States, industry executives hope to contain (at least) four initiatives that involve more regulation and higher taxes. First, there's the Hedge Fund Transparency Act. This bill is an amendment to the Investment Company Act of 1940. Senators Charles Grassley (Iowa) and Carl Levin

(Michigan) introduced the Hedge Fund Transparency Act, which would require hedge funds, private equity, and other private funds with $50 million or more in assets to register with the SEC. These funds would have to file an array of information with the SEC to qualify for certain exemptions from registration for privately offered funds. As $50 million is not a lot of money for a private equity or venture funds these days, just about everyone is affected.

A companion bill, the House Hedge Fund Advisor Registration Act is an amendment to the Investment Advisers Act of 1940. Representatives Michael Capuano (Massachusetts) and Michael Castle (Delaware) have introduced this bill. The Mutual Fund Directors Forum blog reports that the bill effectively closes an exception to SEC registration for advisers who have a limited number of clients. The bill will require all investment advisers with even a single U.S. client—including advisers of hedge funds, venture capital funds, private equity funds, and CDOs—to register with the SEC. This registration regime commits advisers to a range of restrictions and duties to which advisers of regulated pooled investment vehicles are currently subject.

A third front is led by Treasury Secretary Geithner. It espouses the Obama administration's overall views on financial regulation as outlined in the Treasury Department's white paper, *Financial Regulatory Reform: A New Foundation*, issued in June 2009. At 89 pages, the document is long but comprehensive. It covers the range of financial regulatory issues, from banks to insurance companies, regulatory agencies to regulated industries, domestic to international. It lumps private equity and venture capital funds under "private pools of capital" and says they "should be required to register with the SEC under the Investment Advisers Act." They would be asked "to report information on the funds they manage that is sufficient to assess whether any fund poses a threat to financial stability."

The paper gives good reasons for its recommendations for regulating "funds that trade commodity derivatives," as well as the danger created from "de-leveraging by hedge funds." But it offers no rationale for regulating private equity and venture capital, other than that the information would be useful to assess whether they "pose a threat to financial stability."

The report is a good document. For a country in which legislation regularly subordinates stated policy objectives to trading political favors, it is one of the first clear statements of government policy in recent memory (if not longer). Without commenting on its conclusions, the American public probably wouldn't mind similar documents on other issues such as defense, education, or criminal justice.

It falls short, though, in a few areas. The report should prioritize its recommendations. It covers a lot of topics, and some items must be more important than others. Second, the report evinces further movement along the joint dimensions that have governed American political life: federal-state relationships and the public-private divide. It is a clear directive for federal authority over private initiative. Finally, it prescribes many different solutions, perhaps too many, but leaves enforcement to the job description provided. That's how the system almost went off the rails in 2008. The most heavily regulated industries—the banks and insurance companies—were the ones who caused the greatest problems.

Says Doug Lowenstein of Private Equity Council,

> We are encouraged that policymakers do understand that private equity firms have limited or no leverage at the fund level, that we do not rely on short-term funding, are not deeply interconnected with other financial market participants through derivatives positions, counterparty exposures, or prime brokerage relationships, and that we invest in long-term illiquid assets. In short, when applying the administration's systemic risk factors to private equity, it is hard to see how any particular private equity fund could be considered a systemic risk. But people in Congress are saying, "We don't want to carve out private equity because if five years from now something happens and we don't have a window into your business through some regulation, it will appear to be a serious oversight gap." All that said, the administration has proposed to require that private equity firms register with the SEC as investment advisors. We have testified that we support this requirement, provided it is carefully calibrated.
>
> We support registration under the Investment Advisers Act. But we would be most concerned about registration under the Investment Company Act. It's still problematic, and we're not sure we could operate a private equity business under those rules. The Act was developed to operate in the mutual fund industry and is mostly about investor protection. The one thing that could change the equation regarding how private equity is regulated is if you have a couple of big private equity deals going bust. This will create a different story line around private equity that could undo a lot of the positives around the industry.

Referring to representatives who do not serve on the House Financial Services Committee, Mike Quaranta, chief of staff to Representative Michael Castle, said, "Most members have not yet joined the hedge fund registration debate. Although some members and staff are aware of private pools of capital and the attendant issues, most will focus their attention elsewhere, unless some 'incident' occurs, or until a House vote is scheduled. They hear the words 'hedge fund,' 'private equity' or 'venture capital' and instantly become suspicious. Now many factors fuel that suspicion, and primary among them would be the inability of regulators to even identify some funds and their managers." Looking at the scope of House action, Quaranta feels that any registration legislation will "certainly cover hedge funds. However, the breadth of registration requirements that could be imposed remains unresolved."

Quaranta thinks the main players that will decide the fate of this issue are the obvious ones: "Treasury Secretary Geithner, Representative Barney Frank, and Senator Richard Shelby. The 'unknown' or 'yet to be understood' factor in all of this will be the views taken by Senator Chris Dodd [Chairman of the Senate Banking Committee]. Dodd is presently managing much of the president's healthcare reform package in the Senate and not focused on issues like these."

Senator Dodd also faces a tough reelection campaign in 2010. In a September reshuffling, Senator Dodd ceded control of the committee that handles healthcare reform so that he could focus on overhauling the nation's financial regulatory policy.

In the House, notes Quaranta,

> Congressman Frank says he's going to move pieces of financial regulatory reform out of Committee, perhaps tie them together for full House action, or maybe even move some separately on to the Senate. I think he's keeping his options open, because predicting the House floor agenda months from now is something he knows is difficult to do. He also has to consider what he wants to accomplish, what makes the most sense to package and send to the Senate that gives him the greatest leverage should additional negotiations be necessary. I think it's highly probable that the House will pass a couple of financial reform bills, but it's way too early to tell what the Senate might do with any or all of this. The Democrats have made it clear that the economy and unemployment, healthcare and energy reform issues will dominate the agenda. Although financial reforms like these are important to "get right" for many good reasons, pollsters tell us they're simply not the issues voters consider come Election Day.

A Washington-based consultant said privately that he expects some action, but says it's still too early to see exactly what comes out. "My prediction is that Congress will get pieces of legislation: systemic risk, orderly resolution of nonbank financial institutions, and different industries by the end of the year. We will see heavy congressional action later this year. Even if the financial crisis recedes, there's enough pressure to keep these issues alive. The politicians are getting great mileage out of it.

He adds, "The Federal Reserve Board will be the new systemic regulator. We'll see how the financial regulatory framework will work, how much more these entities will be regulated. How far Congress gets into private equity remains to be seen, though. I would doubt that it goes beyond making the big groups more transparent. They have to make quarterly reports, etc. to the FRB. All sorts of provisions—such as the confidentiality of the reports—have yet to be worked out."

STATE POLITICAL ISSUES

The soul-searching in Washington notwithstanding, there's another issue that has largely bypassed the private equity and venture capital community. Namely, what do state trustees of public pension plans think of the decline in returns? After all, the hard-working police officers, firefighters, and teachers are really the ones absorbing the stress in the industry. So far, the trustees have said little if anything. California trustees, in fact, increased their allocation to alternative assets in June 2009. Whether that will continue and for how long remains an open question.

One subject that has generated headlines, however, is how public pension fund assets get allocated to private managers. As this book went to press, the New York state attorney general was expanding his probe into how state pension funds were being accessed. The state is examining the use of placement agents to steer state funds into specific private equity funds. Using placement agents is standard practice; but the "pay-to-play" scandal centered on whether state officials received kickbacks for investing pension assets in their clients' funds is not.

The attorney general has issued more than a hundred subpoenas to investment firms and intermediaries who brokered deals with public pension funds. The attorney general claims that the payments are essentially bribes or kickbacks disguised as legitimate business payments. He said a preliminary review by his office found that as many as half of the intermediaries in pension fund transactions in New York State and New York City were not properly licensed and registered with a broker-dealer, as required by federal securities laws. Being licensed by the state seems a no-brainer, but apparently not. The investigation is also targeting pension funds in California and New Mexico.

Under way for two years, the inquiries have focused on the millions of dollars that friends, relatives, and aides of New York State's comptroller,

Alan Hevesi, may have earned by gaining access to the $122-billion New York state pension fund. Three aides and a Dallas investment adviser have already been indicted. At the center of the case is a campaign strategist who was the top political adviser for Hevesi. (Hevesi has not been charged.) As the *New York Times* reports, "It's an uncomfortable moment in the spotlight for placement agents, which have long operated behind closed doors."

The investigation is serious, as evidenced by The Carlyle Group's agreeing to pay $20 million and to stop using placement agents to gain business from pension funds nationwide. Another private equity group, Riverstone Holdings (a Carlyle joint venture partner), settled with the attorney general for $30 million in June 2009. As part of the deal, Carlyle executives and the firm will not face any further action, including criminal prosecution, by the New York state attorney general. According to the *New York Times*, Carlyle manages $1.3 billion and generates $13 million in annual fees from the state pension fund.[1]

"Pay-to-play" has been going on for some time, according to industry experts. Many placement agents simply took their lumps and did business elsewhere. Those who haven't may soon find themselves on the attorney general's subpoena list.

EUROPE AND THE UNITED KINGDOM

The *Wall Street Journal* reports that the U.K.'s financial regulator, the Financial Services Authority (FSA), and the British Treasury Ministry have expressed less interest in tightening regulation of private equity funds than their continental counterparts. British officials' more laissez-faire attitude toward private equity seems to stem from their conclusion that private equity funds are not "too big to fail."

The U.K.'s FSA has produced the *Turner Review*, a report issued in March 2009 that recommended regulatory responses to the financial crisis. It argues that since "hedge fund activity in aggregate can have an important procyclical systemic impact," many such funds should be subject to capital, liquidity, and other restrictions. The *Turner Review*'s policy proposals, however, did not identify private equity funds as financial institutions that pose system-wide risks. In this respect, at least, the *Turner Review* seems to agree in principle with the European Private Equity and Venture Capital Association's (EVCA) assertion that neither private equity's funding models nor the portfolio companies in which private equity typically invests pose systemic risks to financial markets.

In April 2009, the European Union offered its response, the Directive on Alternative Investment Fund Managers (AIFM). It is intended to create a comprehensive regulatory framework across the 27 member states and specifies capital, reporting, and organizational requirements. Jim Brundsen of the *European Voice*, which reviewed a draft of the EU proposal, wrote that the legislation would require private equity funds with assets under management in excess of €250 million to maintain a minimum capital requirement of €125,000, plus 0.02 percent of the amount by which the funds' portfolios exceed €250 million. Funds whose assets remain below the €250 million threshold would be excluded from the new regulatory requirements.

An article in the *Guardian* reported, "The EU plans to impose tough new regulations on hedge funds. Private equity and their managers are in disarray because of a political row within the European Commission. The argument raging between economic liberals in favor of light-touch rules and social democrats demanding a clampdown could delay legislation until next year."[2]

Senior socialist members of the European Parliament denounced the draft legislation as "almost worthless" and "filled with loopholes" and accused José Manuel Barroso, the European Commission's president, of a lack of leadership on the issue. Poul Nyrup Rasmussen—president of the Party of European Socialists (PES) and author of European Parliament reports demanding strict cross-border supervision—said, "The current proposal has more and bigger holes than a Swiss cheese."

Forces digging in their heels against the measures demanded by the PES and its allies are being marshaled by Charlie McCreevy, EU internal market commissioner, and his senior officials. PES's Rasmussen said, "Either Barroso's goal is to prevent this parliament debating the financial regulation it demanded or he cannot unite opposing views within the EC."

Hedge funds and private equity groups, which favor a stricter but still voluntary code of conduct, have lobbied fiercely on the issue, insisting they are not responsible for the financial crisis. McCreevy endorses their view that they could be part of the solution to the turmoil, which the International Monetary Fund says has caused $4 trillion of losses. Private equity also insists it should be treated differently from hedge funds, as it poses no systemic risk.

By September 2009, the disagreement had turned into a slugfest between the more market-driven U.K. and the more regulatory-inspired countries on the continent. Boris Johnson, mayor of London, which is home to 60 percent of Europe's private equity industry, was blunt in a September 2009 interview in the *Guardian*: "The directive as it is currently drafted will have enormously damaging consequences for London, for the U.K., and for Europe too. There is no suggestion or evidence that investment funds were in any way to blame for the financial crisis, and it is difficult to see the justification for this level of regulation."[3]

For the continental socialists, the question isn't the systemic risks but who benefits from private equity. In their eyes, the employees (labor unions) are left holding the bag when a corporation is merged into or was purchased by another. Their solution is to stipulate a series of stringent disclosure and reporting requirements when a private equity fund acquires more than 30 percent of an EU company.

Jonathan Blake, senior partner at the law firm SJ Berwin in London, offers a broader perspective: "Over the last few years, for the first time ever, there's been a sense that private equity are the bad guys. They have been pushed on the defensive."

Blake places the blame on the coverage given to the larger deals. "I think it's very much linked to the growth in mega-deals involving household name companies and high leveraging, but it isn't as if they were the cause of the financial crash. Private equity has wrongly been increasingly linked with those deals rather than the mid market where it continues in a much less high-profile manner.

"David Walker and the disclosure requirements were probably right," he says. "What's now happening with the proposals for regulatory reform coming from the EU is very concerning and is largely misplaced—it won't bring any benefit, but it risks killing the industry for no reason, because they haven't properly understood the industry and haven't distinguished it from hedge and other funds, which have different issues. Part of it is a backlash against the market economy and enterprise by people who would prefer a different system."

At press time, discussion on the proposed Alternative Investment Funds Managers Directive remained lively. The directive is scheduled to become law sometime between December 2009 and spring 2010.

Looking at the regulatory front in both the United States and United Kingdom/Europe, governments' beef with private equity and venture capital isn't totally logical. If anyone should be concerned, it would be their limited partners. They are the ones investing in illiquid investments and receiving poor returns. As Blake notes, even on the mega-deals, the private equity and ventures houses were casualties, not causes. By and large, the industry improves and builds the companies they invest in. Did the mega-funds take advantage of the liquidity bubble? Yes, but the limited partners supplied the equity capital and agreed to the fees. Banks provided the loans. Failing any systemic risk that the funds pose—and there don't seem to be any—the general partners should be queried by the limited partners and banks not the government on their fees and other grievances.

There is, of course, the argument for employees of companies that have been acquired by private equity who have been made redundant or have been laid off in a failed deal. Clearly, during the liquidity bubble, private equity firms paid unsustainable prices for companies. The GPs then overleveraged the acquired companies while taking out fees and dividends, which in hindsight proved bad decisions, if not simple greed. But that money came from somewhere—the banks and limited partners—which is one reason that the financial system is still not out of the woods in 2010 and institutional investors have seen portfolios values drop 20 to 30 percent. Everybody, not just employees, paid a price.

In other instances, jobs have been eliminated by private equity's drive for efficiency. The world is a different place than it was 20 years ago. Industrial economies in the United States and Western Europe face systemic challenges not only from reckless financial institutions but from companies with lower production costs and different work rules. The United States and EU can pass tariffs and otherwise threaten these countries, but these other countries can do the same. Their markets are growing while Western markets are flat. In essence, the West's economic supremacy is not what it once was. Keeping dysfunctional or poorly managed corporations alive through subsidies or government cash may work in the short term but can only fail in the future.

Ultimately, the answer can best be found in societies' (governments') defining longer-term objectives and projects that will put people to work in a productive way. The answer does not lie in "stimulus programs" or "government bailouts," which may work short-term but do not contribute to rebuilding the economic base. For better or worse, by optimizing large companies or funding new ventures, private equity and venture capital buttress those goals.

Whether the government wants to turn insolvent financial institutions over to private equity is another story. In August 2009, the FDIC announced new rules governing private equity's purchase of troubled banks. The rules are more liberal if the firms team up with banking industry partners. But not many volunteers with the cash and human resources have stepped forward to value toxic assets and nonperforming loans. To date, the Treasury Department's PPIP initiative has not generated huge interest. If funds get involved, they expect to make a profit. Clearly there are those private equity partners who are capable and others who aren't. That's a fair call for the regulators to make, but different from one that casts suspicion over the entire asset class. See also "The Public Face of Private Equity," later in this chapter.

TAX ISSUES: THE CARRY—CAPITAL GAINS OR ORDINARY INCOME?

Of equal if not greater concern is whether the private equity and venture capital fund managers are paying their taxes. The most pressing tax issue is how the carried interest (the "carry") should be taxed. Again, the carry is that percentage (usually 20 percent) that the fund manager receives from the sale of portfolio company shares once the limited partners have been paid back.

In the United States, the issue of whether or not to tax the carry interest, and if so, how, remains alive. A Private Equity Council fact sheet says,

> Capital gain treatment is intended to reward those who invest in capital assets and realize capital gains. Our tax system has long recognized that a taxpayer may be entitled to capital gain treatment with respect to the sale or exchange of property where the gains are attributable in whole or in part to the taxpayer's own personal efforts. The key criterion for capital gain treatment is not whether the gains are attributable to capital or to labor. Rather, the key criterion is whether the taxpayer has made an entrepreneurial investment—of capital or labor—in a long-lived asset, the return for which depends entirely on the value of the asset.

Representative Sander Levin (Michigan) introduced legislation in early 2009 to tax carried interest compensation at ordinary income tax rates. Currently, fund managers are able to receive compensation for these services at the much lower capital gains tax rate rather than the ordinary income tax rate, by virtue of their fund's partnership structure. Levin's bill would treat the "carried interest" as ordinary income rather than capital gains. Said Representative Levin,

> This is a basic issue of fairness. Fund managers are receiving compensation for managing their investors' money. They should not pay the 15-percent capital gains rate on their compensation when millions of other hard-working Americans, many of whose income is performance-based, pay ordinary rates of up to 35 percent. This proposal is not about taxing investment, it's about ensuring that all compensation is treated equally for tax purposes. Anyone who actually invests money in these funds will continue to receive capital gains treatment, including the managers. So there is no reason to expect that the amount of capital available for these kinds of investments will be reduced.

Lowenstein says that,

> Taxing carried interest at ordinary rates is in the Obama budget and is very much back on the table. But the environment today is very different than two years ago. We're not the white hats, but we're not the black hats. Looking at $2 trillion deficits, the $23 billion in additional revenue over 10 years isn't nearly as attractive. It is complicated to predict how this plays out. It is likely that the House will include it as a revenue raiser in some legislation. What will happen in the Senate is unclear. I think many people in the industry expect that taxes on carried interest will go up, but the weak economy has changed things so the certainty that something would happen is not as great.

Lowenstein argues, "We think that carried interest is a capital gain. What's different now is that two years ago it was the highest priority in the tax debate. Now, it's just doesn't have the kind of impact it did because of the economy, concerns about stimulating new investment, and the fact that the deficits are so huge. This raises relatively little revenue, and even less than hoped for because there is so little carry being generated."

Much has been written on the subject, from 50-page law review articles to five-page fact sheets. Even more has been said by industry representatives in Washington. The issue is not simple: company (including portfolio company) shares are capital assets. Thus they should nominally be taxed as such by the authorities. But the inquiry doesn't end there. Why do general partners receive portfolio company shares (representing the carried interest) upon a successful exit? The shares are granted as a form of additional compensation to incentivize them to perform. That should make any income taxable, in part, as ordinary income. One GP notes, the question really revolves around, "How much risk is the participant in the carry really taking? In our firm, the cash compensation at the salary level is really very low. Taxing the carry at capital gains rates just means that there's a genuine incentive." He admits that those who argue "compensation" rather than "risk" aren't totally off base.

He suggests, then, that the carry should be considered much like stock options. Assuming that they are granted at fair market value, he says, there's no tax. "Instead of a carry, you could give the GP options in the company. If they are held in the partnership, then the tax flows through. That's the alternative for a fund." But if there's no ordinary income tax when the options are exercised, then nothing changes. So the philosophical argument between "compensation" and "risk" remains. The government may want to propose a different metric (see the following discussion).

Alan Patricof has suggested another test: a sliding scale, based on the holding period. Funds making investments in companies that have previously raised less than $50 million would be eligible for special treatment on the shares representing their carry. (Patricof points out that the SBIC uses this dollar amount as a cutoff for defining small businesses.) The tax rate decreases depending upon how long the investment is held. Thus, if a fund holds an investment for five years, the general partner receives capital gains treatment on his shares. If the fund holds the investment for one year, gain on the sale of the GP's shares is taxed at ordinary income rates. In between, the tax rates are adjusted pro rata. Either way, as Lowenstein suggests, "The question is what and when, not if."

But these regulatory and tax questions are just the beginning. The industry also faces a number of internal structural and economic issues that, one way or the other, it will have to resolve. Some of these issues have already been presented.

NO CREDIT

This issue has been discussed throughout the book and remains crucial to private equity's future returns. Richard Slocum says that "Credit markets are key to private equity markets: not only to provide leverage, but to facilitate a more dynamic M&A market and even IPO market. For distributions to come back in any meaningful way, credit needs to come back first."

The price of debt has come down from its crisis highs, but the banks have been unwilling (as of September 2009) to lend large amounts in levered deals. One indicator of perceived credit risk is the TED spread, which measures the difference between three-month U.S. Treasuries (risk free) and the three-month Eurodollar contract (risk of lending to a commercial bank). In September 2009, it was about 16.5 basis points, well down in its normal 10 to 50 basis point range.

In Australia, Justin Reizes, KKR member, says, "Financing will be difficult to get for a while. We will just have to be creative. Solutions include using pieces of the existing debt structure and raising funds from providers that are not part of the traditional structure."

In Asia at least, one deal may prove a template for future transactions. In May 2009, Anheuser-Busch InBev said it agreed to sell its South Korean Oriental Brewery to a joint venture between KKR and Affinity Partners for $1.8 billion. The JV partners would be putting in about $800 million, purchasing the company for about 9x to 10x EBITDA. In the past, buyout firms have typically paid around 25 percent in cash and borrowed the rest. KKR's check represents about 45 percent equity. The seller is also offering

$300 million in vendor financing for the deal. The rest of the money came from bank loans, whose interest rate is a hefty LIBOR (London Interbank Offered Rate) plus 600 basis points.

FASB 157: MARK-TO-MARKET

The Financial Accounting Standards Board standard FASB 157 had a big impact on 2H2008 (down) and on 1H2009 (up) valuations. FASB 157 is the accounting profession's dictate that private equity and venture firms have to mark their investments to market. The yardstick is generally comparable public companies.

It's a real issue—no one seems to be happy. Philip Bilden says the timing couldn't be worse.

> We are seeing next to nothing in terms of distributions in 2009. Capital calls have slowed as well except for paying management fees as few deals are being done. LPs are still reeling from draconian write-downs at year-end 2008 in sympathy with the public markets. Although the fundamental relationship between private equity and public markets has not changed, the accounting for that relationship has changed dramatically with FASB 157. The industry adopted the standard in the most volatile year. Many LPs and trustee boards will be confused by the volatility of interim returns and the visibly marked-to-market correlation with listed markets. Ultimately, it is realized returns (cash) that matters after a long investment life cycle. Unfortunately, many LPs will not have the stamina or discipline to focus on the end returns when PE quarterly performance is marked to a volatile public market.

In the end, he says, "The industry will have to offer investors alternative valuation methods. Particularly, since one of the nominal advantages of private equity and venture capital is that they untie their unlisted portfolios from the short term movements of the public markets."

The directive is also an issue for the banks making the loans and impacts their willingness to restructure overleveraged deals. Ralph Parks of Oaktree Capital argues that mark-to-market wasn't intended to cover today's volatility. "The consequences of mark-to-market accounting—producing immediate, cascading downgrades from the rating agencies across the entire finance industry—were never intended. Mark-to-market was not created to meet the situation faced by markets and regulators in the fourth quarter of 2008. What the securities are worth on the last (possibly forced) sale versus their value at maturity ignores the fact that many banks may hold loans until maturity."

David Coulter of Warburg Pincus also believes that banks hold loans to maturity, so they shouldn't be valued on an interim basis. "The whole fair value accounting issue has gotten a bit out of hand. You don't manage a commercial bank entity on a daily mark-to-market basis. It is an important tool to alert management to potential problems. But GAAP [generally accepted accounting principles] is also a well-developed and comprehensive discipline for commercial banks that reflects both the stability of their deposit bases and the hold-to-maturity nature of many asset categories."

DRY POWDER AND THE BID-ASK SPREAD

The industry still has a lot of cash. Sources indicate that the overall figure for private equity is $400 to $470 billion in dry powder. Including real estate, venture, and other, the amount available for investment may be closer to $1 trillion. The numbers for Private Equity Council members are shown in Table 6.1.

As noted previously, the industry initially thought that the downturn would provide once-in-a-lifetime opportunities to invest this capital. To date, that has not happened. Lack of credit is one reason. The other is the bid-ask spread for pricing deals. Target companies have seen the rise in public equity markets and have simply been unwilling to do deals at low multiples.

TABLE 6.1 Private Equity Council Member Firms' "Dry Powder"

	USD in billions as of 6/30/2009
TPG	24.9
Bain Capital	19.1
Carlyle Group	17.3
Apollo Management	15.4
Kohlberg Kravis Roberts	14.1
Apax Partners	12.2
Silver Lake	8.7
Blackstone Group	8.2
Permira	6.7
Providence Equity Partners	6.6
Madison Dearborn Partners	4.9
Hellman & Friedman	NA
Total (known)	**138.1**

Gary Stead of Shearwater Capital Group calls the difference in pricing expectations "price discovery." He says, "Deal flow was slow in 2009 because of a couple of factors. The first was price discovery, the buyer is taking a cautious approach. And access to credit: there's a dearth of providers in this space. When there are major economic dislocations, the gap between bid and ask, buyers and sellers widens. Sellers want yesterday's prices, buyers want tomorrow's prices. This mismatch reflects an ongoing lack of confidence in the market and an inability to value both the debt and equity side."

Harjit Bhatia of Credit Suisse Private Equity Asia says that gap presents a paradox. "We have an enormous credit contraction, but people are also sitting on huge amounts of cash. Maybe a lot more money will come back. People are expecting two or three years, but liquidity could trigger a little quicker rebound." Bhatia notes, "When we talk about valuation, we look at numbers 10 years down the road. People used to say, 'look at my forward numbers.' Now they are saying, 'look at my past numbers.' "

KY Tang of Affinity Equity Partners agrees that there's still a lot of cash looking for a home. "There's a lot of capital waiting on the sideline to buy assets. But they won't, because, given all this volatility, they don't know how to price the asset. It's all sitting on the sideline."

Warren Hellman has been equally surprised by the lack of completed transactions. "We've done some bolt-ons, but we haven't written a check for about a year. The incoming deals aren't much cheaper in terms of cash flow than in 2007. The panic of 1987, with terrible capitalizations, doesn't exist. That's because there is so much dry powder in the industry. The bid-ask spread remains large. The market hasn't retreated."

One reason for the lack of 2009 activity, says Howard Marks of Oaktree Capital Management, is that a lot of forced selling took place in 2008. "The market is pretty quiet in the debt world today. Most people who had to sell sold in the fall [of 2008]. Many are willing to wait until a recovery. Right now [March 2009], things are quiet." Said one LP, "Fourth quarter 2008 was busy. We were busy in the first quarter 2009, but didn't get a lot done. The press has it right: there's still a lot to do, but not a lot happening."

It's a major issue, one that will likely be solved through a number of routes including more equity, vendor financing, reduced multiples, and the cobbling together of enough banks to supply the credit to complete a transaction.

MANAGING FAILURES

This industry touts its ability to close mega-deals, and it's unaccustomed to being on the short end of a workout. The spectacular returns of bygone days have largely dried up, and private equity is sustaining itself on healthy salaries and management fees—not performance fees. There have been many portfolio company problems, some leading to bankruptcy: TPG's investment in WaMu, Apollo's buyout of Linens 'n Things, and Cerberus Capital's write-down of its Chrysler equity stake are among them.

Responses have varied, but one trend seems likely: the heroes of the past 10 years will not likely be the heroes of the next decade. Though high returns may come back, the deals will require more time, thought, and effort to achieve.

Philip Bilden of HarbourVest says managing failures will also require cash. "There's a question of solvency: there will be a lot of equity cures. If those funds are tapped out, there's nothing more to give. They won't be able to raise the funds. There will be new injections from the private equity side that have to come from private equity sources."

As reported in the *New York Times* in February 2007, the 10 largest private-equity transactions were: TXU ($43.8 billion, 2007), Equity Office Properties ($38.9 billion, 2006), HCA ($32.7 billion, 2006), RJR Nabisco ($31.1 billion, 1988), Harrah's Entertainment ($27.4 billion, 2006), Clear Channel Communications ($25.7 billion, 2006), Kinder Morgan ($21.6 billion, 2006), Freescale Semiconductor ($17.6 billion, 2006), Albertson's ($17.4 billion, 2006) and Hertz ($15 billion, 2005).[4]

With the exception of RJR Nabisco in 1988, all these deals occurred in 2005–2007. It's like the kid in the candy store—on his way to the dentist. You can blame the kid (private equity) for buying all the candy, or you can blame his parents (the LPs and the banks) for bankrolling him. The only one who has made out is the candy store owner (target company), who has sold far more sweets than he should have.

FUNDRAISING IN THE NEXT DECADE

It's no secret that fundraising will be difficult. That is not to say that funds were not raised in 2009. Carlyle Asia Growth Partners IV raised $1.04 billion, Keytone Ventures in China closed its first fund at $200 million, and MBK Partners in Korea closed on $1.6 billion for its second Asian fund in July 2009. In the United States, Matrix Partners closed a $600 million venture fund in July 2009, and Khosla Ventures raised $1.1 billion in September. But the amounts were down considerably from previous years: through April 2009, $45.7 billion versus $268.2 billion in 2008.

Gary Bridge says that without additional funding, the GPs will have to make painful choices. "There's the painful issue of triaging their portfolios. There's not enough money in their current portfolios to fund these companies through this period of time. That will have a double whammy effect on their portfolios in terms of (1) the need to triage meaningfully and (2) lowering the value of many companies because of the severe economic downturn."

Describing the state of affairs in early 2009, Philip Bilden says that cash is in short supply. "One response for GPs facing portfolio distress is to set up an annex fund or a separate fund to invest in prior funds' deals where cash is needed. Certain managers are attempting to raise annex funds with mixed results." It's a sign of the times, says Bilden. "There's real distress in the portfolios, cash is needed for equity cures, earnings are diminishing in a recessionary environment, and banks want to put the risk back on the equity. Meanwhile, the exit and refinancing markets remain shut. All of this puts a lot of stress on the GPs. Some managers will respond by slowly easing out of the business as it becomes too hard and less fun. The crisis may well be a catalyst to older GPs handing the keys to the next generation. Tough times will force management company issues to the table."

Toward the end of 2009, one GP reports, "The fund raising environment is really opening up, so maybe there's some confidence returning." LPs like the asset class, and the pension funds have new money. The rebound in the stock market has also helped.

CAPITAL CALLS

Capital calls are another issue. These are the total commitments that institutions have made to the funds, much of which lies in the future as the funds require money to be invested when a deal is completed. There's a big, unfunded capital overhang, as shown in Table 6.2.

Richard Slocum would like to see capital calls lowered. "The market would benefit greatly from more examples of what TPG did—allow LPs to lower their committed capital to a given fund. This would contribute to bringing back liquidity to the private markets, as investors would not be forced to reserve as much for this massive capital overhang." He adds,

TABLE 6.2 U.S. Private Equity Capital Overhang

U.S. Private Equity Overhang (USD Billions)	2007	2008	2009
Equity Invested	320.07	127.22	24.03
Capital Raised by Funds	264.90	268.24	45.74
Overhang (By Year)	(55.17)	141.02	21.71
Overhang (Cumulative)	236.86	377.88	399.59

Source: PitchBook Data, Inc. through 4/2009.

"Given the nearly total halt in distributions in 2008, we saw investors redeeming from their public and hedge fund managers to fund illiquid asset commitments. This includes private equity, real estate, distressed credit, and energy. The effect of this was to contribute to the downward spiral of the public equity markets."

Sheryl Schwartz of TIAA-CREF pointed out that capital calls would be minimal in 2009. "That's because there's no leverage or liquidity. Also, there's a mismatch between buyers and sellers because there's such uncertainty in the market. Therefore deals are not getting done. When that changes, the LPs will have tough decisions to make." Bruce Feldman adds to that: "GPs can't expect existing investors whose private equity exposure models have been turned upside down by market turbulence to commit capital at their historic pace and amount."

There's another reason behind the drop in capital calls in 2009, says Steve Byrom of Australia's Future Fund. "It's more than just LPs not having the capital to give the GPs, but there appears to be a level of disenchantment in the asset class. LPs are now getting more involved with their investments. The LPs have been getting more courageous and talking more among themselves whilst GPs have been trying to play divide and conquer. There are a lot of people who will come back, expecting to raise capital and won't be able to get what they are wanting."

THE PUBLIC FACE OF PRIVATE EQUITY

Private equity is just that—private. Or it was. Just 10 years ago, few if any leaders in the private equity and venture communities felt a need to talk publicly. Says one public relations executive, "I was sitting in Asia in 2004 and saw the increasing volume of private equity. Suddenly, private equity was reported everywhere. I thought, they will want to get known, to help them access deals. But when some of the big U.S. firms arrived, their main comment was, 'We have no reason to talk to anybody. We will keep our own counsel.' "

He notes, "Then, we moved into 2006–2007, when you had the big backlash in the United States and Europe. Private equity was named 'Public Enemy No. 1.' The key players were clearly insensitive to the way in which the outside world perceived them. If you take the stakeholders—NGOs, unions, employees, customers, government, the media—they are all interested. You employ hundreds of thousands of people across dozens of companies with billions in revenues. How private equity firms could believe that they had nothing to disclose when they controlled such chunks of the economy is hard to fathom."

He says, "Things are changing, though. In conversations with a couple of major private equity firms, they now seem to be far more sensitive to these issues than before. They are asking, 'How will this look if we do something?' rather than saying 'Let's not worry about it until later.' They are starting to break out of the privateness of private equity."

He continues, "Senior guys who set up these funds were able to run them privately 20 years ago. Now you have a new generation of leaders coming through. They are asking themselves, 'How will this look publicly? If all of this doesn't smell like roses, how will this impact my fund?' "

What would be some examples of private equity's changed attitudes? He says, "The big firms seem to be waking up to the fact that openness builds trust, and trust is a critical ingredient at a time of crisis. Let's assume you are a private equity player and you have portfolio investments in Asia. How would you react if the papers run a story tomorrow that says one of the fund's portfolio companies uses suppliers that rely on child labor? I would argue that the firms with a track record for transparency will get a far better balanced hearing in the court of public opinion that those who hide behind 'privacy.' "

The considerations are not hypothetical. Consider the January 2006 Sago Mine disaster in West Virginia. A January 14, 2006 article in *New York* magazine reported:

> [F]or a private-equity investor who specializes in collecting underperforming assets in the industrial heartland, it was a nightmare come true. Wilbur Ross, Jr., had just gotten out of bed on January 2 when he received a frantic call: There had been an explosion in a mine he owns in Sago, West Virginia. Thirteen miners were trapped underground—some two miles from the mine shaft's opening—a disaster that would soon command the attention of the international media.
>
> What followed was brutal press coverage that painted Ross as a heartless latter-day nineteenth-century coal baron. The blast shattered an extraordinary streak for Ross. He spent decades as an investment banker. In 2002, Ross started snapping up decaying steel mills, southern textile mills, and mines, vaulting him into billionaire ranks for the first time. This past November, he took over the International Coal Group, owner of the Sago mine. And then: the explosion.[5]

Or take Harrah's casino. A March 2009 article in Bloomberg reported:

> Harrah's casino owners, private-equity firms Apollo Management LP and TPG Inc., are buying debt to protect themselves should the world's biggest casino company fail, people familiar with the matter said. Apollo and TPG, which purchased Las Vegas-based Harrah's in a $30.7 billion buyout last year, have bought about $2 billion of its loans, the people said. They may hold an additional 20 percent of its "second-lien" notes through a proposed debt exchange, according to a March 5 offering memorandum obtained by Bloomberg News. Harrah's reported a fourth-quarter 2008 operating loss of $5.35 billion today, ending a year in which Las Vegas casino revenue fell by the most on record. At least two other casino companies are attempting to restructure their debt this year.[6]

That's not the kind of news that private equity general partners are keen to discuss openly.

Finally, there was a May 2009 newspaper article on one private equity fund manager bidding to buy a small national bank in Missouri. The article and his printed remarks generated a rash of negative comments along the lines of, "What a staggering putz this guy is. So much arrogance but enough humility to recognize that he is indeed a 'lowlife.' "[7]

By its own admission, private equity is an industry that makes important contributions to the economy. It would seem justified for it to generate better PR for itself. So why doesn't it? On the one hand, private equity partners make *a lot* of money. One way they do it is not to tell everyone their secrets. That's certainly fair, but then you can't expect the man on the street to like it, especially when the private equity partner upstairs enjoys tax advantages that are not open to the janitor sweeping the lobby floor.

When you're worth hundreds of millions if not billions of dollars, involved in multibillion-dollar transactions, and have the government knocking on your door to purchase troubled banks and mortgages, keeping your own counsel should not be unexpected. Yet these partners now control very large economic entities, impacting the lives and fortunes of many. Hiding behind the "private" of "private equity" no longer seems an expedient course.

The industry is changing. The large firms set up an industry trade association, the Private Equity Council, in 2006. It is increasingly responsive to requests for comment—all steps in the right direction. But old habits die hard.

Quite curiously, venture capital is the opposite. The National Venture Capital Association was founded in 1973, 33 years earlier. Visit the websites of any major venture firm, and you will find pictures of its partners, their bios and e-mails, and even the names of their assistants prominently displayed for one and all. They still may not return calls or answer e-mails. Many VC partners are worth hundreds of millions of dollars, yet no one seems to bother them. There's a lesson in here somewhere.

SUCCESSION

Succession has become an important issue in the private equity and venture capital world. The time to pass the torch to a new generation is fast approaching (if not already here). Most U.S. private equity and venture firms are in their first generation. That also goes for Europe, though there are a number of private banking firms that have survived for two or three hundred years. Asia is similarly situated: there are families that have invested for many decades. On an institutional level, private equity and venture have been around for only 30 to 40 years. Will the founding partners take the money and run? Or will they stick around to build multigenerational institutions? How will they pass the mantle of leadership to a new generation?

At the start, succession was far from the minds of those who began investing. They were looking for promising companies and high returns but the industry has evolved, says Warren Hellman. "There are a couple of points on this issue. First, the founders of the industry were ambivalent. Was this simply an opportunity to make investments or are we trying to create an institution that has some longevity? If we are trying to create an institution, then we should always think about succession. I have focused on succession ever since we started the place."

The industry has grown and prospered. Once two-or-three-person offices, industry firms now have billions of dollars under their belts and large staffs to handle the business. Hellman says that how a firm handles succession depends upon the firm's business model. "You have to ask yourself, 'What business are we in: assets under management business or the investment business?' The answer shapes your response to, 'Who's next?' "

Will Schmidt of Advent International emphasizes that LPs will have an important say in the matter. "The most important constituents are the investors in the fund. They will ask, 'Do portfolio companies have the right stewardship? Are private equity firms doing what is necessary to help management teams improve operations and create value?' "

If the team isn't right, they will not be able to raise another fund. Says Schmidt, "The issue of succession is very different from whether private equity will be around in a hundred years. The raw material for private equity will be here for a very long time. It's not like the industrial holding companies of the 1960s. Still, the fund managers must convince investors that they are able to continue producing attractive returns. Now more than ever, the GPs have to demonstrate that they have a differentiated and consistent approach to generating value for their investors."

What do LPs look for in the next generation? Schmidt thinks,

> The LPs look for consistency: they really require top-quartile performance from their general partners, not just from one fund but across multiple funds and investment cycles. Attribution used to be a key criterion; that is, will the people who led the deals still be there? That's still important, but the private equity industry is more institutionalized—the firm or partnership does the deals, not the individuals. The more institutionalized the organization, then free and open sharing of information to make the best decisions is essential. Hierarchy, size, and ego can limit the flow of communication. That can limit the kind of energy that you need to have spontaneous creation of ideas.

Developing the right culture is also important. Mentoring the next generation contributes to that environment. "Many private equity firms are small companies, reliant on certain individuals," notes Schmidt. "If the senior team has developed young people and a culture that can carry forward, they will be able to convince their investors that the firm will continue to deliver solid returns. If the older partners haven't developed that structure, convincing investors of consistent teamwork and performance will be a lot harder. Longevity comes from the development of an investment culture, an experienced management team that will stick together. Those with very high-profile individuals who make all the decisions themselves may not have developed such a strong culture."

That said, private equity and venture capital require different skill sets. Yoshito Hori of Globis Capital looks at the succession issue. He thinks succession in venture capital is difficult.

> Private equity and venture capital are different. Private equity is more of a "commodity." Entry and exit valuation is decided by auction process, so there's not much room for differentiation. Venture capital is different. The entrepreneur keeps his shares when they finance equity, so that they tend to choose a VC who adds value rather than selling to buyers with a higher valuation. Therefore, a VC can differentiate himself based on value-added supports. Thus, venture capitalists are required to have very different and unique sets of skills, experience as well as intuition. Therefore, the succession of VCs is not easy. It is more like craftmanship rather than an institution.

Joncarlo Mark is of the same mind: "It's hard to replace iconic figures. How many times has there been a smooth succession? There are a number of firms in the 15- to 20-year cycle whose founders are getting old. It has nothing to do with the financials. Can there be a fairly benign transition?"

Gary Rieschel is more optimistic about transitioning a venture firm, but he says they "have done a very bad job on succession planning. You have to love working with entrepreneurs, but have to put yourself on the edge to do that. There are a lot of guys in venture who are working 30-hour weeks."

Furthermore, he emphasizes, "Senior people need to bring people along. Venture firms haven't pushed themselves as hard as they have their portfolio companies. They wouldn't tolerate a CEO in their shops for five years without results. Succession has to be rigorously planned. Senior people have to be ready to pass on their own relationships. And, to the extent they can, able to support the younger partners." There's an even more fundamental problem: "If growth goes away for the next decade, how do you keep people excited?"

Bringing on the next generation is, indeed, a hard task. Leonard Harlan of Castle Harlan says, "We are all struggling on how to do it." He cites the example of the firm's Australian affiliate. "The founders of CHAMP have set up a successor company to manage the next fund that is being raised right now. The existing company continues to manage the portfolios of the previous funds. This is a move to institutionalize the business. They will sell stock to senior executives, create a board of directors, and institute corporate governance mechanisms. These moves mean that we are willing to delegate authority to the next generation. The new company will have all the same components as the founding entity, except it starts with an institutional framework."

Says Harlan, "Most of us old-timers enjoy the business and want to hang in there. Some probably want to be carried out on a stretcher. So we have to create an environment so that guys like me can stick around while leaving room for the next generation." He agrees that succession is "an issue on the minds of most LPs. The LP community is saying, 'We want to make sure that these younger guys are going to be around for a long time.' "

To a certain extent, the issue solves itself. Partners who are doing well and feel they are not being rewarded, quit and set up their own firms. Firms that are not doing well cannot raise their next fund and go out of business. Of course, GPs may not be able to raise their next fund, but the current fund has a long life before it expires.

But for the mega-firms and those firms that expect to carry on, the issue is real and the succession mechanisms difficult. Firms will need to solve these issues not in the calm waters of 2003–2007, but in the stormy conditions that will likely prevail over the next several years: heavy debt that needs to be refinanced, tight credit and difficult exits. Lewis Rutherfurd, cofounder and managing director of Inter-Asia Venture Management, says industry executives have to ask themselves, "Will I continue to train for triathlons? That's one way of asking the question, 'How much longer do I expect to be part of the business?' " If the answer is "Not as long as I would like," then they should start thinking about ways to move on and finding a successor.

ADAPTING TO GLOBALIZATION

Twenty years ago, private equity firms focused on their countries for companies to acquire, while venture capital was strictly a local business. That has changed dramatically over the past two decades. Although the results have not always been successful, few if any firms can afford to look at only their own domestic markets for funding, deals, or talent.

Private Equity

Only a handful of funds, mostly American, truly operate worldwide. There are several regional firms in Europe and Asia, with offices throughout these continents. Then there are country-specific funds around the world. Venture tends to be more local, though that is also changing. Now many Silicon Valley firms have offices in China and India, though not in Boston or New York. More Boston and New York firms have opened offices on the West Coast. East Coast firms also like Israel, where a number are sourcing deals.

As this book suggests, the world and its markets have grown irreversibly global. The mega-firms have been reasonably successful in growing their overseas offices: TPG, Carlyle, KKR, Bain, and Blackstone. Carl Ferenbach of Berkshire notes, "One of the challenges for the middle market folks is that firms are increasingly interested in having international capabilities. Europe was first. We are now seeing efforts in Hong Kong, Beijing, Shanghai, Mumbai, and Singapore."

All of the mega-funds raise capital globally but they also invest globally. "Until recently, there used to be national models," says Peter Cornelius. "You had a family-owned company in France that had difficulty finding an investor. The pool of prospective buyers was likely national. Typically, a national or regional intermediary served as an intermediary. But that has changed. Today both the industry interest and capital could be provided by GPs and LPs from elsewhere."

Private equity had its genesis in American-Anglo culture. It features a corporate governance model that can happen anywhere certain basic ingredients exist: an equity funding mechanism (limited partnerships), availability of debt (well-capitalized banks and mezzanine funds), reserves of experienced management (from corporations or past deals), and viable exit markets (M&A and trade sales). Different governments and regulatory regimes exact their own prerequisites. The Chinese government, for example, has unstated preferences for minority stakes and local funding. The Indian government likes to say when and where a deal will happen. Cultures such as those of Germany, Japan, and Korea remain skeptical about private equity's ability to deliver fundamental value. International firms doing local deals should understand these differences.

For global private equity firms, good things—and disaster—can happen anywhere. Carlyle, based in Washington, DC, watched the value of its stake in China Pacific Life soar while its $22 billion London-based Carlyle Capital Fund was forced into liquidation in March 2008. KKR, headquartered in New York, reported a 30-percent drop in the value of its Amsterdam-listed fund for 2008 while profitably exiting from its 2007 purchase of Cleanaway in Australia. TPG's cofounder, David Bonderman, describing the firm's 42-percent stake in BankThai as "the worst underwriting TPG has ever done," exited profitably from its stake in Shenzhen Development Bank in 2009 at close to a 5x return.

Venture Capital

Dr. Ta-lin Hsu of H&Q Asia Pacific observes that times have changed. "Twenty years ago, Silicon Valley dominated the technology venture world. There was no competition. With globalization, technology spread around the world, and as a result, technology has now become a commodity."

NEA managing director Peter Barris concurs. "We believe that the practice of venture capital is becoming and will become a global practice. You have to play globally or have to be very specialized."

If Silicon Valley is no longer the epicenter of the venture world, Sonny Wu of GSR says others will take its place. "The Valley is different now than it was 10 or 15 years ago. A lot of innovation has become more dispersed. The valley is becoming more and more virtual. The negative way is to say it's becoming more and more marginalized. If you can do everything in Israel or China, why do it here?"

But is Silicon Valley out of ideas? Has the technology world moved on? Dick Kramlich of NEA says no. "The Valley is still the wellspring of innovation: the sun and water are here; we have the educational systems and a very refined technology infrastructure."

Dr. Hsu agrees: "I have a selfish hope that Silicon Valley's existing infrastructure, good weather, and favorable immigration policies continue to make it a strong cluster point for technology ventures. It still remains an attractive place to showcase technology to the world."

Yet neither Kramlich nor Dr. Hsu really answers the question: has the Valley simply run its course? The Bay Area features the ecosystem that entrepreneurship requires: great universities, financial wealth, work ethic, and America's legal and regulatory infrastructure among them. The sun, mountains, and great weather don't hurt. Having shown the way, though, are others just saying, "We can do it, too"?

Arguably, Sand Hill Road was so successful that it provided the impetus for innovation elsewhere. And as many of the innovators were originally Chinese or Indian or Korean, it should come as no surprise that new ideas are coming from Asia. In her book *Silicon Dragon* (McGraw-Hill, 2008), journalist Rebecca Fannin says it's not that the Valley has disappeared; it's just that the rest of the world has caught up. Smart and ambitious entrepreneurs abound. They can do it less expensively elsewhere. She profiles a number of Chinese entrepreneurs who have made the leap.

Innovation may not depend on the apparatus that Sand Hill Road requires. There are hundreds of new ideas every day. The Valley's cash, costs, and regulatory framework can also be a negative. Sonny Wu observes that, "There's no manufacturing in the Valley. Everything related to stem cell research is not there. Everything related to TV is not happening there. Will manufacturing come back to the United States? I would argue that the easiest way to rebuild the economy is to rebuild at $8 an hour and not at $29 an hour."

Whether venture capital has transitioned to a global model will remain controversial. Len Baker argues that the Valley has yet to prove itself overseas. "The Silicon Valley model hasn't successfully transplanted itself into another country. It has failed in Europe. I think that China and India will adopt their own structures. Analog models in Shanghai and Beijing will not work out. Those doing more indigenous types of businesses will succeed. The dilemma for VC firms: how do you go global? It's very hard to have the branch plant model, where you have firms around the world."

WHAT BUSINESS ARE WE IN?

The mega-funds are as much in the asset management business as they are in the transaction business. In addition to private equity, they have multiple divisions handling all aspects of the investment business—real estate, hedge funds, and capital markets, to name three. LPs have to ask themselves whether this is the business in which they have invested. Again, the answer is one of returns: how has the specific fund performed in the market?

Will Schmidt thinks the industry should stick to its knitting. "The governance model—of buying a business, incentivizing management and providing advice and resources to implement operational improvements—is where private equity has earned its keep. Yes, we're an investor, but we're an active owner. The owner wakes up at 3 A.M. everyday and asks, 'How can I make this company better?' The general consensus today is that the only way for private equity to generate top returns is by driving operating improvements. We are entering a period where private equity will need industrial capability as well as financial skills to create long-term value in a business."

Warren Hellman points out that both private equity and venture capitalists started out as opportunistic investors. But they have evolved into an industry that seeks to improve the businesses in which they had invested. "We can really help our companies. They bring real substance to the company." To which he adds, "Private equity has morphed from a number of recovering investment bankers to firms that can make a real contribution to the companies in which they are investing. We and others have learned that we are there to help and support the guys."

He emphasizes that the key investment criterion is more than getting a deal done. "A lot of people in our industry were investment bankers: anything that comes in, let's figure out how to make this work. Private equity is exactly the opposite: you are guilty until proven innocent. I start out saying, 'I don't want to do this.' It's the quality of the business, it's how we can make this business run better. What's the purpose of private equity? We're not permanent capital. We're not Warren Buffett—we don't want to own See's Candy for a hundred years. We invest in a company as temporary owners."

FUND STRUCTURE: IS THERE A BETTER WAY?

That raises another issue for both private equity and venture capital: how long should private equity be "temporary owners"? The industry has two major flaws, says Len Harlan. "First, we're out of business every four to six years (once the fund's money is invested). Second, if you find a great company, you should really be holding onto it for more years than that. But the private equity business model says you have to sell it. It frequently gets sold too early so that the fund can show returns."

Traditionally, private equity funds are of a fixed duration from seven to 10 years. Anil Thadani thinks this time frame is too short and stops the industry from taking advantage of its strengths.

> Does the traditional fund structure remain the right model for volatile and high growth environments like we have in Asia? A fixed term fund is actually not the best structure. It's good for stable, low growth economies, where value in these deals is created by financial engineering and leverage. Where you have real growth, and you superimpose an environment of volatility, then timing becomes a much more critical variable than it normally might have been. A fixed life fund puts a needless premium on timing of investment and disinvestment. It also forces you to sell perfectly good investments which still have attractive growth left in them. If you have the time, you can generally fix a problem. If you're forced to fix it within a predetermined time frame, then you could have a problem.

Len Baker agrees. "The biggest thing is the time horizon. Fund structures are overlapping: it forces a fairly short investment cycle. On the margin, carry goes down. If you're in a fund that doubles your money, on the margin you're working for a 10-percent carry. Overlapping fund structures incentivize a short investment horizon. A different time horizon would incentivize people to do the rational thing: to build companies over a longer period of time."

Thadani thinks that Warren Buffett has provided an enviable model. "Private equity firms should organize along the lines of Berkshire Hathaway, where you do not have any time limits for investment or divestment, and the GP is the wealthiest guy in the group with lots of skin in the game. Investing in Berkshire Hathaway means you pay no fees, no carry. You just ride along with the principal."

He notes that Buffett's company offers investors "a listed investment vehicle which gives the investment manager the time he needs to maximize the value of his investment. At the same time, it gives investors liquidity and the opportunity to either cash out, or indeed increase their stake, by trading their shares on the stock exchange. The problem is that most investment vehicles of this type tend to trade at a discount to their true value. However, I think as the market realizes the benefits of this structure, which is relatively new, this discount will disappear."

Thadani hopes that the economic crisis will lead the industry to rethink some basic assumptions. "What is the best way for GPs to invest? How do you compensate them? Many of the most egregious funds were the so-called hedge funds. Basically, the term 'hedge fund' allowed the general partner to charge fees and carry instead of a nominal fee for portfolio investment, which is what many of them were doing anyway. Where will the industry end up? Probably somewhere in the middle, but definitely with more regulation and oversight."

GOING PUBLIC

For general partners to go public in an industry that is essentially driven by private investment sounds like an oxymoron: if private equity has the answers, why list them publicly? One reason is that it provides an evergreen source of funds, solving the GP's perennial fund raising issue. A second reason is that it's a vehicle to monetize the fees that private equity firms charge.

Like others, Peter Cornelius says there are inherent conflicts. "On financial intermediation, will this 'going public' trend that we saw in 2005–2007 regain momentum? KKR announced that it wanted to follow Blackstone, but the market turned against them in 2008. In July 2009, KKR announced that it will merge with its European affiliate, which is listed on the Amsterdam exchange. LPs will need to examine carefully whether there are any potential conflicts of interest arising from being a shareholder in a private equity firm to whose funds they commit capital."

There are also financial issues aside from the philosophical questions. In March 2007, S&P launched an index of 30 private equity funds. Among them are Blackstone, Onex, and Jafco. The Index had a value of 100 in November 2003; hit a high of 201.4 in June 2007 and a low of 30.5 in March 2009; and traded at 66.9 on June 1, 2009. Looking at the list of underlying companies, none of the shares are trading at or above their issue price or net asset value. A listed private equity firm is certainly subject to overall market levels, but they have only occasionally been sound financial investments.

Blackstone may be unique, but it nonetheless highlights the issues. The firm launched an IPO in June 2007 at $31 per share, raising a total of $4.13 billion for the fund. The two cofounders walked away with a combined $2.33 billion, according to a Bloomberg article. One cofounder took home an additional $702 million in compensation for 2008, though Blackstone says the sum reflects the partnership interests he contributed to the firm. In September 2009, the stock traded at $12.00 per share, just over one-third of that value. In fact, analysts' worst nightmare was realized: the partners cashed out and investors lost money, while only a small amount was raised for the fund.

OTHER EUROPEAN INDUSTRY ISSUES

Most funds are headquartered in London, where the government has taken a more benign attitude towards the private equity industry than have the continental capitals. Distress investing is a U.S. skill set, but secondary funds in London and elsewhere are active. Venture capital remains embryonic, so the question of whether Paris or Munich is "out of ideas" is moot. European governments have actually taken an interest in venture capital, but thus far their support has been mostly to sponsor conferences and trade missions.

The issues are largely those that have been discussed in previous chapters: a culture that values safety rather than adventure; fractured legal and financial systems; and governments used to setting work rules rather than promoting entrepreneurial activity. The lack of credit, bid-ask spread, and succession issues are as prevalent as other issues, such as fund raising and public profile.

ASIAN INDUSTRY ISSUES

Asian funds have been hit by limited credit and the different price expectations of buyer and seller. By and large, they have been immune from the regulatory and internal issues that have impacted the United States and European funds. Moreover, Asian deals have never been as levered as U.S. or European transactions. The balance sheets of Asian financial institutions are relatively clean. The main problem is that most of the commitments to the buyout industry were made by international banks—those with the NPLs and toxic assets. Local banks have made loans but in much smaller amounts. Steve Byrom says, "In Australia, credit has been topping out at \$250 million. You need seven banks to lend you \$30 to \$40 million each to get that."

Of course, each Asian country has its own particular set of issues. China is promoting venture and RMB funds and is not keen on foreign control buyouts; Japan has many large companies but remains tied to cultural norms that promote stable relationships and protect existing management; Korea is dominated by its *chaebols* and prefers long-term investors over "punters," India has high growth but an overinvolved government, and Australia is still facing the constraints of the credit crisis. Asia may exist on Western maps, but it is 16 (or more) separate governments with an equal number of social norms and regulations to follow. Most of those investing in Asia have seen the speed bumps and slowed down to traverse them successfully.

MIDDLE EAST ISSUES

The Middle East is largely unbothered by most of these issues. It's a region whose investment tempo has been largely set by the price of oil, but one with large cash reserves and an infrastructure that remains in the early stages of development. Families and governments control most of the wealth. Public markets recorded big losses, but the vaults are still full. To date, they have acted very conservatively and pulled back after the crisis hit. But private equity has gained a foothold, and that foothold will grow as the markets recover and open to further development. Venture capital exists in very small pockets, but it too has a future.

LIMITED PARTNERS

The issues confronting limited partners were set out in Chapter Three. Will LPs acquiesce to questions of access, or will they confront a compensation structure that, in the face of declining returns, does not meet their objectives? Will Schmidt says he has already seen changes. "Access to fund managers is clearly not the issue now. Hardly anyone is hitting their fund-raising targets. About one-third of LPs have temporarily frozen new commitments, another one-third has liquidity or allocation issues, and there's one-third for whom it's business as usual."

He predicts, "During the next set of fund cycles, it's unlikely you will see the big step-ups in fund sizes that the industry has experienced since its inception. Some funds may be downsized because of the environment, and in many cases the LPs will be in the driver's seat. For the 'right-sized' funds that still have strong performance, there might still be an access issue."

Leonard Harlan, however, thinks that LPs have other issues to resolve. "I don't see the LPs becoming more active in our space. There are more LPs who want to be co-investors. But when they are given the opportunity, they often take a pass. They are more focused on the 'fair market value' of portfolio investments than they have been in past, though. I think that's crazy, because valuations can lead to all sorts of distortions. The true value is determined only by a sale."

LP issues will be critical. If the market does not recover quickly, they will have to ask themselves the questions that they ignored in the boom years: Do I want to invest in the asset class? How will I get my returns? If the public market rally erases many of the losses, will the LPs be more demanding on the next go-around? All are good questions, though it seems in the interests of both GPs and LPs to find a common ground.

What lies ahead for private equity and venture capital, and where are the opportunities? Our story continues in the next chapter.

CHAPTER 7

The Next Decade: A Future Scape

Reading the crystal ball is always a difficult and risky task. Difficult, because knowing what will happen is impossible; risky, because what you think will happen won't necessarily happen. To not attempt such a reading ignores the predictive powers of precedent and leaves one totally surprised when the inevitable occurs. So, in the hope that some of what I predict here will actually happen, this chapter is a look into the future of private equity and venture capital.

The investment landscape for the next decade may not look a lot different from what it is today, but it will be different. A "new normalcy" will emerge. The global economy will start with an estimated trillion dollars less of consumer demand and trillions of dollars less of market capital and bank lending. The United States and Europe will struggle to maintain high cost structures and to replace jobs that have been lost. Earnings will be driven as much by cost cutting as by higher revenues. Housing sales will recover gradually but reflect lower sale prices. The economic environment will feature emerging stars and aging heroes. China, India, and other Asian countries will rise. Wall Street will offer new products but be met with increased skepticism. Large corporations will prevail, but the creative instinct will find a home in smaller, yet successful companies.

Warren Hellman welcomes news of an improving economy and higher stock prices, but says,

> I'm part of the 80 percent that think things will keep going the way they have been: revenues will flatten, but earnings will look very good because people are really focused on costs. Part of what has fueled the stock market rally is that corporate earnings are better than the terrible earnings people were expecting. What I don't understand is, what does the federal deficit mean? What is the effect of that? At some point, does that return to haunt us? If you have a $1 trillion deficit per year, what does it mean for the currency? Is inflation inevitable? Does the U.S.

become Brazil 2—will the dollar be worth some fraction of what it once was?

The general partners have tough decisions to make. There is still money in the till, yet time and human resources will be devoted to portfolio company survival and debt restructuring. Deal flow has been good, but the pricing gap between buyer and seller has proven stubbornly resistant to deal making. Venture capital faces a world of new technologies and products. Many will come to pass, but how they do, who finances them, and what returns they generate are open items. Market forces will shape the response of private equity and venture capital models to the new environment. The next generation of industry leaders may well share the same goals but with different styles.

This chapter focuses on the future. With all that's happening in the world, how will private equity and venture capital firms be structured and where will they find their investment strategies?

FORWARD TO THE FUTURE

As private equity and venture capital adjust to the new world, several trends have become apparent. Mirroring the general economy, Philip Bilden of HarbourVest sees the industry becoming smaller. "I would see a contraction of this industry in 2010–11. The crisis is a catalyst for the inevitable elimination of marginal players across the food chain, including LPs who will soon recognize that it is greatly challenging to select fund managers in the top quartile with consistency."

Harjit Bhatia of Credit Suisse also believes the industry will contract. "For the past three or four years, there has been a surge of smaller private equity and hedge funds. This downturn has hurt quite a few of them. That will lead to a consolidation of private equity and hedge fund players. In the longer term, that's not such a bad thing."

Though the industry will contract, equity checks as a percentage of transaction value will be larger. The banks will insist. Some firms are even touting the "all equity" transaction, the "UBO—unleveraged buyout." Equally novel is vendor financing, where the seller takes back a note or equity ownership against the purchase price. Berkshire's Carl Ferenbach admits, "We would rather not do a UBO. Our feeling is that if it's a business we really like, we would like to own that return. We would like to help management and make sure they have the resources."

Many private equity money funds raised new money in 2006–2007 on the back of earlier results. Wilbur Ross believes that funds raised during this era will have a tough time showing returns. "Performance will be even more skewed than it has been. Many companies have been over-leveraged. In the case of a mistaken investment, they will have a zippo return on money. In the case of additional infusions of capital, the returns will be negative."

Andrew Liu of Unitas Capital says that monitoring portfolio companies will consume a lot of GP time at the expense of making new investments. "We will be spending time on portfolio monitoring. We want to make sure that management is doing everything it can: taking costs out, continuing to drive operational improvement, running businesses on the assumption that both equity and credit markets will get worse this year." Tina Ju concurs, saying that KPCB China will pay close attention to their investments. "Everyone is focused on strengthening their portfolio companies. In an economic downturn, quality companies emerge as leaders. Now more than ever, KPCB has dedicated resources to building and supporting the companies we have invested in."

The mega-funds will also have to refinance large amounts of debt in the coming years and sort through other issues outlined in the next chapter. It will not be an easy time, but the firms that come through this will find themselves stronger and in more clearly defined positions.

The issue of struggling LPs is significant. Dan Carroll of TPG notes that liquidity for the industry is based on the liquidity of its investors. Maintaining solid LP relationships will be important. Looking ahead, he predicts, "Those groups which have maintained their firms' focus and managed their LP relationships will do well through this period."

In terms of investments, OMERS' Martin Day is confident that the funds will figure out a way to complete transactions. "GPs will find ways to get around the credit crunch. They are certainly looking at deals—deals done without credit. People will find a way to transact. By definition, the multiple is so low on deals that are being looked at that the buyers are comfortable with returns on multiple expansion. Or they can take advantage of existing leverage; for example, minority stakes. We are seeing a lot of buy-and-build strategies, where they don't need so much leverage to start with." But there has been far more looking than actual investing—as the 2009 results have shown.

For venture capital, NEA's Dick Kramlich says the industry must begin returning capital. "Returns for venture have been minimal for the past eight years. For 1998, 1999, 2000, the returns were pretty spectacular. 1994 and 1995 vintage years were the best. The 1999 vintage year was the worst. It rebounded somewhat in 2005–2007. Venture capital is super cyclical. But if you take any 10-year cycle since 1960, the venture industry has outperformed all other asset classes."

THE PRIVATE EQUITY FIRM OF THE FUTURE

What will the private equity firm of the future look like? Different types of firms are already emerging. Take Carlyle and KKR. According to Carlyle's website, the firm has 66 funds spread across four investment disciplines (buyouts, growth capital, real estate, and leveraged finance). Carlyle also has an investor services group, one of the largest in the industry, that handles an array of administrative services including accounting, compliance, and external affairs.

Or consider KKR, which has a number of divisions including asset management and capital markets. The firm runs an in-house consulting team, KKR Capstone, a team of operational consultants who work exclusively with portfolio company management teams to strengthen operations in portfolio companies. In late July 2009 the firm announced an IPO for one of its portfolio companies, Dollar General, which sells inexpensive appliances and private-label food. Taking on a new role, KKR acted as one of the lead underwriters, hoping to tap its institutional clients as well as its recent alliance with Fidelity Investments. (See Chapter Eight for more.)

Joncarlo Mark of CalPERS sees tomorrow's private equity firm as more versatile and perhaps more focused. "The private equity firm of the future will evolve to a more flexible structure. The money is there. They have the resources to hire the people from the investment banks and the hedge funds. You will also see some spin-offs of the big firms by top-performing partners who want to start their own firms."

Private equity firms of the future will likely be smaller with fewer partners. The reasons are simple: they will not be able to borrow as much debt, and, as Mark suggests, partners who feel unloved by their share of profits will move out on their own.

Another reason firms may become smaller, says Steve Byrom of Australia's Future Fund, is that it may enable better contacts with investors. "A lot of people could leave the GPs and set up smaller funds. It might drive a closer relationship with LPs. Under that scenario you could see a slightly different private equity manager: a smaller manager with a smaller number of LPs where LPs have a greater say. There may even be a shakeout in big names. All this may drive an even greater divergence between those doing pure play private equity and those doing alternative asset management."

Harald Quandt Holding's Fritz Becker sees the advantages of the "trend towards smaller and mid-sized GPs. A lot of investors are focusing on smaller and mid-sized teams because they are more hands-on, instead of just doing financial restructuring."

But this will also test the creativity, stamina, and leadership of the managers of today's firms. As we noted in the last chapter, this is an industry in which the top guys don't quit until someone calls an ambulance. Yet if private equity (and venture) are to realize their potential in the years ahead, they will have to pass the infrastructure on to the next generation. Much has been learned and built over the past 40 years. Private equity will require leaders with the same smarts and work ethic as the previous generation, but one that can also adapt to and profit from a different set of economic and corporate constraints. That is the challenge and the opportunity.

Authentic Private Equity

As the industry considers its options, one alternative is to redefine its parameters (and the salaries of its partners and managing directors). These parameters may be redone anyway by market forces, but one path is to focus on fewer transactions. PEP's Tim Sims calls it "authentic private equity."

He applies this term to a resilient and distinctive subset of the industry; he also calls them "unlisted performance engineers." He bases his observations on the study of long-term private equity performance in the U.K. which is a large, well-established market. Says Sims, "In a sense there are two extremes of private equity: 'the bandwagon' and 'authentic private equity.' In the U.K., 75 percent of all private equity funds failed to achieve a 20-percent annual returns between 1984 and 2002—a very disappointing statistic given the average market conditions over that time. What that says is that 75 percent of PE funds did not achieve the accepted risk margin over public equities in the same period; worryingly, such returns as they did achieve were accounted for by multiple expansion on exit and by leverage in different market conditions where these returns evaporate or reverse." "For the elite performers, the value engineers" he says, "the excess return is explained by enhanced performance. Less than 10 percent of the firms have consistently increased profits by the significant levels."

Sims says the strategy has a number of benefits.

> In the enormous shifts we've seen, if you could define a perfect rational investment response it would be to chose to buy control of a carefully selected company, off the back of thorough diligence, with a team of performance specialists, who agree a business plan, follow strict ROI guidelines, have long-run objectives and reporting obligations, and only get paid if they succeed. This is authentic private equity or unlisted performance engineering. Public markets provide the target substrate for this alternative; they are fraught with conflict, short-term objectives, and incentives and commission leakage as brokers churn and play the stock for short-term gain.

"In our experience," he says, "authentic private equity or unlisted performance engineering require the calm understanding of long-standing team relationships, good local market knowledge, and a team that has served a genuine long-term apprenticeship in working with management to produce superior results over time." Sims outlines a four-step process that brings all this together:

Resourcing: A qualified team and careful diligence up front.

Execution: The right kind of management and an agreed five-year plan.

Incentives: Support with annual fees that sustain a significant resource effort. The core research needs to be executed and owned by the investment team themselves, with no false incentive to deal, invest with the investors, and then share profits above a threshold return after the investors have received their capital and a respectable base return.

Outcome: Selling into a well-prepared and compelling outcome.

Sims's methodology is a good one. Some would say it's idealistic. But the more closely private equity teams approach this model, the more likely they are to produce consistently attractive returns for their investors and themselves. At the same time, they will build a group of industrial enterprises that provides sustainable rewards for its employees and for the community at large.

VENTURE CAPITAL FIRM OF THE FUTURE

The profile of the venture capital firm of the future will also evolve. Unless markets change dramatically, the bigger firms will need to become more specialized and tap greater skill sets. Kleiner Perkins promoted a precursor to this idea with its "*keiretsu* strategy" involving the exchange of services and funds between its portfolio companies. The changing financial landscape will lead to further changes: how will firms generate returns if they can't exit through the market? How will they handle the demands of larger deals, with longer time frames, involving some form of government participation? And how will they resolve succession issues as well as those involving partners who've simply had enough? These are all difficult questions whose answers will not likely be known for several years to come. On an institutional level, venture capital firms may well have to scale up in size to meet the competitive demands placed on them.

Certainly, there are many types of venture capital firms, specializing in deals of different sizes and structures. The industry will have to ask itself, what types of bets can we make that will generate the returns we expect? NEA's Peter Barris thinks the industry will need to seek outside help. "Where we are impacted is wherever you have capital-intensive bets—the semiconductor and energy sectors, for example. In the absence of some type of help, there will be a reluctance of venture capital firms to fund capital-intensive industries."

Venture capital will continue to diverge from private equity, though it may adopt some of private equity's organizational structures. Dixon Doll, who recently served as chairman of the NVCA, is more precise:

> We make our money in very different ways than private equity. Venture capital is about job creation, innovation, and applied science. At the end of 2008, 12.1 million jobs in the U.S. were attributable to venture-backed companies. Revenues generated by these companies corresponded to 20 percent of GDP on annual venture capital investments representing 0.2 percent of U.S. GDP. Even more amazing is that 92 percent of all the jobs that are created by venture-backed companies happened after the company goes public. We think that you can look at the U.S. VC industry as one of the most important and productive engines of job creation and job growth today.

Doll points out ways that venture is different: "Venture capital investors don't rely on significant amounts of debt for financing our companies. In general, we are creators and builders of sustainable companies over the long term. Private equity is best known as efficiency-optimizers. They either take an entire company or a division thereof and spin it out; then clean it up and sell off parts or try to take it public again. Frequently, some of the efficiencies are created as a result of job elimination and job reduction."

Venture capital, of course, founds new businesses and funds new technologies. Many of these have been game changers: Intel, and the semiconductor; Apple, and the personal computer; Google, and search; Starbucks, and a good cup of coffee; Facebook, and social networking; and many more.

Doll was the main driver behind the NVCA's 2009 Four-Pillar Plan. The plan is aimed at addressing four main concerns that its leaders see in today's markets. The first pillar calls for increased collaboration and healthy competition among all partners in the venture capital ecosystem. These partners include VCs, entrepreneurs, investment banks, accounting and law firms, buy-side securities firms, and securities exchanges. The intent is to encourage collaboration and shared economics between major and boutique investment banks, and to inspire the creation of new boutique banks and a new set of tech-oriented buyers for high-quality IPOs. The industry can then jointly help a critical number of smaller companies, particularly those who want to raise $50 million to $75 million through the public offering process.

Second, revitalizing the venture-backed IPO market is critical. The NVCA hopes to offer small venture-backed companies an enhanced distribution system for the sale of initial stock. (See the discussion in Chapter Eight.) Third, the NVCA wants to preserve the existing capital gains tax rules as well as new tax incentives that encourage company creation. Finally, the NVCA would like to see Congress review regulations such as Sarbanes Oxley. The NVCA supports protecting investors where necessary but does not believe in a "one-size-fits-all" regulatory approach.

As venture faces the challenges of the future, though, it will have to add ancillary skill sets, including government relations and, perhaps, some form of permanent capital to undertake larger transactions. Private equity is already there.

European Venture Capital

William Stevens of Europe Unlimited says that fragmented legal and financial markets are major impediments to developing a European venture capital market.

> One of the key problems in Europe for investment is that it's really dependent upon the legal context. That is a very fragmented market, which goes from board of directors' meetings to minutes to contracts. It is more difficult to invest in Germany if the minutes have to be in the local language. Preparing minutes in Dutch or French doesn't help an English investment. If the company is in Paris, you still have to do all the bylaws in French. But more and more people are setting up in the U.K. If you're investing in Germany, you take the company to London.

"The fragmentation of legal systems is accompanied by the fragmentation of the financial markets," he adds. "In Europe, we are working at a quarter of U.S. volume. That means you have fewer funds around. One reason the U.S. is successful is that everyone is working with the same language and same culture. For a specialized fund, it's not easy to find investors."

Will this change? Stevens is not optimistic in the short term. "Looking ahead two or three years, I don't think it will grow very much. Very few institutional funds are willing to put up the money. There is an issue of returns. Not many institutions can put the funds on the table to create a \$100-million to \$150-million fund. Nor are they willing to lock up their money for five to seven years."

Will Schmidt of Advent International is more direct. "All of the Europeans have wanted to copy the Silicon Valley model, but there's always something missing. Nothing else, except maybe Boston or Israel, comes close to Silicon Valley."

Stevens says the banks are the biggest suppliers of medium-term money, but "they have been really shaken by the crisis. Most of the venture money came from the banks, so in the short term, for the next three or four years, it will be tough to raise venture funds. It's simply not a priority for them. It's the same with the insurance companies: it's not a priority."

In terms of his own business, matchmaking for venture in Europe, Stevens says, "We work a lot with regional or local governments, who play a bigger role than in the United States. With real venture investment, government is responsible for maybe 50 percent of funding in Europe. We are getting orders from governments to put our investors in front of people. Governments are keen to get more out of their research and development funding. They want to see more technology transfer."

Corporate Venture Capital

Intel Capital, the venture arm of Intel corporate, maintains a very active venture program. In 2008, there were 62 new investments and 102 follow-on investments. Most of Intel's investments are in the \$3 million to \$5 million category.

But the company has the ability to go higher. Take, for example, its investment in the WiMAX carrier Clearwire. Intel has made three investments: \$20 million in 2004; \$600 million in 2006; and \$1.0 billion in 2008. Says Sriram Viswanathan, managing director, Intel Capital and general manager of the WiMAX program office,

> Looking at the project holistically, it was really driven by the notion that spectrum is a valuable asset. Intel was the early lead investor in this deal. Intel's interest is in making ubiquitous broadband happen fast, since it is a huge bottleneck to growth of the whole PC area. If broadband wireless is available universally, it creates new usage models that lead to new business models.
>
> We had two choices in terms of spectrum. We could have waited for 700 MHz auctions to happen in various geographies and their encumbrances to get cleared over a period of time, or we could have

gone with 2.5 GHz spectrum that was available in the United States in one large chunk. We went with the latter, since there was abundant spectrum available that was an order of magnitude more than 700 MHz. When the last deal was done in 2008 with Clearwire, that was literally months before the global economic turmoil hit all capital markets. As we looked at the stock market taking a huge dive, it became apparent to the investors to mark-to-market their holdings of various public securities, not to mention it met certain criteria of regulatory requirements as well. [In 2008, Intel wrote down $1 billion on their Clearwire investment.] It is our belief that the underlying value of the spectrum is still quite strong. Over time, when the business delivers operational results on this, our expectation is that the stock price will truly reflect the underlying value.

The spectrum continues to be a huge asset. We are building it in Portland and then in Atlanta followed by Las Vegas and other cities. It takes time to build the network. They must have some percentage of the market built out before launching the service in the market. It's a laborious task, but not something they haven't done. It takes approximately $4 to $5 billion to get the whole country built out. Clearwire has a significant amount raised, but will need more capital, perhaps another $2 billion to build out the system. It's not like you have to keep digging the hole. You can do it market-by-market. The revenue source for the company is broadband network access that gets priced anywhere from $20 to $50 per user. Then you can layer other revenue sources on top of that.

PRIVATE EQUITY: WHERE ARE THE OPPORTUNITIES?

In an October 2009 interview with Bloomberg, David Rubenstein says he sees private equity coming back "stronger than it was."[1] It is a central thesis of this book that he is right, but the opportunities in the near future will be different from those of the past. Acquisitions will be smaller, and there will be greater partnering with strategic buyers. Three particular areas will also stand out: distressed situations, secondary positions, and growth capital (minority positions).

Distressed Situations

The basis of distress investing is simple, says Howard Marks. "When the face amount of debt exceeds the value of an asset, the loan is underwater.

Servicing the debt will continue to eat into the capital of people who own the asset. In bankruptcy, the equity is wiped out, and the old creditors become the new owners."

If private equity cannot purchase the shares, it will look at acquiring corporate control through the debt portion of the balance sheet. Harjit Bhatia thinks the market has room to grow. "In the United States and Europe, activity will be in the distressed space. The funds will get active, but with less leverage. The fund size will become much more sensible."

The government has invited private equity to participate in distressed situations. These are represented by the $1.25 trillion PPIP programs that the U.S. Treasury has enacted. European governments have taken on the mantle themselves, but the U.S. government is seeking to let private enterprise lead the charge. BlackRock, PIMCO, and Wilbur Ross have applied to participate in the program. But most private equity firms have kept their distance.

The corporate sphere, however, will serve up its own opportunities. In a May 2009 article in the *Financial Times*, Henny Sender reports that in 2004, "'door maker' Masonite caught the eye of KKR, which purchased the company for C$3.3bn. Four years on, in March 2009, with housing markets ravaged by subprime defaults and the wider crisis those triggered, Masonite finally filed for bankruptcy protection. KKR borrowed $1.5 billion from the banks and issued an additional $770 million in high-yield bonds to help gain control. But most telling of all is who Masonite's next owners may be: they are likely to include Oaktree Capital."[2]

"Creditors are about to become the owners of many companies," says Howard Marks. "Equity owners will be wiped out. When you buy with borrowed money, there are some environments you can't withstand." He continues, "The end of the boom brought a halt to the ownership drive by private equity that used cheap debt to acquire ever larger companies, paying a big premium over the public market. In 2005–2007, the industry spent almost $2 trillion on deals, according to Carlyle Group. Now, the transfer of part of the west's corporate landscape to investors in distressed debt is just beginning."

In Europe, these failures include Edscha (a robot construction company for automobile producers), which was owned by Carlyle. Edscha was declared insolvent in March 2009 despite a full order book until 2012. Carlyle stands to lose its $180 million investment. Kiekert (a handgrip producer for automobiles) was purchased by the U.K.'s Permira. Permira lost approximately 130 million equity on an enterprise value of over 500 million. Two hedge funds, Bluebay and Silverpoint (supported by Morgan Stanley), took over and are still in the restructuring process. TMD Friction (a brake pad producer) was purchased by Montagu in 2000 for 776 million. Several hedge funds took over in 2006 through a debt-for-equity swap, but the company was declared insolvent in December 2008.

There are and will be many more examples. The bottom line is that many of the highly levered deals closed by private equity during 2005–2007 will be restructured. What does this mean for the private equity firms involved? For the larger firms, it will mean a black eye but not the end of the industry, as the investments are structured around vintage year funds. Vintage funds in 2006 and 2007 may show zero to negative returns. Earlier funds will likely show low returns. The market rally has masked the opportunity, but as large chunks of debt become due, the banks will have to decide which ones to support. Those they let fail will spell a busy time for the distressed funds.

Secondary Positions

Jeremy Coller believes there will be two trigger points for change in 2010: "First, an uptick in GP investment in the primary market will mean a flurry of capital calls, which will cause acute liquidity issues for LPs. Second, for some LPs at least, asset allocation decisions will be a trigger: trustees and CIOs will tell managers they have to sell assets to realign the make-up of investment portfolios with asset allocation policies. It's definitely not just liquidity issues that will drive the secondaries market, though. Many investors will want to reshape their portfolios to take account of today's new economic realities."

Coller says that valuing both the debt and equity portions of secondary positions is crucial. "We are taking the recession seriously and being extremely conservative. The credit crunch has made valuations very difficult. You can't just look at the equity; the debt really matters, too. It doesn't impact your ability to finance, but it does affect the credit quality of portfolio companies."

Growth Capital

Much of private equity will invest in growth capital, significant but less than majority stakes. Private equity's objective is to tap the company's economic potential without exercising control. This is achievable through a number of means including board seats, veto rights, and different classes of stock.

Growth equity has had a long history in Asia, where family-run companies own most of the businesses and have been reluctant to give up control. That began to change after the Asian financial crisis of 1997, when these corporations were forced to divest noncore businesses or to sell unprofitable divisions. Over the past several years, however, purchasing minority stakes has come back in style. The investors are now seen as adding value to the equation rather than being simply along for the ride. Funds have been granted various rights that give them more control at the board level and a say in exits. Growth capital plays especially well in Asia, where developing relationships over time is as important as the price tag.

VENTURE CAPITAL: WHERE ARE THE OPPORTUNITIES?

Venture capital as an institutional investment form is at a crossroads. The NVCA's numbers confirm the wreckage. Just 40 venture capital funds raised $4.3 billion in the first quarter of 2009. This level represented the smallest number of venture funds raising money in a single quarter since the third quarter of 2003. The industry contracted further in the second quarter: 25 funds raised $1.7 billion. During the same quarter, venture capitalists invested $3.7 billion in start-ups, down from $7.6 billion in the period a year earlier. Investment is on track to shrink by half for 2009 to less than $14 billion, a level last seen before the dot-com bubble.

No venture-backed IPOs occurred in the first quarter of 2009. There were, however, five venture-backed IPOs and 59 M&A exits totaling $2.6 billion in the second quarter. Deals returning less than the amount invested accounted for 54 percent of the first quarter's total, compared to 29 percent in the comparable period of 2008.

Yet the lifeblood of venture capital is constant change and innovation. Someone, somewhere *always* has a new or better idea. Finding and monetizing that idea is venture's quest.

Even in Europe, venture is moving slowly but happening, says William Stevens. There are "some new technologies, including energy management and cleaner materials. We are also investing in applications, industrial biotech for biodegradable products, and techniques that offer superior products." What are the leading geographies in Europe? Says Stevens, they include "Scandinavians, with Denmark leading, then Sweden and Finland. The reason is that they have a culture of high transparency and high ethics. For international people, it's easier to do business with them. Switzerland is like Scandinavia, but more aggressive commercially. The Portuguese, even the Greeks, who have highly educated people, are interested in internationalizing and have things to offer. Before, it was confined to hot spots. But now it's cheap to travel and easy to Skype."

In Asia, Walden's Lip-Bu Tan notes, "A few industries will go through consolidation. Being a contrarian investor, we also like recession-proof companies such as online gaming companies in China. We also consider companies that offer healthcare services or focus on organic vegetables. It doesn't necessarily have to be high tech." And he adds, "We continue to look for opportunistic investments in China and India. In the U.S., we continue to look for investments that have a strategic link to those two countries."

What are some of the new industries where venture capitalists are putting their money? The principal areas seem to be alternative energy, mobile platforms, digital media, consumer goods, biotech, money-saving devices, and education. One aspect of all these new ideas is that they increasingly involve more than just producing a machine or device. They involve ongoing services, training, and sensitivity to consumer tastes, and they signal adapting to a more long-term investment model for venture capitalists.

Mobile Platforms

Kevin Fong of GSR Ventures sees opportunity in the interplay between word processing and mobile phones. "The major trends are the smart phone merging with the PC; and, how that change in form factor changes the Internet. iPhone and BlackBerry sales are still very strong. Users are exchanging laptops and desktops for netbooks. The big thing is the $350 netbook. You can't quite do documents on iPhone or BlackBerry, but then you have all the restaurants and movies that you need to find. It will be interesting to see how the intersection between the smartphone and the netbook turns out and what that product will look like."

That new media has fundamentally altered journalism is no secret. Says Fong, the question is, where will it lead?

> I got a Kindle over Christmas. The problem with reading media on a Kindle is the DRM [digital rights management] and its closed nature. Can you solve that with a netbook and still be able to protect content? Still, I'm a great believer in the form factor of the cell phone, which resulted in the smartphone. I had a Palm and a RAZR and now have a BlackBerry Bold. Now, BlackBerry has figured out how to do a good phone. There is a large range of products you can create between a standard cell phone and a netbook. The question for this form factor is: what kind of tradeoffs between screen and keyboard size will sell?

Kleiner Perkins' Ted Schlein also likes mobile platforms. "Another area is mobile as a platform, the things we carry around in our pocket. Asia got there before the United States." He points to "the amazing evolution of the iPhone and number of applications that exist. People want to use these as platforms. We have numerous companies in this area. For example, Pelago, which is creating a mobile community-based search and discovery application, and ngmoco:), a creator and publisher of games for the iPhone."

Digital Media

Digital media is another active area. Music, movies, newspapers—everything seems to be moving to the digital space. Pat Kenny, executive vice president of Qiosk.com, a pioneer in digital magazine delivery, says that magazines will have to change if they are to survive. "Print titles cannot migrate to the Internet in the same format as they exist on the newsstand, but they will have to adapt to what's happening in the magazine space. Either that or become extinct." Amazon's Kindle offers users digital books and can also deliver magazines. Once the price drops and color graphics are added, digitally delivered magazines could grow exponentially. Many titles will be designed for web delivery, becoming more than an exact replica of the print edition.

In China, GSR's Sonny Wu likes digital media and alternative energy. "We will selectively and strategically make some bets in the new materials, new energy and wireless Internet as well as other high tech oriented areas. Less will be spent on consumer and retail areas." In terms of specifics, he says, "The technology space has been hit badly, but upstream components will get purchased first. Interesting areas include digital TV, new energy, and the upstream supply space. We believe that some of the energy-saving devices will get picked up."

Wu says the digital TV space in China is wide open. "There's the whole network TV area, YouTube, network applications, personalized content, and digitization. New energy saving and TV-centric products, such as LED backlit TVs and networked TVs, are in demand. The media space in China is still young, early, and small. As the economy grows, it will as well."

KPCB China will continue to focus on its core sectors, says Tina Ju. "Our core competencies have traditionally been high tech, green technologies, life sciences, and consumer goods. We will deepen our investment in renewable energies as well as energy conservation and materials. We have just invested $15 million in China's largest biology contract research organization (CRO). In addition, we will continue to look at consumer companies with quality brand value, including financial services and retailing operations."

Green Tech and Alternative Energy

Ted Schlein agrees with his partner Tina Ju's approach. "We're looking at three main areas: life sciences, information technology (digital), and green tech. Just saving power on your PC is a goal. Or take a company like Fisker Automotive, which is working on the first plug-in hybrid power automobile."

Schlein is also a big proponent of green tech. "You can pay people to recycle. Most individuals would like to recycle. At KP, we have a systemic commitment to green the consumer and to green the enterprise. And figuring out new ways to generate energy. There are numerous investments around fuel cells. All of these could be very, very interesting."

On the energy side, Schlein says the challenge is that the many projects are capital intensive. "You may need to build a plant. It's difficult to get project finance in this environment. These are trying times, but from that comes opportunities. Our job is to identify those opportunities. In green tech, there's a reasonable-size debt portion. You have to get creative about that."

According to NEA's Peter Barris, the firm is "very excited about what's happening in the energy/clean tech space, notwithstanding that many investments are capital intensive. There's a huge problem set that the world now recognizes we have to solve. The third leg to technology and health services is now clean tech."

Barris's partner Scott Sandell emphasizes that government support will be important to the success of green tech.

> Industries showing growth include clean tech. It's still in the very early phases, but it has enormous potential. The industry is dependent upon aggressive government subsidies to make up the difference between today's costs and current market prices. As has been shown in countries like Japan, however, such government subsidies can facilitate the development of technology which ultimately requires no further subsidy and produces cleaner power more cheaply than traditional sources. Such government support is starting in the United States, and we think it will facilitate the creation of a large new industry complete with new jobs and tax paying companies. It feels like the IT industry 25 years ago. We have been investing since 2003, and a number of our early investments are maturing to the point where we expect liquidity soon.

Vinod Khosla is another apostle of clean tech and alternative fuels. A former partner at Kleiner Perkins, he set up Khosla Ventures in 2004. In September 2009 he closed his Fund III at $800 million and a smaller fund to seed very early-stage ideas at $275 million. CalPERS invested $200 million and Khosla put $150 million of his own money into the larger fund. CalPERS also invested $60 million in the smaller fund.

In a *New York Times* interview, Khosla said the smaller fund is "really geared toward science experiments. The goal there is very much to take risks that nobody else will take." To which he added, "We're really about reinventing the infrastructure of society, which is the only way we'll get the carbon footprint down, and we're not afraid to fail."[3]

Is clean tech too limited an industry for institutional venture to participate in? Joncarlo Mark doesn't think so. "It includes materials, bioplastics, biofuels, alternative energy, and lighting. There are tons of things that fall under the clean tech umbrella which impact energy, water, housing, construction, and consumer markets. So, if you can come up with a new technology—cleaner, lighter, more durable—there's huge upside. There's been a lot of hype around alternative energy. The public market is likely going to be willing to support that as much as—if not more than—another software product."

Yoshito Hori of Globis Capital sees potential growth in "the renewable energy area, fuel cells, batteries, electric car, and environmental technology that give opportunities for growth. Also, the nuclear area is promising. There are only two countries, Japan and France, that have vast nuclear technology. Japanese companies such as Canon also specialize in precision engineering."

Hori also suggests, "There are certain areas where the venture community will not be able to participate, because the expenditures are so large, such as nuclear sectors. But Japanese midsized companies that have been run by mama-papa management where they each have more than 20 percent of the global market share can all be modernized and consolidated." In general, he says, "Other sectors like the Japanese service sectors that are still low in terms of productivity, such as agriculture and recycling business, have room for improvement. Also, there's a new generation of gaming and entertainment coming with multi platforms."

Hori thinks that Japan can play a leading role in developing energy efficient batteries. "There are quite a few areas, such as components for lithium batteries. The lithium battery is dominated by Japanese companies at this moment. They will be used in electric cars, not just mobile phones. As such, in terms of growing sectors in global economies, Japanese technology will play a major role in the ecosystem."

While the world needs alternative energy, however, there's a real question on how countries will replace legacy energy systems that are premised on fossil fuels: Who will pay for it? How long will it take?

In its "Annual Energy Outlook 2009 with Projections to 2030," the U.S. Energy Information Administration predicts that biomass and renewable energy as a share of total energy sources will grow from 7 percent in 2009 to 12 percent in 2020. Meanwhile, natural gas will range from

25 percent to 28 percent while coal will remain constant at 30 percent. Many factors are obviously involved, but the bottom line is the same: renewable energy sources will still provide only a small percentage of America's energy needs in 2020. Alternative energy is certainly a promising area, but its growth as a profitable venture investment remains an open question—subject to many variables, including government subsidies, overall economic conditions, and, most important, whether it can become a profitable source of power for its suppliers.[4]

Consumer Goods

Themes of an emerging middle class and its desire for consumer products are evident throughout Asia. Scott Sandell is a strong believer in the investment potential of Asia's rapidly emerging middle class.

> Our long-term thesis for China and India is to invest in products and services which serve emerging middle class consumers. The companies that did that in the United States from 1950–1980 are the household names of today. Prior to the emergence of a sizable middle class, these companies did not have large markets to pursue. The middle class in the United States grew rapidly during those years on the back of a low cost manufacturing economy initially fueled by exports and later by domestic consumption. Companies like Visa, Wal-Mart, CNN, Motorola, Walt Disney, and FedEx all pioneered products and services which served these groups. We are trying to find companies pioneering new products and services for middle-class consumers in China and India today.

Dick Kramlich mentions Red Baby, the Amazon of China. "They started out as an online ordering system for baby products, then expanded to health and beauty aids, and then to home products. The cost of customer acquisition is virtually nil. It should do well."

Kramlich also sees opportunities in consumer finance. "UPG is a microfinance company that started in Hongzhou. They are a loan guarantee company. In the first year, they analyzed 600 companies and picked out 11 to work with. They were profitable their first year."

Money-Saving Devices

The economic downturn also represents an investment theme, says Ted Schlein. "There is also an opportunity in anything that makes energy or saves you money. That's what a recession does for you. Consumers have identified identity theft protection. Then there is Chegg, which rents textbooks. After tuition and housing, the next most expensive purchase [for college students] is purchase of textbooks. It uses the Netflix business model, but applied to textbooks."

Barris agrees. "This environment has created lots of enterprise focus on cost efficiencies—business processing, software as a service, web-based Internet services that will be offered to corporations by third parties."

Education

Education has provided another area for investment, says Jean Eric Salata, CEO and founder of Baring Private Equity Asia. "We're very value-oriented. We have invested in education—our largest exposure. In India, the infrastructure area is still looking pretty good." In Dubai, Khaled Al Muhairy, CEO, Evolvence Group, has started the American Community School through Evolvence Education Holding. "Our investments into education are based on our belief in the powerful attributes this sector holds for the communities in which we operate. Our focus is on social entrepreneurialism—to continually strive to develop the quality of our services and support the community. We have formed partnerships with prestigious international schools to provide high-quality education in the region."

Life Sciences

NEA is looking at life sciences, says Peter Barris. "We are investing in healthcare areas such as biopharma and medical devices. With an aging population in the United States and around the world, they have great potential." Dick Kramlich thinks that China's regulatory agencies will facilitate the growth. "There's no FDA in China, and IP protection is limited. There's no reimbursable health insurance. But they do have an SFDA, which is twice as effective as the FDA at one-tenth the cost. As far as IP, that's a 'prospective statement.' China will be one of the IP bastions in the world."

What Is Different About Today

Much of the great technology and services in which venture is investing will not be built in the United States or Europe: prototypes and designs, yes; large-scale manufacturing, no. Or if it is built in the U.S. or Europe, it will be only a fraction of the finished product. Whether it is a flat screen or a lithium battery component or a handheld platform, the technology may be state-of-the-art, but the device will be made in China or Southeast Asia or India. The reasons are pretty simple: even with currency appreciation, manufacturing costs in that part of the world remain one-quarter to one-eighth of what they are in the Western world. Lower costs translate directly to less investment and quicker time to market. Sonny Wu says, "With the reset, a lot of deals aren't happening in the U.S. The best is yet to come for technology finance in China!"

Then there are the Asian consumer markets that potentially dwarf those in the United States or Europe. Dr. Hsu thinks it's especially important for "the United States to encourage R&D and technology innovation to offset our labor cost disadvantage." The United States and the European Union represent huge markets. They will consume and buy, but it will be competitively challenging for them to make.

In August 2006, Focus Ventures managing director Jim Boettcher wrote a white paper entitled *The China Paradigm Factor*. In it, he points out that one U.S. telecom chip start-up he tracked needed about $85 million over five years to get to break-even. A similar company in China requires only three years and less than $15 million. He estimates that in 15 years (2025), China will have a middle class of 520 million people, larger in itself than the population of the United States or the European Union. The troubling implications of the accelerating shift in manufacturing base from West to East—in terms of exacerbating the West's unemployment problems, increasing its national debt, and swelling its trade deficits—are readily apparent.

As bright or problematic as the future may be, we are just at the beginning of the human experience. Scientists estimate that our species has been around for 250,000 years. They expect the sun to explode in about five billion years, obliterating the earth. Financial crises will come and go, but a lot will happen between then and now. The industry will be there.

So with one eye on the future and another on today's issues, private equity and venture capital are preparing for what comes next. They confront hostile markets as well as internal issues. Both will battle government efforts to increase regulation, taxes, and oversight. Why, then, do I believe the future of private equity and venture is still a bright one? That is the subject of the next and final chapter.

CHAPTER 8

Toward a New "Corporate Norm"

Throughout this book, I have suggested that private equity and venture capital represent a new model for corporate governance—a game changer for the way in which corporations are organized and managed. It is now time to deliver the details.

Corporate theory, as the name suggests, explains how corporations behave. Although they are ever present in modern life, corporations are legal fictions. They are legislatively designed to look like a person so that they can carry on business and governments can tax them. Before corporations, individuals and families engaged in economic activity on their own. The corporation allows its owners to multiple their economic results a hundredfold.

Once corporations became established, the "corporate norm"—a pyramid of rights and responsibilities—was created. At the base of the triangle are the shareholders, next comes the board, and at the top are the CEO and management.

This final chapter poses the question of whether this accepted corporate norm remains the only viable legal structure. That is, has private equity created a "new" corporate norm that alters both the concept and the parties involved in corporate governance? If so, what does the "new norm" look like, and what are the implications for corporate theory?

As befits its legal origins, corporate theory has been written mostly by lawyers and judges, seeking to set out the limits, responsibilities, and privileges of corporate activity. They do this mostly in briefs and court decisions, and it's a very large volume. Others, mostly academics, have written about corporations in a less formal though patently rigorous way, mostly discussing the attributes and reach of corporate activity.

In the United States, at least, modern corporate theory has its origins in 1932. As mentioned in the Introduction, in that year two Columbia University professors, legal scholar Adolf Berle and economist Gardiner Means, published *The Modern Corporation and Private Property*.[1]

When the book was written, the economy of the 1920s had collapsed and America had entered the Great Depression. Franklin Roosevelt had just been elected president and was in the process of building his administration. The world stage was populated by figures including Stalin, Hitler, and Mussolini. The United States had been plunged into economic depression, totalitarian leaders were on the rise in Europe and Asia, and the prospects for class war were real if not realistic.

Although looking back on this from the year 2010 we might not think so, that was a perilous time for American—and world—democracy. Private corporations formed the backbone of the American economy. Says law professor Steve Diamond, "How do you put in place a system of corporate governance? If people can overthrow kings, why not overthrow directors? Berle and Means were searching for a governance mechanism to get this under control."

Berle and Means provided a landmark book, which held that the advantages of the modern corporation hinged on its separating owners (shareholders) and managers. The corporation wasn't new, but widely held public corporations were. The movement from family-owned to publicly owned firms was in its infancy. Though the number of Americans owning shares was still relatively small, it had increased. As shareholders were widely dispersed, they relied on the board of directors to represent their interests. Over time, management could better grow the company in line with the corporation's needs. But they also dominated the boards of directors, who nominally controlled the corporations, to further their own interests rather than those of the shareholders.

Mark Mizruchi, professor at the University of Michigan, elaborates: "Berle and Means began by arguing that capital in the U.S. had become heavily concentrated during the previous few decades and that this vested a relatively small number of companies with enormous power. As these firms grew, it became increasingly difficult for the original owners to maintain their majority stockholdings, and stocks became dispersed among a large number of small shareholders. The consequence of this dispersal, Berle and Means suggested, was the usurpation, by default, of power by the firm's managers, those who ran the day-to-day affairs of the firm."

According to Mizruchi, Berle and Means believed these managers had interests not necessarily in line with those of the stockholders.

> Whereas owners preferred that profits be returned to them in the form of dividends, for example, managers preferred to either reinvest the profits or, in more sinister interpretations, to further their own privileges, in the form of higher salaries or "perks." Removed from the pressures of stockholders, managers, for Berle and Means, were

> now viewed as a self-perpetuating oligarchy, unaccountable to the owners whom they were expected to represent. Berle and Means's concern about the separation of ownership from control was not only about managers' lack of accountability to investors. It was also a concern about managers' lack of accountability to society in general.

Lost in the debate has been the second half of the book's title: *and Private Property*. It's also important to note that their book was equally aimed at "the relation which corporations bear to property." Say Berle and Means, "[M]en are less likely to own the physical instruments of property and more likely to own pieces of paper. Power over industrial property has been cut off from the beneficial ownership of this property, that is, the legal right to enjoy its fruits." Understanding this separation of ownership and control of property is important because "it is precisely this separation of control and ownership which makes possible tremendous aggregation of property" through an open market in its securities.

Berle and Means point out that the meaning of "property" had also changed since the country's early days. The men who wrote the Constitution had read *The Wealth of Nations* and incorporated Adam Smith's ideas into their political blueprint. For Smith and his followers, private property was a unity involving possession. Berle and Means wrote,

> Whatever the answer as to the fruits of property, it is clear that in dealing with the modern corporation, we are not dealing with the old type of private property.
>
> Side by side, these two forms of wealth exist: passive wealth (impersonal and involving no responsibility) and active wealth—great, functioning organisms dependent for their lives on their security holders, workers, consumers, but most of all on their "mainspring—control." In the still larger view, the modern corporation may be regarded not simply as one form of social organization but potentially (if not actually) as the dominant institution of the modern world.

Berle and Means were making several points: first, that the evolving nature of "property," separating passive from actual ownership, had given birth to the modern corporation; and second, that once established, management had actual control over a corporation's physical assets. That is, through the means of passive wealth, they owned the actual means of production. Further, failing any accountability to the shareholders or to the board, managers could legally use this property as they chose.

A FALSE DICHOTOMY?

Steve Diamond, however, questions whether we really ever had the Berle and Means corporation. "They were both wrong," he says. "What they missed is the fundamental dynamics of capitalism. Capitalists compete. They survive by increasing the productivity and profitability of their companies or they go out of business. There's always constant, dynamic change in a free market." Diamond says, "I think there are just capitalists. There's a kind of working relationship between owners and managers, not a new form of financial engineering. It represents a more stable form of making capitalism work."

In sum, he says, the owner-manager paradigm paints a poor picture of the corporate world.

> I think we are not well served by the idea of owners versus managers: that's been the framework for 70 years. It sets up "inside owners" and "outside managers." But this assumption—that shareholders own the company and the CEO works for them—is just not reality. It's not an effective way of getting to what is happening. Private equity tried to eliminate that type of divide by saying the goal here is to increase value, productivity, and profitability. It's a joint management of the business by the general partners and the CEO and his management team. It posits a governance model that says there is one ownership team that will improve the way the company does business.

In fact, that "one ownership team" is what distinguishes the private equity model from the corporate model.

Mizruchi says that much of the analysis involves means by which owners can provide effective monitoring mechanisms. The last line of "shareholder" defense is the board of directors. The actual power of the board is a regular question among jurists, academics, and the media. He says, "In 2010, everything is dwarfed by the crisis and how companies are impacted by that." But he notes, "Though boards are usually picked by the CEO, they are still in a position to sanction management if something goes wrong. The extent to which they can do this is affected by how close and loyal they are to the CEO, and how willing they are to provide independent oversight. The other problem relates to matters of time. We're talking about people who are often full-time CEOs at other companies. There are just limits on their ability to process information." Today, however, "CEOs have to answer to shareholders, especially institutional owners, in a way that they did not have to in earlier years."

Leonard Harlan emphasizes that the responsibility for governing a company rests with its board of directors, and that the board must be an active one. "Everyone who owns stock should exercise their rights," he says. "In the private equity model, management has an owner that it must satisfy. And that owner demands performance. What gets lost in these large companies is, there's no owner. It's not the size alone, but who holds management accountable? In large companies, the substitute for owners is the board of directors. And who proposes the board? Management does." Harlan argues, "In the mid-market, we buyout guys are the owners. We work with management and demand that they perform."

There are differences between the U.S., Europe, and Asia in terms of corporate governance. Peter Cornelius says the European model is highly concentrated. "There's a difference between the U.S. and Europe: how do you control managers? In the U.S., there is very dispersed ownership. It's difficult to control management. Ownership in Europe is more concentrated in banks and wealthy families. Berle and Means were relevant for the U.S. market, where there's widely dispersed ownership. In Europe, ownership is much more concentrated." What the European model also does is recognize the role that debt holders play in corporate governance.

Asia is also different and considerably less contentious. The Chinese concept of the "mandate from heaven" has governed the region over the past 5,000 years. That is, once decreed, the ruler has the right to demand obedience, whether that ruler is the emperor, the Communist party, a military junta, or self-established. That mandate can be used wisely or ruthlessly, but it's legitimate. And that obedience extends into the corporate sphere. Thus the separation between government and business has never been great. Yes, there is a private sphere, but the government is as much a part of that realm as the public sector. Whether it's India or China, Japan or Vietnam, Hong Kong or Singapore, that unity exists. Hence the separation between ownership and management has never been a serious concern: he who has the mandate, rules over all—including owners, managers, and employees. Certainly, different governments have different briefs, but the distribution of authority remains the same.

THE INDUSTRY MODEL

This corporate governance theory bears a direct relationship to the model endorsed by private equity and venture capital. Private equity's continued success depends on its ability to solve a number of issues. First, it will have to attract good people, the lifeblood of any organization, and it will have to respond to succession and organizational objectives. It will have to come to grips with the concerns of its LPs: either distribute the returns they've been promised or alter the payout arrangements accordingly. It will have to source and manage properly its investments, then exit profitably. Finally, it will have to deal correctly with the public face of private equity in an era that increasingly demands accountability to society commensurate with corporate reach. That means convincing the public and government that their partnerships are appropriate stewards of the task they have assigned themselves: restructuring or growing companies to generate above-average returns for their investors while still contributing to the public good.

Similarly, venture capital faces major challenges ahead: it has largely picked the low-hanging fruit of advances in the computer, IT, and Internet fields. Ahead lie investments in industries that will require considerably more capital, time, and government involvement: alternative energy, clean tech, and life sciences, to name a few. Dealing with the globalization of talent and markets will become important issues. There will always be the innovator in the dorm room or garage with a great idea. But he or she will face greater financial and marketing challenges. One response for venture capitalists is to create firms whose specialties reflect their partners' judgment of where the opportunities lie. That transformation is actually under way at several firms. And that evolution will mean integrating a set of talents and skills that have previously operated separately.

This author, however, modestly believes that the private equity and venture capital industries are up to the challenge—because the basic model is a sound one. That model has reunited investors and managers along with the means of production—both active and passive wealth. Rather than using cash flow to embark on extraneous acquisitions or nonessential activities, they use it to pay down debt and to reward those who have successfully kept the company focused on its core strengths and markets. In an economic downturn, such as we have now, that debt can be overwhelming. Private equity then works to renegotiate the debt, find a buyer, or place the company in bankruptcy. In the last instance, the company can then be purchased at a significant discount from the amount paid by another fund or distressed-asset investors. In a way, this restructuring is the private equity equivalent of a "down round" in venture capital.

The industry also requires the ongoing involvement of the owners—the general partners—as part of a team that determines the success or failure of the business. Good private equity and venture capital firms can all do this. Congress, the European Parliament, and the public are focused on the mega-funds, those that make headlines. We live in an era in which governments routinely throw around tens and hundreds of billions of dollars through multiple "stimulus programs." But a billion dollars is a very large sum of money.

Most of the industry, certainly in terms of deal numbers, does transactions that rarely cross the $1 billion threshold. The real importance of private equity is in those deals. According to Preqin, in 2008, 46 percent of the dollar volume, but only 4 percent of the number of deals were over $1 billion.

A mid-2009 report prepared by Preqin and Dealogic stated that more than two-thirds of buyout deals in 2008 were valued at less than $100 million. Out of all buyout deals, 26 percent were within the $100 million to $499 million band, which accounted for 22 percent of the number of deals. Interestingly, during 2008 there were no buyout deals valued at $10 billion or more, whereas during 2007 there were eight deals falling into this deal size bracket.

Jonathan Blake of SJ Berwin believes that private equity's true importance lies in these mid-sized transactions:

> I did have misgivings on the way in which the highly public-eye deals were, for the last few years, becoming synonymous with private equity. Private equity is much more about the middle market. There private equity plays a very critical role. That's where it's adding value in the emerging economies. Private equity will help bring Western economies out of recession as a means of restructuring. It creates a resource that is otherwise hard to find.
>
> So I think there will be a return to basics, and that will probably be a good thing. The clock will be turning back, not 10 but maybe five years, and we will see private equity much more involved with the mid market and with growth capital transactions.

Have private equity and venture capital written a new chapter in corporate theory? This book argues that they have: the general partners are implementing a new corporate norm, a model that is still seeking its limits, but which could well have implications not only for the industry but for the corporate world and the global economy at large.

A NEW THEORY

A good place to start is Diamond's observation that the accepted dichotomy between owners and managers really doesn't exist in private equity. That is, the parties actually are all part of the same team. The private equity GP focuses on financing and bringing in the right team, while the managers concentrate on running the business. The limited partners provide the equity, while the banks provide the debt. The board of directors engages the GPs,

CEO, limited partners, and the banks. Potentially, the employees are represented as well through their relationship to management.

This model differs from the accepted corporate norm: the shareholders, board, and management forming a pyramid with the CEO at the top. In the private equity world, this triangle no longer exits. There are two or three large equity owners, a board composed of the owners and managers, a management team, and the employees. There are also the limited partners, who stand to gain disproportionate returns if the general partners are successful—different from what corporate shareholders can expect. And there are also the banks, who exercise their rights through the lending agreement covenants.

Although not a perfect graphical representation, this organization is best described as a "+" not a Δ model. The vertical line of the "+" represents the GP at one end, the CEO/management at the other. Share-owning and non-share-owning employees are both included in management. The horizontal line represents the limited partners and the banks at respective ends. They all meet in the middle, where the board of directors sits. And they are all centered on the success of the parties working together toward a profitable transaction in which they have a vested stake.

HOW DOES THIS TRANSLATE TO LARGER CORPORATE THEORY?

This new corporate theory has certain fundamental implications (as well as others that remain to be explored). First, it suggests a nonhierarchal, multidimensional relationship among all the stakeholders—owners, managers, limiteds, debt providers, and staff. That is, the owners are still in charge, but their success is directly dependent on the participation and contribution of the other parties. There will always be someone with ultimate authority, but here the responsibilities are divided among two or three parties.

Second, it suggests that companies should be smaller. One complaint about private equity is the "slash and burn mentality"—that is, the firms fire people and sell assets to get high returns. That they do, but then maybe that's the point. The invested companies have simply grown too large to be effective. Downsizing and then resizing are very much part of private equity's task. Rather than growing the size of the company, private equity's responsibility is to focus on a core mission and to optimize the company to the task at hand. That may well mean laying off employees or selling assets. Not only are bureaucratization and inefficient size harmful to a company's ability to generate profits, but they are also deadly for employees who live and work in this environment. There are, however, certainly decent and humane ways to downsize, such as giving employees a fair notice period, outplacement services, and appropriate severance.

There is another aspect of optimizing a company's results by making the company leaner: the outsized salaries that are paid to CEOs and top management, particularly in the United States. In fixing a CEO's compensation, the operative question is, "Who made the corporation's results happen?" not "Did they happen on the particular CEO's watch?" The CEO provided the leadership, but he or she had help. Namely, the firm's many employees who did the actual work. How is the CEO's salary related to the average employee's salary? Should employees be entitled to some portion of the CEO's reward?

Private equity and venture capital acknowledge this issue by giving employees (mostly management) stock options, effectively a call on the corporation's success (or failure). These options provide a performance incentive, but also a noncash portion of an employee's salary. Many corporations have stock option programs; many others do not. Should these option- or profit-sharing programs be put in place? How can they be made meaningful; for example, what is the ratio in salary between what top management receives and what employees get? These incentive programs have contributed to the results of the private equity and venture capital model while avoiding the excesses of CEO compensation.

The model also offers a new yardstick for corporate performance. Wilbur Ross says, "Cash flow has become the important criteria for measuring a company's performance, not earnings per share. For example, if you build inventory, that's good for EPS, but it's bad for the company's cash flow." Although not perfect, EBITDA generally measures true cash flow, the lifeblood of any corporate organization. EBITDA can still be fudged through several methods, including accrual accounting. For example, when is a sale booked—that is, when does cash constitute earnings and not a receivable? But EBITDA is a far better barometer of corporate health than earnings, which can be as creative as the auditor who constructs them.

Another issue is exits. Neither private equity nor venture capital want to own the company forever. With IPO markets currently shut and trade sales slow, how can the industry facilitate returns for its investors? The proposed June 2009 collaboration between KKR and Fidelity to dispose of KKR's private equity interests is one way. Except in Hong Kong and China, few investors are buying IPOs these days. Concerning whether or not this arrangement will work, "The devil is in the details," says DCM's Dixon Doll."From a Fidelity standpoint, the main reason to do so is that Fidelity can get bigger allocations on more favorable terms. From a KKR perspective, the Fidelity relationship will increase the overall demand for securities of the companies in which they invest. Fidelity is sophisticated enough to do their homework and decide which companies they want to invest in."

Doll notes, "The venture industry is talking about setting up new exchanges. Several that are discussed include SecondMarket and Inside Ventures, firms that have different approaches in matching up companies with institutional investors in advance of the IPO." The idea is that investors will get to know a company well enough so that they stick with them on the public offering. Other possibilities include expanding NASDAQ portals to high-net-worth individuals and to private corporations. Founded in 2004, secondmarket.com claims to be the largest centralized marketplace for illiquid assets, such as bankruptcy claims or limited partnership interests.

Other aspects of the model remain unexplored. For example, in the United States, banks rarely sit on corporate boards. But given the new financial environment and the amount of money that banks have lent, that may not be a bad idea. As noted earlier, in Europe, banks play a much more powerful role and are traditionally board members.

LPs sit on advisory committees for the partnerships in which they have invested. Maybe they should play a more active role. Obviously, LPs cannot watch over every transaction in their portfolio, but then maybe this responsibility argues for a more limited and focused investment program.

THE NEW THEORY AT WORK

Different companies have been affected in different ways by the economic meltdown. AIG and Citibank in the financial sector and Chrysler and General Motors in the automotive sector have all been affected negatively. Then there are public companies that have carried on business as usual; for example, McDonald's and Wal-Mart.

United Technologies, a conglomerate, continues to be profitable (though second quarter 2009 earnings were down). Of course, private equity doesn't always succeed. There are multiple factors at work in each situation. Whether size or organization alone is definitive is doubtful but corporate governance does provide an important and possibly critical dimension. Let's briefly review the histories of these companies, look at their governance models, and then consider why they have weathered the storm (or not) so differently.

Citibank

Citibank has a long history, dating to its founding in 1812 as the City Bank of New York. In the 1960s, the bank entered the credit card field. In the

1980s, Citibank began to grow its mortgage business. As a result of the huge losses in the value of its subprime mortgage assets, Citibank was rescued by the U.S. government. In November 2008, in addition to initial aid of $25 billion, a further $25 billion was invested in the corporation together with guarantees for risky assets amounting to $306 billion.

AIG

The history of American International Group, Inc. (AIG) dates back to 1919, when Cornelius Vander Starr established an insurance agency in Shanghai, China. He continued until 1949, when he fled to New York in advance of Mao's forces. The company went on to expand, often through subsidiaries, into other markets, including other parts of Asia, Latin America, Europe, and the Middle East. In 1962, Starr asked Maurice "Hank" Greenberg to take over the company's U.S. holdings. Greenberg shifted its focus from personal insurance to high-margin corporate coverage and focused on selling insurance through independent brokers rather than agents to eliminate agent salaries. In 1968, Starr named Greenberg his successor.

In "The Rise and Fall of AIG's Financial Products Unit," published in March 2009, authors Zachary Roth and Ben Buchwalter tell the story of how AIG's Financial Products (AIGFP) unit used credit default swaps to almost wipe out the company in 2008.[2]

AIGFP was enormously profitable but failed because it grossly underestimated the risk on credit insurance policies written on subprime mortgage bonds that it believed would never default. As pointed out in Chapter Three, AIG were only sellers, not buyers. In October 2008, AIGFP had $2.7 trillion worth of swap contracts and positions and 50,000 outstanding trades with 2,000 different firms. In March 2009, AIG, once the world's largest insurer, said it lost $61.7 billion in the fourth quarter, the biggest quarterly loss in U.S. corporate history.

General Motors

General Motors (GM) was founded on September 27, 1908. In 1940, Alfred Sloan took charge of the corporation and led it to its postwar global dominance. This unprecedented growth of GM would last into the early 1980s, when it employed 349,000 workers and owned 150 assembly plants. In late 2008, GM became dependent on government loans to avoid bankruptcy resulting from the recession, record oil prices, and competition from abroad. GM's higher labor costs compared to its competitors, resulting from its union agreements and crushing healthcare and pension benefits costs, contributed significantly to its financial problems. GM had 22 subsidiaries as of early 2009, including stakes in international divisions, parts suppliers, and a finance subsidiary. From 2006–2009, the company sold off many of these parts. In February 2008, GM announced a $39 billion loss, the biggest loss of any U.S. automaker.

As of April 2009, GM had received US$15.4 billion in loans from the U.S. Treasury. GMAC, a financing company held 49 percent by GM, had received US$5 billion in loans under the same program; GM has received an additional US$1 billion loan to buy more equity in GMAC. In May 2009, GM took in another $4 billion from the U.S. Treasury. GM filed for bankruptcy on June 1, 2009, the fourth largest in U.S. history.

Chrysler

Chrysler was first organized as Chrysler Corporation in 1925. The company had its first go-around with bankruptcy in the 1970s, but was rescued by U.S. government loans and the leadership of Lee Iacocca. From 1998 to 2007, Chrysler and its subsidiaries were part of the Germany-based Daimler-Chrysler AG. In May 2007, DaimlerChrysler announced the sale of 80.1 percent of Chrysler Group to Cerberus Capital Management, although Daimler continued to hold a minority stake. In April 2009, Cerberus Capital Management agreed to purchase Daimler AG's remaining stake. On April 30, 2009, Chrysler filed for bankruptcy under Chapter 11 and announced a partnership with Italian automaker Fiat. The Fiat partnership was approved in June 2009. Chrysler had only about a third of the divisions that GM has, but they are also spread across the parts and financial subsidiary.

McDonald's Corporation

McDonald's Corporation is the world's largest chain of fast-food restaurants, serving nearly 47 million customers daily. McDonald's revenues grew 27 percent over the three years ending in 2007, to $22.8 billion. 2008 saw global sales increase another 6.9 percent. The business began in 1940 with a restaurant in California owned by the McDonald brothers. But the present-day corporation dates its founding to April 1955, when Ray Kroc opened a franchised drive-in in suburban Chicago. Kroc later purchased the McDonald brothers' equity in the company and led its worldwide expansion. McDonald's Corporation earns revenue as an investor in properties, a franchiser of restaurants, and an operator of restaurants. As of 2008, only 20 percent of McDonald's restaurants are owned and operated by McDonald's Corporation directly. The remainder are operated by others through a variety of franchise agreements and joint ventures.

Wal-Mart Stores

Wal-Mart Stores, Inc. runs a chain of large, discount department stores. The outlets' name was updated to "Walmart" in 2008, with a new logo, although the corporate name remains the same. It is the world's largest public corporation by revenue, according to a 2008 study by *Fortune* magazine. Founded by Sam Walton in 1962, it was incorporated in October 1969. Wal-Mart's operations primarily comprise three retailing subsidiaries: Wal-Mart Stores Division U.S., Sam's Clubs, and Wal-Mart International. The company does business in nine different retail formats. The company is nonunion in the United States, unionized elsewhere.

United Technologies

United Technologies Corporation is a multinational conglomerate corporation. It researches, develops, and manufactures high-technology products in numerous areas, including aircraft engines, helicopters, heating and cooling, fuel cells, elevators, escalators, fire and security, building systems, and industrial products (among others). UTC is also a large military contractor, producing missile systems and military helicopters (most notably the Black Hawk).

WHY HAVE SOME SUCCEEDED, OTHERS FAILED?

There are many, many factors that influence a corporation's success or failure: leadership, product mix, market demand, and capital structure, to name a few. To explain the results for the corporations just described would require considerably more research than this book can undertake. But if small is better, a focused strategy crucial, and accountable management imperative, how can the success and failure of these corporations be explained? And if private equity offers a superior corporate organization, how does the increasing number of private equity failures fit the model?

Certainly there are many differences between poor performers such as AIG, Citibank, GM, and Chrysler on the one hand, and successful companies like McDonald's and Wal-Mart on the other. AIG and Citibank were largely profitable, but brought down by one unit or business activity that took on too much risk. There was a board of directors in both instances that could have acted but didn't. GM and Chrysler were taken down, in part, by unsustainable salary and benefits packages. Their corporate structures were large and unwieldy, their managements unresponsive to the competitive demands of the marketplace. When GM and Chrysler executives showed up in private jets for a Congressional hearing on whether they deserved financial aid, astute observers knew that was the end of the line.

McDonald's and Wal-Mart have done well for many reasons, not the least of which is that they have a unified structure with a focused strategy. Moreover, McDonald's is 80 percent owned by local franchisees that have a direct stake in the business. The corporate offices have purchased several noncore businesses, but these acquisitions were quickly divested. Wal-Mart is also very locally oriented, though it doesn't have franchisees. Wal-Mart also has a profit-sharing plan that extends to all employees.

United Technologies suggests that a large company with multiple, disparate businesses can succeed. Of course, whether the business would be more profitable or better managed if broken into its constituent parts is an unanswered question.

The private equity failures stem from one source: overleverage in an era of declining profitability. If the corporate failures were attributable to malfeasance, the private equity failures were due to negligence (or simply a case of owners whose eyes were bigger than their wallets). Private equity is premised on a certain model that is a function of both operational improvement and capital structure. Its practitioners relied heavily on bank debt to price their investments; that is, the more money the banks were willing to lend, the more money they paid for an acquisition. The few deals that are being closed today and those that will be done in the future will (it is hoped) reflect a chastened industry whose debt loads are attuned more to the risks of operating a business than to what they can get from lenders.

Clearly, private equity's failures represent a breakdown in the model's ability to perform in a downturn. That certainly weakens the model, but it doesn't invalidate it. In its current guise and most successful form, it offers investors, if not a guaranteed return, at least one that has beaten the public averages for the reasons suggested: a unified owner-management team, properly incentivized, with a defined goal to return profits.

And it is a model that offers an alternative plan of corporate governance to the traditional corporate norm. The corporate norm hands the company's business over to management, whose incentives are different than those of widely disbursed owners. With exceptions, existing models frequently promote a decision-making process that is accountable to an organization chart, not to shareholders. Any accountability to owners (shareholders) mostly occurs when the business doesn't go well. Private equity is a full-time, 24-7 alignment. Managers and employees report to a board on which they are represented. Their financial stake in the business requires their paying attention to what's happening. New laws and regulation will certainly affect the private equity model but will not change its fundamental character.

The private equity model is easily transportable, though its precise profile will change across continents. Cultural norms will continue to play a role in how corporations organize and function. Whether a new model is practical for most public corporations is another question. It is probably a difficult transition for most U.S. and European companies. It may not be for corporations in the developing world, notably China and others. Criticizing the excesses of private equity and venture capital is easy. It is far more difficult to impugn a model that at its best has produced stunning successes for its owners and managers.

THE NEW MODEL AND OTHER MARKET FACTORS

Going forward, the banks will not extend the loans they did during the 2004–2007 period. Portfolio company failures will certainly occur, but they will not pose the type of risks to the financial system that the derivatives, subprime mortgages, and, most egregiously, poorly managed financial institutions and industrial corporations did. The private equity and venture industry will find its own solutions: the distressed and secondary funds will purchase failed companies or portfolio company positions at discounts and make the necessary changes. And with the "+" corporate governance model, all the stakeholders potentially have a say in their own gains or losses.

Private equity took advantage of market conditions, but it did not cause them. While banks will take write-downs on overleveraged balance sheets, the losses will come out of private equity's pockets as well. By comparison with the multiple trillions of dollars involved with cleaning up the system, these losses will be small.

Though the economy is on the mend, there were many reasons behind the economic crisis. The book has looked at these in detail (Chapter 3), but ultimately, the United States government needs the fortitude to ask itself, "Who is really to blame, here?" The Clinton administration removed restrictions on the mortgage market, revoked Glass Steagall, and passed changes in the futures and commodities laws. The Bush administration ignored the build-up in derivatives, stood by as the Federal Reserve brought down interest rates, and looked the other way when common sense standards were routinely flouted. Congress watched while all this happened, doing nothing until the horse had long since left the barn.

The industry will change of its own accord. If the "+" model is valid and is improved on—by bringing the banks and limited partners into the decision-making process—then private equity's governance model will only grow stronger.

SHAPING THE GLOBAL ECONOMY

In Asia, private equity has been around for 40 years, but came into its own after the 1997 financial crisis. Previously, the industry was given the minority stake crumbs from families who did their own deals. The 1997–1998 financial crisis changed that. It created distressed sales throughout the region, which private equity saw and purchased. TPG's investment in Korea First Bank and H&Q Asia Pacific's investment in Good Morning Securities, to cite two examples. Companies were forced to focus on core strategies, which created unwanted subsidiaries for sale. There has been a general recognition by a new generation of Asian dealmakers that this American-Anglo model had relevance to the region.

TPG's Newbridge raised its first Asian fund in 1995, and Carlyle set up its first Asian fund in September 2000. But the industry really took off in 2004, after the SARS crisis. KKR, Blackstone, and Bain joined Asian names such as Affinity, CDH, ChrysCapital, HSBC Asia, Hony, ICICI, JAFCO, Symphony, Unison, and Unitas to give the industry its critical mass. At the same time, Australia emerged from its geographic seclusion to take advantage of its global skill sets, enabling investors to profit from deals such as PEP's Just Jeans and CHAMP's turnaround at AUSTAR. The rapid growth of China's venture capital industry and its emerging private equity business are well documented. India's private equity industry rose to global prominence in the post-2004 period, with local and international funds raising capital devoted to Indian investments. Japan, Korea, Taiwan, Hong Kong, and Singapore have all seen increases in private equity and venture capital activity.

Europe's private equity industry began with 3i's post–World War II investment. What they proved to a wary populace was that their investment style enabled "ordinary blokes to get really, really rich." Large funds—including Permira, CVC, and Cinven—led the charge. Private equity grew gradually, then exploded in the first decade of the new millennium. European private equity was and remains a largely U.K. phenomenon, though funds exist on the continent. The market fragmentation that lies beneath the European Union has been a challenge. Another constraint is the rise of a pan-European bureaucracy, which remains indifferent to the free-enterprise philosophy that private equity espouses. Could that change? It could, but there seems to be little effort by those in charge to do so.

Finally, private equity and venture capital (assuming some needed changes) very much conform to the economic system envisioned when this country was created. The men who wrote the Constitution recognized that economic prosperity was a precondition to political stability, and, in turn, that political stability was essential to economic progress. Responding to a postwar recession that bottomed in 1786, the Constitutional Convention envisioned a commercial system founded on free markets and a level playing field. The country's early leaders were firmly committed to the ideas of free trade and open markets, but they also expected government to play an active role in ensuring a fair and competitive economy. James Madison noted that the question was not regulation of commerce "among the several states" but the "degree of that regulation." The principles of free markets and limited but direct government participation in the economy are now playing out in the current administration and Congress. There are bad apples in every barrel, but America's success has come from its reliance on private individuals and groups to make market decisions.The men and women in private equity and venture capital make these decisions. There have been abuses, but they write checks rather than waiting around for the monthly payroll. Government should intervene where necessary and appropriate, but it has rarely (if ever) supplanted private enterprises' ability to create value.

In offering the financial markets a new corporate governance model, private equity and venture capital have challenged the accepted wisdom. Too often seen as a niche investment strategy, its lessons go far beyond an opportunity for a select few to get rich. It replaces the idea that owners and managers are antagonistic with one that stresses accountability and cooperation between the two. Its model more closely resembles corporate cultures that have worked together rather than those that accelerated or succumbed to the economic downturn.

IS THIS THE BEGINNING OR THE END?

We are at the end of our story. Private equity and venture face many hurdles. They also have many opportunities. Does the economic crisis signal the end of the art form? Or are private equity and venture just coming into their own?

For the next several years, I believe the Western world will come to grips with large unemployment figures, tight credit, an unresponsive economy, and limits on what governments can do.

The United States is in a particularly tough spot. The national government has proposed an expansive social agenda in a country whose national debt and recurrent deficits have soared to unprecedented heights. State and local authorities are bordering on insolvency. The country's basic social and economic infrastructure has been ignored for decades. Though most corporations will be profitable, they will continue to consolidate and cut costs. The public equity and debt markets will remain volatile. For now, most of the money the government has spent in stabilizing the financial sector resides on their balance sheets. What happens when the Treasury turns off the "stimulus taps" or banks begin to spend the funds they received is unknown.

The European Union is in an analogous position, though the amounts are far more manageable. Whether European's cultural bias toward a safe and managed society will be a help or hindrance is unclear. Asian economies will continue to grow, albeit at a slower rate. Asia will necessarily move toward expanding consumption and building infrastructure. The rest of the world will watch as wealth moves inexorably in their direction.

Private equity's ability to structure deals with less debt, create new exit markets, and rebuild the relationship with LPs stands out among the many themes this book has explored. New partners with a global perspective and a greater sensitivity to the industry's public profile will take charge. Venture capital will transform itself if it is to play a meaningful role going forward. There will always be a role for entrepreneurship, but it will happen globally. Different types of deals and new partnerships will evolve. The old generation will be carried out feet first, and the next generation will begin its stewardship of the process. The wise GPs understand the transition and have already begun to prepare.

Governments will want to be more involved. But aside from changes in tax rates, they will not prove a burden—because, I believe, the industry will be recognized as an important and valuable contributor to a market economy. Recharged private equity and venture capital industries may well emerge as cornerstones of the financial industry. Those who founded the industry several decades ago and participated in its early growth will be surprised at what they have created. The industry has evolved over the past 40 years. At its best, its leaders have grown from opportunistic buyers to unique and important contributors to the global economy.

Beyond the mega-deals, the vast majority of private equity and venture capital transactions are aimed at optimizing good companies with unrealized potential or rebuilding those with troubled balance sheets, and creating new businesses out of great ideas and great people. Private equity's and venture capital's "+" model of corporate governance distinguishes the industry from today's corporate norm. Though the industry has many issues to solve, therein lie the true roots of its future success. To the extent its model is considered and adopted by the corporate community at large, private equity and venture capital will have done more than build an industry. They will have indeed contributed their experience and capital to shaping a renewed and transformed global economy.

Notes

Chapter 1

1. Stephen F. Diamond, "Beyond the Berle and Means Paradigm: Private Equity and the New Capitalist Order," School of Law, Santa Clara University, February 9, 2009.
2. Boston Consulting Group and IESE Business School, University of Navarra, *Get Ready for the Private-Equity Shakeout: Will This Be the Next Shock to the Global Economy?* December 2008.

Chapter 2

1. Vipal Monga, "That Worrying Wall of Debt," *The Deal*, June 5, 2009.
2. Alan Feuer, "A Study in Why Major Law Firms Are Shrinking," *New York Times*, June 5, 2009.
3. William Pollak, "Random Thoughts," *Bill's Blog*, August 3, 2009; http://us-blog.incisivemedia.com/2009/08.

Chapter 3

1. Securities Industry and Financial Markets Association, press release, http://www.sifma.org/.
2. Peter Schiff, "Obama's Opening Salvo," February 16, 2009, http://www .321gold.com/editorials/schiff/schiff021609.html.
3. Wilbur Ross, "The Financial Crisis in the United States," conference remarks, May 9, 2008, www.policytoday.com.
4. Adam Davidson, "How AIG Fell Apart," Reuters, September 18, 2008, http://www.reuters.com/article/newsOne/idUSMAR85972720080918.
5. Heather Landy, "The Stock Slump of 2008: Wrecking Ball to Wealth," Special to the *Washington Post*, January 11, 2009.
6. Silvio Contessi and Johanna L. Francis, "U.S. Commercial Bank Lending through 2008: Q4: New Evidence from Gross Credit Flows," Federal Reserve Bank of St. Louis, March 2009.
7. David Enrich, Robin Sidel, and Deborah Salomon, "Fed Sees Up to $599 Billion in Bank Losses," *Wall Street Journal*, May 8, 2009.
8. Paul Kedrosky, Senior Fellow, "Right-Sizing the U.S. Venture Capital Industry," Ewing Marion Kauffman Foundation, June 10, 2009.

Chapter 4

1. Leslie Wayne, "California Pension Fund Hopes Riskier Bets Will Restore Its Health," *New York Times*, July 24, 2009.
2. Katie Zezima, "Data Show College Endowments Loss Is Worst Drop Since 1970s," *New York Times*, January 26, 2009.

Chapter 5

1. "Japan Needs a Breath of Political Fresh Air," *Independent*, July 14, 2009.
2. "It's Stupid to Be Afraid," *Der Spiegel*, August 8, 2005.
3. "Facetime with Victor Chu," CNN, November 9, 2007, http://edition.cnn.com/2007/BUSINESS/11/08/chu.interview/index.html.
4. Stephen Castle and Alan Cowell, "Center-Right Parties Gain in Europe," *New York Times*, June 8, 2009.

Chapter 6

1. Danny Hakim, "Carlyle Settles with New York in Pension Case," *New York Times*, May 14, 2009; "Riverstone to Settle Pension Fund Inquiry," *New York Times*, June 11, 2009.
2. David Gow, "EU Deadlocked on Financial Regulation Crackdown," April 21, 2009, www.guardian.co.uk.
3. Hélène Mulholland, "Boris Johnson Warns of Threat from EU Regulation Plans," September 2, 2009, www.guardian.co.uk.
4. Andrew Ross Sorkin, Dealbook, "The Top 10 Buyouts," *New York Times*, February 26, 2007.
5. Greg Sargent, "Wilbur Ross's Distress," *New York*, January 14, 2006.
6. Jonathan Keehner, Caroline Salas, and Jason Kelly, "Harrah's Owners Said to Hedge Against Bankruptcy," Bloomberg.com, March 13, 2009, http://www.bloomberg.com/apps/news?pid=newsarchive&sid=aJzJ_THa9Pck.
7. Eric Lipton, "As Investors Circle Ailing Bank, Fed Sets Limits," *New York Times*, May 5, 2009.

Chapter 7

1. Lindsey Arent and Jason Kelly, "Rubenstein Sees Private Equity Firms Getting Stronger," Bloomberg, October 1, 2009, http://www.bloomberg.com/apps/news?pid=20601087&sid=amXzzQP4IrG4.
2. Henny Sender, "Creditor to Predator," *Financial Times*, May 15, 2009.
3. Claire Cain Miller, "Venture Firm's 'Green' Fund Tops $1 Billion," *New York Times*, September 1, 2009.
4. Annual Energy Outlook 2009 with Projections to 2030, Energy Information Administration, March 2009, http://www.eia.doe.gov/oiaf/servicerpt/stimulus/aeostim.html; International Energy Outlook 2009, Energy Information Administration, May 2009, http://www.eia.doe.gov/oiaf/ieo/highlights.html.

Chapter 8

1. Adolf Berle and Gardiner Means, *The Modern Corporation and Private Property*, tenth edition (originally published 1932, copyright 1968; Harcourt, Brace & World, 2009), pp liii, 8, 6, 305, and 306.
2. Zachary Roth and Ben Buchwalter, "The Rise and Fall of AIG's Financial Products Unit," March 20, 2009, http://tpmmuckraker.talkingpointsmemo.com/2009/03/the_rise_and_fall_of_aigs_financial_products_unit.php.

Private Equity and Venture Capital

THE CLASS OF 2010

(PEOPLE INTERVIEWED IN THE BOOK)

Joe Bae
Managing Partner
Kohlberg Kravis Roberts & Co. Asia, Hong Kong

Len Baker
Managing Director
Sutter Hill Ventures, USA

Peter Barris
Managing Director
New Enterprise Associates, USA

Fritz Becker
CEO
Harald Quandt Holding, Germany

Harjit Bhatia
Managing Partner and head of Credit Suisse Private Equity Asia, Hong Kong

Philip Bilden
Managing Director
HarbourVest Partners, Hong Kong

Jonathan Blake
Senior Partner
SJ Berwin, UK

Wim Borgdorff
Managing Partner
AlpInvest Partners, The Netherlands

Photo courtesy of Ton Kastermans, Fotografie

Gary Bridge
Managing Director
Horsley Bridge
Partners, China

Dan Carroll
Managing Partner
TPG, USA

Matthew Chanin
Senior Managing
Director
Prudential Investment
Management, USA

Victor Chu
Chairman and CEO
First Eastern
Investment Group,
Hong Kong

Patricia M. Cloherty
Chairman and CEO
Delta Private Equity
Partners, USA

Jeremy Coller
CEO and CIO
Coller Capital, UK

Peter Cornelius
Economist
AlpInvest Partners,
The Netherlands

David Coulter
Managing Director
Warburg Pincus
(former CEO, Bank
of America), USA

Martin Day
Managing Director
OMERS Private
Equity (vice-chair of
the Institutional
Limited Partners
Association), Canada

Ashish Dhawan
Managing Director
ChrysCapital, India

Stephen Diamond
Professor of law
Santa Clara
University, USA

Dixon Doll
Cofounder and
General Partner
DCM, USA

Lindel Eakman
Director
University of Texas
Investment
Management
Company
(UTIMCO), USA

Bruce Feldman
Director
of alternative
investments
State Employees'
Retirement System,
Commonwealth of
Pennsylvania, USA

Carl Ferenbach
Managing Director
Berkshire Partners,
USA

Joseph Ferrigno
Managing Partner
Asia Mezzanine
Capital Group,
Hong Kong

Bill Ferris
Executive Chairman
CHAMP Private
Equity Group,
Australia

Dr. Ernst von Fischer
Senior Adviser
Sal. Oppenheim
Private Equity
Partners, China

Kevin Fong
Special Advisor
GSR Ventures,
China

Leonard Harlan
Chairman, Executive
Committee
Castle Harlan, USA

Warren Hellman
Chairman and Cofounder
Hellman & Friedman, USA

Yoshito Hori
Founder and Managing Partner
Globis Capital, Japan

Dr. Ta-lin Hsu
Founder and Chairman
H&Q Asia Pacific, USA

Jay Jordan
Chairman and Managing Principal
The Jordan Company, USA

Tina Ju
Founding Managing Partner
KPCB China, China

The Honorable Paul Keating
Former Australian Prime Minister and Treasurer, Australia

Grant Kelley
Founder and CEO
Holdfast Capital, Hong Kong

Patrick Kenny
Executive Vice President
Qiosk.com, USA

Gulpreet Kohli
Managing Director
ChrysCapital, India

Dick Kramlich
General Partner and Cofounder
New Enterprise Associates, USA

Jae Woo Lee
Founding Partner
Vogo Investment,
Korea

Andrew Liu
CEO
Unitas Capital,
Hong Kong

Douglas Lowenstein
President and CEO
Private Equity
Council, USA

Joncarlo Mark
Senior Portfolio
Manager
CalPERS, USA

Howard Marks
Chairman
Oaktree Capital
Management, USA

Daniel Mintz
Founding Managing
Director
Olympus Capital,
Hong Kong

Luis Miranda
President and CEO
IDFC Private Equity,
India

Mark Mizruchi
Professor
University of
Michigan, USA

Photo courtesy
of d.c.goings

Khaled Al Muhairy
CEO
Evolvence Group,
UAE

Stephen Pagliuca
Managing Director
Bain Capital, USA

Ralph Parks
Chairman
Oaktree Capital
(Hong Kong),
Hong Kong

Alan Patricof
Founder
Greycroft Partners,
USA

Michael Pralle
Former Global CEO
GE Real Estate
Investing and
Lending, USA

Mike Quaranta
Chief of Staff
Representative
Michael Castle (DE),
U.S. House of
Representatives, USA

Tom Quinn
Managing Principal
The Jordan
Company, China

George Raffini
Managing Director
HSBC Private Equity
(Asia), Hong Kong

Justin Reizes
Member
Kohlberg Kravis
Roberts & Co.,
Australia

Gary Rieschel
Founder and
Managing Director
Qiming Venture
Partners, China

Stephen Roach
Chairman
Morgan Stanley Asia,
Hong Kong

Wilbur Ross
Chairman
W L Ross & Co, USA

David Rubenstein
Cofounder and
Managing Director
The Carlyle Group,
USA

Maarten Ruijs
Managing Partner
and CIO
CVC Asia Pacific,
Hong Kong

Lewis P. Rutherfurd
Cofounder and
Managing Director
Inter-Asia Venture
Management,
Hong Kong

Jean Eric Salata
Managing Partner
Baring Private Equity
Asia, Hong Kong

Scott Sandell
General Partner
New Enterprise
Associates, USA

Ted Schlein
Managing Partner
Kleiner Perkins
Caufield & Byers,
USA

Will Schmidt
Managing Partner
Advent International,
UK

Sheryl Schwartz
Managing Director
Alternative
Investments,
TIAA-CREF, USA

William Seidman
Former Chairman
FDIC and Resolution
Trust Corp, USA

Jeffrey Shafer
Vice Chairman
Global Banking,
Citigroup, USA

Betty Sheets
Senior Investment Manager
Private Investments, IBM Corporation, USA

Tim Sims
Founder and Managing Director
Pacific Equity Partners, Australia

Joseph Skrzynski
Managing Director
CHAMP Private Equity, Australia

Richard Slocum
Director of Private Investments
Robert Wood Johnson Foundation, USA

Arvind Sodhani
President
Intel Capital, USA

Dr. Kareem El Solh
CEO
Gulf Capital, UAE

Dr. Adnan Soufi
Managing Director
Financial Investments Group
Saudi Economic and Development Company (SEDCO), Saudi Arabia

Gary Stead
Managing Director and Cofounder
Shearwater Capital Group, Australia

William Stevens
CEO
Europe Unlimited, (formerly Secretary General, EVCA), Belgium

Georges Sudarskis
Formerly Senior Investment Controller
Abu Dhabi Investment Authority (ADIA), UAE

Lip-Bu Tan
Chairman and Founder
Walden International, USA

KY Tang
Chairman and Managing Partner
Affinity Equity Partners, Hong Kong

Teo Ming Kian
Former Permanent Secretary
Singapore Ministry of Finance, Singapore

Anil Thadani
Chairman
Symphony Capital Partners (Asia), Singapore

Sriram Viswanathan
Managing Director
Intel Capital, USA

Paul Waller
Managing Partner
3i, UK

Peter Wiggs
Managing Partner
Archer Capital, Australia

Sonny Wu
Managing Director
GSR Ventures, China

Biao Xing
Head
Private Equity Division Team, National Council for Social Security Fund, The PRC, China

Yichen Zhang
CEO
CITIC Capital Holdings, China

Not Pictured

Steve Byrom
Head of Private Equity
Future Fund, Australia

Henry Kravis
Cofounder and Managing Partner, Cochairman and co-CEO
Kohlberg Kravis Roberts & Co., USA

Index